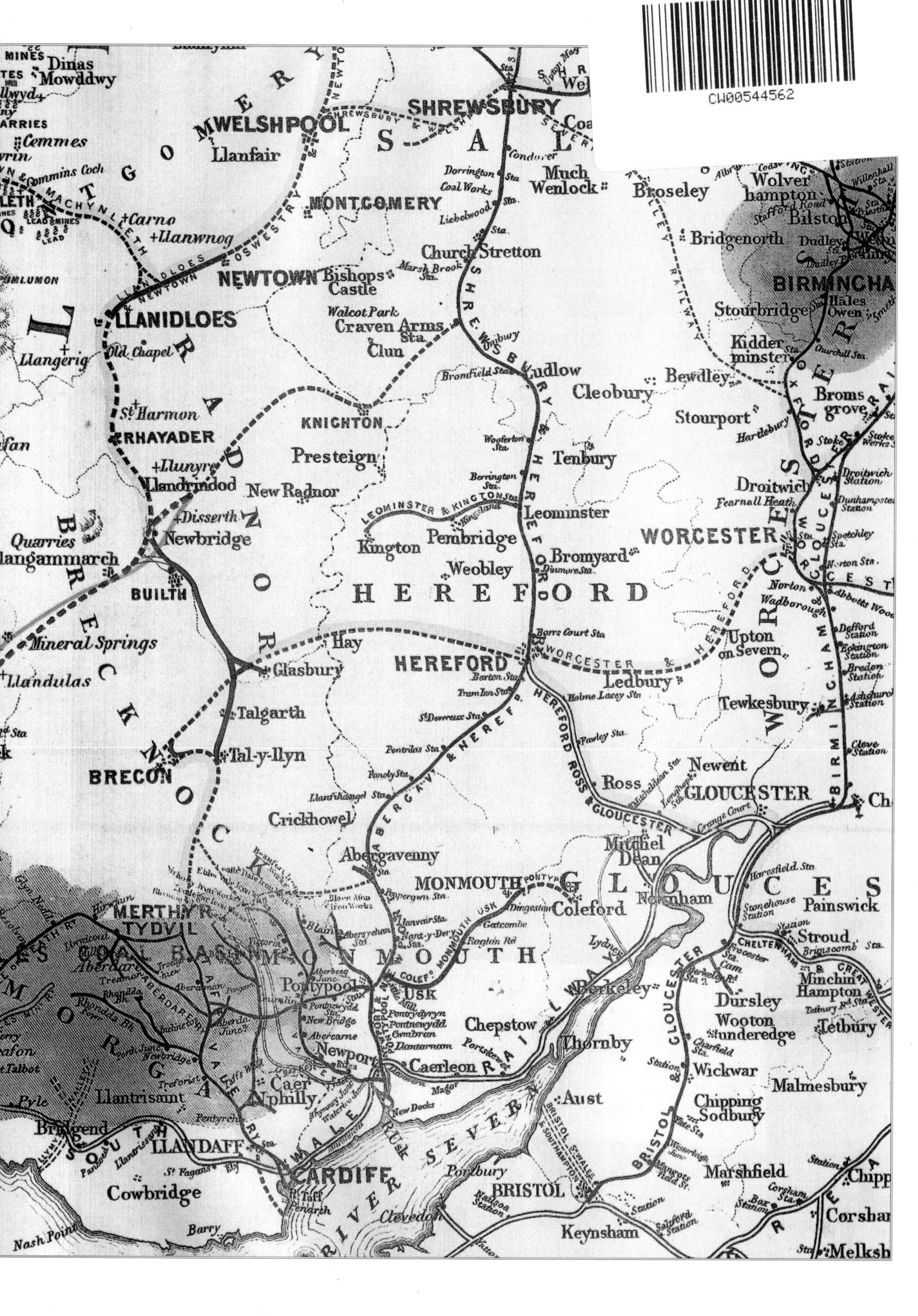
Dinas Mowddwy
SHREWSBURY
WELSHPOOL
Llanfair
Cemmes
Commins Coch
Carno
Llanwnog
MONTGOMERY
Much Wenlock
Broseley
Wolverhampton
Bilston
Dudley
Bridgenorth
Church Stretton
NEWTOWN
Bishops Castle
PLINLIMMON
LLANIDLOES
Llangerig
Old Chapel
Walcot Park
Craven Arms Sta.
Clun
BIRMINGHAM
Stourbridge
Hales Owen
Kidderminster
Ludlow
Bewdley
Cleobury
Broms grove
St. Harmon
RHAYADER
KNIGHTON
Stourport
Presteign
Tenbury
Llandrindod
New Radnor
Droitwich
Disserth
Newbridge
Leominster
Quarries
Llangammarch
Kington
Pembridge
Bromyard
WORCESTER
Weobley
HEREFORD
BUILTH
Mineral Springs
Hay
Upton on Severn
Glasbury
HEREFORD
Ledbury
Llandulas
Talgarth
Tewkesbury
Tal-y-llyn
BRECON
Ross
Newent
GLOUCESTER
Crickhowel
Abergavenny
Mitchel Dean
MONMOUTH
Coleford
Newnham
Painswick
MERTHYR TYDVIL
Aberdare
Stroud
Minchin Hampton
Pontypool
Usk
Berkeley
Dursley
Wooton underedge
Tetbury
Chepstow
Thornby
Newport
Caerleon
Wickwar
Llantrisaint
Caerphilly
Aust
Malmesbury
Chipping Sodbury
Bridgend
LLANDAFF
CARDIFF
RIVER SEVERN
Portbury
BRISTOL
Marshfield
Cowbridge
Clevedon
Keynsham
Corsham
Nash Point
Barry
Penarth
Melksham

THE ORIGINS OF THE LMS IN SOUTH WALES

In about 1935 a LNWR Webb 0-8-0 struggles with a mixed freight on the severe gradient approaching Gellifelen tunnel between Abergavenny and Brynmawr.

Original by GBJ. Courtesy WIMM

The Origins of the LMS in South Wales

Gwyn Briwnant Jones

and

Denis Dunstone

Industrial smoke and mountain drizzle merge near Blaenavon. Early 1920s.
J.M. Dunn/LNWR Soc.

First impression—1999

ISBN 1 85902 676 1 (softback)
ISBN 1 85902 671 0 (hardback)

Printed in Wales by
Gomer Press, Llandysul, Ceredigion

CONTENTS

Acknowledgements		7
Preface		9
Chapter 1	Introduction	11
Chapter 2	Early Skirmishes	22
Chapter 3	Over the Top to Cardiff and Newport	51
	Up to Brynmawr	51
	Three Ways to Newport	74
	Chums with the Rhymney	88
Chapter 4	The Merthyr Tangle	95
Chapter 5	The Hard Way to Swansea	121
Chapter 6	The Midland Mops Up	159
	Hereford headache	159
	Where next?	177
	Swansea at last	186
Chapter 7	The Harvest	214
Bibliography and Sources		251
Index		253

Although at 1,200 ft above sea level and the highest town in Wales, Brynmawr was a centre of LNWR activity. This view, facing east, from the station shows the Abergavenny line curving away to the left while the line to Blaenavon is just visible between locomotive number 40145 and the signal box; 1950s.

R.M. Casserley

ACKNOWLEDGEMENTS

One of the pleasures of researching railway history is the unfailing courtesy and helpfulness of the staff at the Public Records Office, the House of Lords Record Office, the National Monuments Record of Wales (NMRW) at Aberystwyth, and at County Archives. Staff at Brecon Museum, Swansea Museum, Carmarthen Museum, Cyfarthfa Castle Museum at Merthyr Tydfil, and at the Welsh Industrial and Maritime Museum in Cardiff have also been most supportive.

The competition to find previously unpublished photographs, particularly of the pre-grouping age, has increased, and the authors have been fortunate in receiving help from a number of sources. Photographers and collectors are credited in the text, but the following have been particularly helpful: Gwilym Davies and Malcolm Thomas of Old Bakehouse Publications, Abertillery, Nigel Lewis, Keith Evans and the late John Beardsmore of the Abergavenny Steam Society, Alan Jarvis and John Miles of Cardiff, Trevor Owen of Aberystwyth, Michael Lloyd of Hereford, Tudor Watkins of Upton-upon-Severn, Nigel Wassell of Swansea, R.M. Casserley of Berkhamsted, W.G. Rear of Conwy and Ian Wright of Whittlesford, near Cambridge. Chris Dean, Trefor David, Paul Reynolds, the Revd Bernant Hughes, R.J. Doran, Malcolm James, R.H. Marrows, Sir David Mansel Lewis and the family of the late Huw Daniel have also been very helpful. We have drawn upon the extensive resources of the National Railway Museum, the LNWR Society and, perhaps surprisingly, the National Tramway Museum.

In some cases previously published photographs have been used, either because of their direct relevance to the text, or because they provide a unique record. It has been necessary on occasions to use photographs of less than top quality and, for the sake of recording locations, to use photographs taken in BR days. For the same reason, it has even been felt justifiable on occasions to include scenes containing GWR locomotives.

The spelling of Welsh place-names generally follows that of the railway companies even though their interpretations were often cavalier or idiosyncratic.

St. Thomas Station Swansea, in July 1955.

Real Photo K2612/NRM

A view up the Tawe at Swansea with the approach to St. Thomas Station on the right, *c.* 1950.

J.E. Martin/WIMM

PREFACE

The first punishable offence at school committed by one of the authors was to draw in an arithmetic book a former LNWR 'coal tank' in the space provided for a tedious set of additions. The locomotive was visible from the schoolroom window where the line from Abergavenny Junction to Brecon Road Station crossed the Old Hereford Road. There was fascination in the LMS presence in the heart of GWR territory with its surprising line up the Clydach gorge, rising from the tranquillity of the Usk to the industrial valleys over the mountain. From the farm at Gilwern it was possible to discern on the southern skyline the silhouette of workings and machinery and to climb up the steep slope of the pastures to see the trains. The writing of this book was stimulated by those images and by the oddity of the LMS position, and is in particular an attempt to answer questions raised during research into the authors' previous book, *The Vale of Neath Line* (1996), concerning the LNW's decision to drop its association with the Newport, Abergavenny & Hereford Railway in 1854.

To deal with the LNWR and to ignore the Midland would have been to leave seriously incomplete what is in a sense one story, that of the invasion of south Wales by English railways. By including the Midland we also have the benefit of a more complete coverage of Swansea, and the appeal of the fascinating stories of Brecon and Hereford. Purists may object that Hereford is not in Wales, but its role is too critical to the theme to be ignored.

Because the railway companies were the first national organisations, it has been illuminating to observe the process by which companies grew, how management practices developed, and how the motivation of railway ownership changed. Initially industrial entrepreneurs sought transport cost savings, like the founders of the Merthyr, Tredegar & Abergavenny (MTA) and the Swansea Vale (SV). Then came those hoping to grow richer by seeing their line become part of a trunk line, like the owners of the Hereford, Hay & Brecon (HHB) and the Neath & Brecon (N & B). Finally, came those for whom recovering potentially lost value by accepting merger with the large English companies was the only way out; such were the Llanelly, and as late as 1891 the Central Wales & Carmarthen Junction (CW & CJ). The interaction between these men and the two large English companies, each bent on tapping the mineral wealth of south Wales, is the theme of the following chapters. As a conclusion, an attempt is made to review what it achieved.

The LNWR bridge over the Old Hereford Road in Abergavenny, *c.* 1970.

DD Coll.

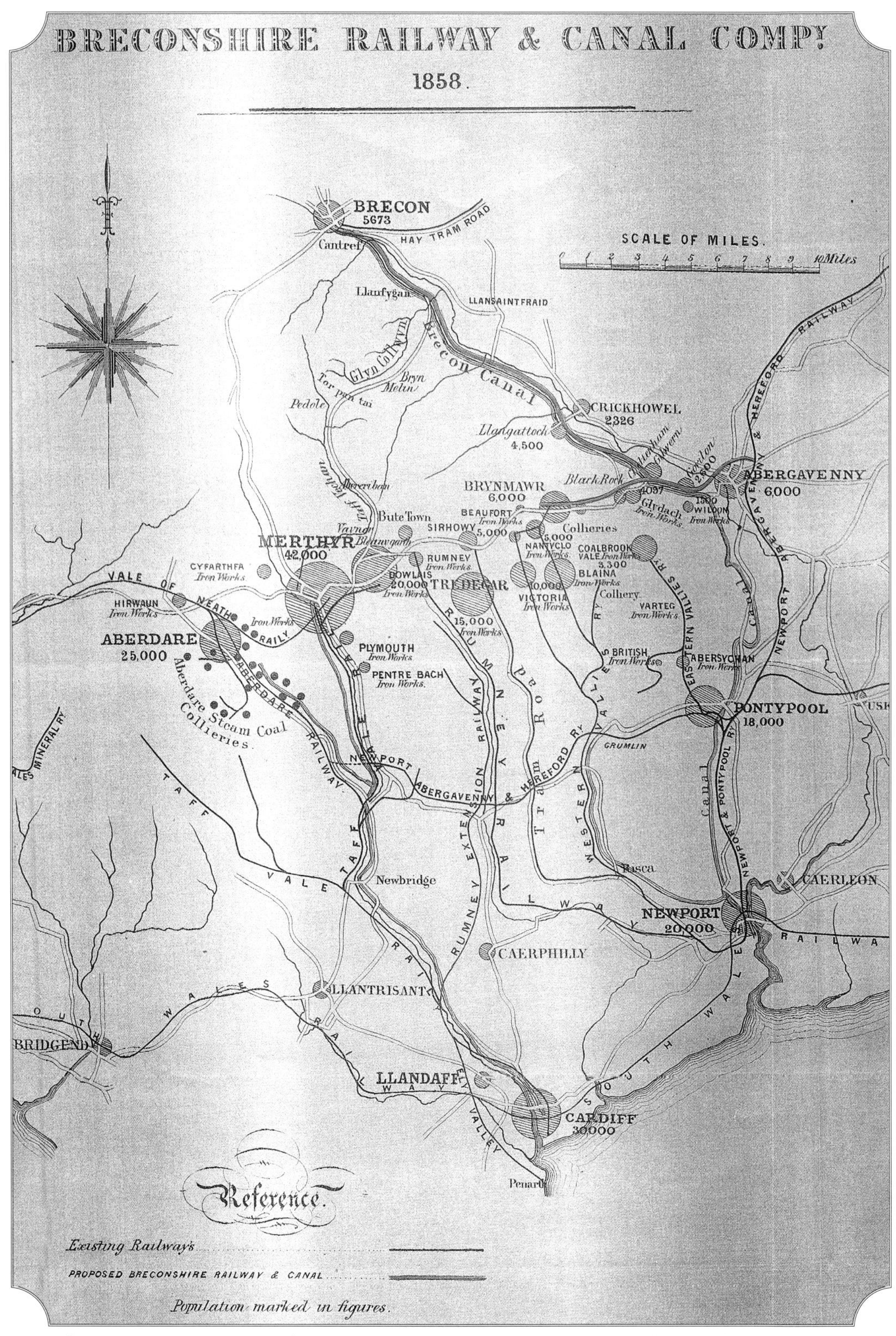

Map of south-east Wales prepared for the abortive Breconshire Railway & Canal Co. project of 1858, to build a railway from Abergavenny to Brecon.

Brecon Museum

Chapter 1

INTRODUCTION

In 1845, when the story begins, the view of south Wales from London and Derby would have been hazy. Separated from the south of England by the Severn and from the north by a lovely but extensive series of mountain ranges, it was not altogether surprising that south Wales had been by-passed by the first round of railway construction. Indeed, the first railways in south Wales were independent of those in the rest of Britain, the Llanelly in the south-west, and the Taff Vale, between Cardiff and Merthyr Tydfil. Both were primarily mineral lines, successors to canals and tramroads, and built to carry minerals to the sea for shipping. One was to play a part in the entry of the LNWR, the other remained staunchly and profitably independent until 1923.

South Wales is an imprecise description but, for the purpose of this book, is the area bounded to the south by the Bristol Channel and on its northern edge by two rivers, the Tywi flowing westward to Carmarthen, and the Usk flowing east to Abergavenny and south to Newport. Oddly, the catchment area between the two rivers was never crossed by a railway. A motorist driving east from Carmarthen along the A40 has the pleasure of a constantly changing skyline on his right, as the Black Mountain, Carmarthen Fan and Fforest Fawr give way first to the Brecon Beacons, and then to the great rampart of Mynydd Llangynidr, and the imposing and formidable mass of the Blorenge towering above Abergavenny.

The nature of the high mountain terrain is well illustrated in this view eastward from the point where the Brecon & Merthyr line crossed the MTA near Dowlais Top. The rust on the rails testifies to the recent closure of the line; 17 August 1959

Alan Jarvis

The mass of the Blorenge Mountain screens the industrial world of Blaenavon. The MTA bridge over the Usk lies alongside the old road bridge. Just beyond can be seen Llanfoist Church in whose graveyard Crawshay Bailey lies buried.

GBJ Coll.

Below the pass over Fforest Fawr, near Cray, a Brecon-bound train descends in BR days; August 1960.
Alan Jarvis

This does not look like prospective railway country, yet the LMS inherited from two of its constituents, the LNWR and the Midland, two lines which found a way into the mountains and presented to the traveller superb mountain views of breathtaking drama; this was entirely incidental to their main purpose which was the carriage of minerals and coal. In the following pages we shall trace the early awakening at Euston and in Derby to what lay behind these magnificent mountain ranges, and then attempt to follow the faltering and intricate progress by which, first arm in arm, and then independently the two companies contrived to establish themselves in the far south-west at Swansea, and in the case of the LNWR, at Newport, Merthyr, Cardiff and Carmarthen as well, none of them short of rival railway company activity.

The route of the Neath & Brecon Railway, which conveyed Midland Railway trains across Fforest Fawr, presented travellers with splendid views as they approached the summit of the line near Penwyllt. Carmarthen Fan (2,632 ft) is prominent to the north-west; 1996.
DD

The way from the midlands and north of England into this then remote and mountainous area lay through towns which in the early 1850s endured some of the most violent and vituperative battles between rival railway interests. Wolverhampton and Shrewsbury saw the GWR and LNWR in hot dispute for territory for their two gauges, the broad and the standard respectively. Gloucester, further south, provided in 1846 evidence for the Gauge Commission of the inconvenience caused by transferring goods and passengers between trains on two different gauges, but it had been impossible for Parliament to resolve the debate, and two-gauge towns were to be created around the Welsh Marches, at Newport, Merthyr, Aberdare, Hereford and Wolverhampton. Worcester was mixed gauge for a short time, but Shrewsbury, oddly, escaped, and was arguably the point on the GWR network from which the broad gauge carpet was gradually rolled back. Further west, Carmarthen was for a time a mixed gauge town as were Swansea, Neath and Llanelly.

The landscape recovers, after the ebb of the tide of industry, though the path of the railway up the Clydach gorge survives. In the distance, the Sugar Loaf (1,995 ft) towers above Abergavenny; 1996.

GBJ

Sunshine and snow near Penwyllt. Locomotives 844 and 3706. Date uncertain.

WIMM/GW Coll.

An elevated view up the south side of the Clydach gorge, looking towards Brynmawr. Clydach viaduct, station and tunnel entrances are prominent in the foreground. Date uncertain but post the Second World War.

John van Laun

Shrewsbury was in a key strategic position, midway on the north-south divide of the Welsh Marches; it stood and still stands as a gateway to mid-Wales and was to serve as the principal jumping-off point for the LNWR as it moved towards Hereford, Abergavenny and Cardiff, and then, through territory mainly outside the scope of this book, to Swansea and Carmarthen. In the case of the Midland, who had to make the best of what was left in a narrow field, Hereford was the key starting point, linked as it was to Worcester.

In 1850 the Midland was recuperating after the trauma of the Hudson débâcle, prior to which it had seemed as though nothing could stop its hegemony spreading over the whole of the eastern half of Britain. One of the beneficiaries of Hudson's fall was the Great Northern who in 1850 opened a line from south Yorkshire to London. This broke the stranglehold the London & Birmingham and its successor, the LNWR, had had on access to London from the north. The Midland and LNWR had successfully constrained the somewhat undisciplined Manchester, Sheffield & Lincolnshire, and had, with the Lancashire & Yorkshire, created an agreement to prevent price-cutting. The new boy on the block, the Great Northern, posed a threat to this and to the lucrative coal traffic from Yorkshire to London, to which the Midland and LNWR reacted by growing even closer together, to the extent that by 1852 they were seriously discussing merger. Parliament was, however, suspicious of large combines forming monopolies.

The massive movement of coal in the Tawe valley is reflected in this impressive line-up of waggons at the Tareni Colliery of the Primrose Colliery Co. This view, looking north towards Ynysygeinon Junction, shows the well-worn, single main line along the right of the complex; 1912.

GW/WIMM

'Black gold' is an expression usually applied to oil. For the Midland Railway coal was gold. Tareni Colliery and sidings, looking south towards Swansea; 1912.

GW/WIMM

On the southern and western flank the GWR presented a threat, for the company was still determined to create a broad gauge network, even looking as far north as the Mersey, and there was no shortage of points of conflict between them and the LNWR, at the time under the management of a particularly clever but aggressive general manager, Captain Mark Huish. The impoverished Oxford, Worcester and Wolverhampton (OWW) was to be torn between them.

In Wales, links with the railways of the rest of Britain were being forged along the north coast by the Chester & Holyhead and along the Bristol Channel coast by the broad gauge South Wales Railway. In acquiring the Birmingham & Gloucester and Bristol & Gloucester, the Midland made for itself a continuous link between the north midlands and the south-west, the first of several strategic leaps into alien territory whereby it

A general view of the locomotive depot at Upper Bank; 23 March 1947.
W.A. Camwell/John Miles Coll.

Along Swansea Bay the LNWR was almost on the beach, here viewed from the 9:45 a.m. train to Shrewsbury on 25 April 1963.
Alan Jarvis

was eventually to reach Carlisle, Southend-on-Sea and Swansea, and, by means of joint lines, points as far apart as Great Yarmouth, Portpatrick and Poole. As early as 1845 shareholders were told of a project to build a line from Worcester to Swansea.

This was the Welsh Midland, a standard gauge scheme which had a brief but eventful life, and casts interesting light on the problems of railway promotion. With a star-studded list of backers, including directors of the London & Birmingham and the Midland, it envisaged a line closely resembling an amalgam of the eventual LNWR and Midland routes to Swansea from Worcester through Hereford and Brecon. Branches to Kidderminster, and Llandovery, Llandilo and Carmarthen were initially canvassed but not submitted to Parliament, and there had even been a suggestion of a branch from Hereford to Pontypool and Quakers Yard, along the later route of the Newport, Abergavenny & Hereford. The line was to end at Oystermouth on the shores of Swansea Bay, and was to absorb the oldest public passenger railway in the world. It proposed, among other remarkable engineering works, a tunnel under Swansea and two in the Tawe valley, one of 1,261 yds and another of 3,230 yds. On either side of Brecon, around

Swansea Bay Station on the occasion of the last day of the Mumbles Tram, successor to the Oystermouth Railway, 5 January 1960.
Huw Daniel

A general view of the N & B route out of the Tawe valley, looking towards Brecon, 1998. The road in the foreground marks the track of the Swansea Vale and Neath & Brecon Railway, just south of Abercrave Station. The path of the railway towards Fan Gyhirych in the distance (left) can be followed along the top of the distant sunlit hillside. Beneath Fan Gyhirych the small patch of sunlight indicates the location of Penwyllt.

GBJ

which the line was to skirt to the north, were three more tunnels, one of 1,430 yds, one of 590 yds and another of 2,101 yds.

Behind this fine façade was a combination of arrogance and incompetence which led to the scheme failing on Standing Orders in the House of Commons. The engineer responsible, Stephen Hall of Swansea, was sick at the time of the submission of the plans to Parliament. When he recovered, he found a number of errors in the drawings and submitted a revised set. The question was whether these were admissable. Parliament took a strong line. After a long hearing at which the opposing broad gauge party took every opportunity to dig up mistakes in both the drawings and the Book of Reference, it was held that Standing Orders had been breeched and accordingly the Welsh Midland application was dismissed. The slump following the Irish famine prevented its revival.

One of its promoters, the deputy chairman, J. Palmer Budd, moved to the Newport, Abergavenny & Hereford (NAH), and in a later committee hearing demonstrated a rather unattractive blend of disdain and conceit, when he blithely told the committee that the NAH had done a lot of foolish things before he joined

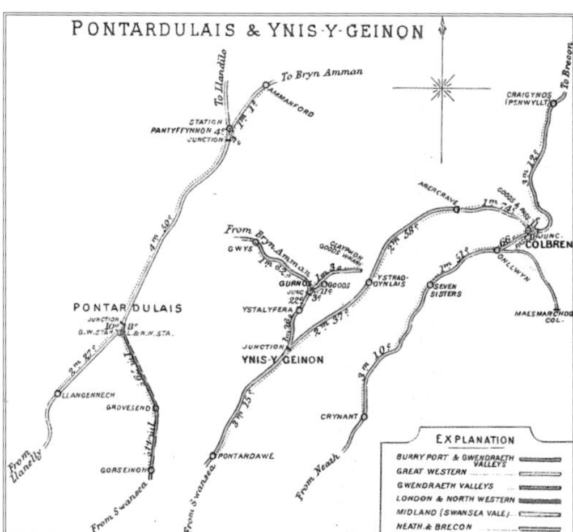

The vital link between Colbren Junction and Ynysygeinon Junction which J. Palmer Budd had foreseen in the 1845 plans for the Welsh Midland; 1913.

Railway Clearing House

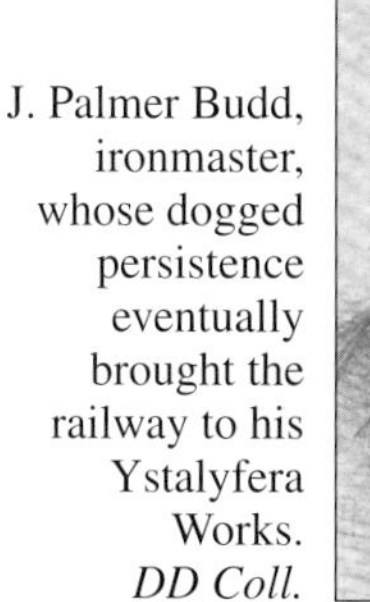

J. Palmer Budd, ironmaster, whose dogged persistence eventually brought the railway to his Ystalyfera Works.
DD Coll.

them. This was unbecoming comment from a promoter of the Welsh Midland, but he was in no way apologetic about the failure, being pleased to refer to it publicly and to blame it on the battle of the gauges. He had arrived in Ystalyfera in 1838 when aged 35 and was reputed to have a good grasp of metallurgy and economics. He came from a local family, his father E. Budd having been a coal owner. He was an able and conscientious man but difficult, opinionated and interfering. His wife was much respected in the community and it is she who earned a memorial in the local church. He successfully built up the Ystalyfera ironworks which by 1846 had six blast furnaces; the 12 furnaces in the associated tin-plate works made it the largest at the time in the world. His is an example of an ironworks which failed to convert to steel making. He reappears throughout this narrative, dogged but flawed.

Ironically, if the Welsh Midland had succeeded, there might have been a rather less complex story to tell of the entry of the LMS constituents into south Wales, but its idea persisted, and was revived in 1853 by the LNW and NAH as the Swansea Junction Extension. It finally became a reality in 1873 when the Neath & Brecon and Swansea Vale linked at the head of the Tawe valley.

The Welsh Midland's demise coincided with other priorities for the Midland. For the time being they negotiated running powers from Stoke Junction on the Birmingham & Gloucester to Worcester over the OWW; these powers were to prove the key to eventual progress towards south Wales.

The LNWR's coverage was at first glance more clearly focussed than the Midland's, even though Peterborough and Cambridge were to give it an unexpectedly eastern flavour. Its outlandish appearance in south and south-west Wales at the end of extended and broken links can be traced back to 1846. In October that year a committee was appointed to look at the possibility of acquiring the Herefordshire & Gloucestershire Canal; this was seen as part of a possible link with a project (which came to nothing) to build a line from Tring, on the London to Birmingham main line, to Cheltenham. This led to an interest in the OWW and the Worcester & Hereford project.

The penetration of south Wales was to prove difficult for both companies, but since the LNWR took the initiative, it eventually gained the best of what was available. It was left to the Midland to make the most of what remained.

In the course of the next thirty years the LNW, the Midland or their constituents, partners or victims were constantly involved in obtaining parliamentary authorisation to build railways, to convert tramroads, to run trains, to take running powers, to share facilities, or to take over one another by lease or purchase. It may therefore prove helpful for the understanding of this book to dwell on this process and briefly to summarise the means by which Parliament controlled railway promotions.

The first step was for a group of promoters to form a provisional committee to carry out a preliminary survey of the projected route; such promoters were business men or local landowners, normally with some important titles included, though Lord Cawdor who owned half the land over which the Carmarthen line from Llandilo was to run said in evidence, 'I do not think it is the part of country gentlemen to take shares even if the concern is

Starling Benson, the Swansea businessman who admitted the Midland Railway to Swansea. *Courtesy of D.I.L. Bayliffe and J.N. Harding*

Starling Benson (centre) presides over a party at his house; the gentleman seated to the left is John Biddulph who was chairman of the Llanelly Railway and Dock Co. for some 30 years. His wife is the striking figure, fourth from the right.

Courtesy of D.I.L. Bayliffe and J.N. Harding.

Thomas Savin, draper and railway promoter.

WIMM

very flourishing.' On the other hand Sir Richard Green-Price of Norton, near Presteigne was M.P. for Radnor and combined landowning with railway promotion. W.L. Banks was a solicitor in Brecon who became almost fanatically interested in railways. Both suffered serious losses. Henry Robertson was a classic Victorian entrepreneur and an imaginative facilitator who in the role of engineer-in-chief was an energetic influence within the component companies of the Central Wales Line and carefully nurtured the involvement of the LNW in that and in the Shrewsbury & Hereford and the MTA. Starling Benson of Swansea was a key local business man who saw the economic benefit of the railway to Swansea. James Biddulph of the Llanelly was a Swansea banker. The Homfrays of the Sirhowy were ironmasters, like the Baileys, J. Palmer Budd of Ystalyfera and Thomas Brown of Ebbw Vale. Savin the promoter was a salesman of genius with tremendous charisma. These men brought a variety of talents to railway promotion: toughness, vision, enthusiasm, drive, risk-taking, entrepreneurship and sometimes a touch of madness. The LNW and the Midland brought management and muscle.

Once the preliminary surveys had been made, the next step was the preparation of plans suitable for taking forward to Parliament. Such plans would be deposited in the first instance with the county registers for those counties through which the projected line was to run. These deposited plans consisted of a detailed drawing of the line of the railway, set within parallel margins to permit minor variation (or 'limit of deviation' as it was called); these plans showed the parcels of land over which the line was to pass, which were numbered and listed with their owners, tenants and current occupiers in a separate document called the Book of Reference. A separate series of drawings showed the sections of the track with the inclines, river and road crossings, and tunnels. A summary described the project and the engineer responsible signed a statement of estimated cost. These requirements and the subsequent process in Parliament were defined in Standing Orders. One such order was that deposited plans were to be presented for the following session of Parliament by 30 November each year.

By that stage it was required that the promoters had formed themselves into a company. Solicitors (known as Parliamentary Agents) who specialised in preparing and presenting Bills to Parliament would be engaged by the promoters' own solicitors to draft the Bill and arrange for it to be deposited in Parliament.

Former GWR pannier tank takes water at Hollybush on a winter's day in January 1960.
Alan Jarvis

Cynghordy viaduct viewed from an eastbound passenger train; 25 April 1963.
Alan Jarvis

If there was no opposition to the Bill, it would proceed through Parliament as an unopposed Private Local Bill. However, there was frequently opposition to projects, either from local landowning interests or commercial competitors, who, on hearing notice of a Bill, might petition Parliament against it. The House of Commons formed a committee of M.P.s to hear these petitions which acted, not surprisingly, rather in the manner of a law court, since most of the players were lawyers, and witnesses would be called by all the interested parties who would be represented by counsel. They tended to be practised in what became a specialised field and the same names keep recurring in the records. On occasions, petitions would also be presented to the House of Lords where a similar committee procedure was followed. The hand-written reports, being verbatim, emerge from the books of record as though spoken aloud and reveal something of the character of the personalities involved.

As a result of the enormous number of Bills, there was soon developed a standard content for the authorising Acts; these would rehearse the background and reasons for the Act and, after defining what was approved, would list the terms under which the authority was to be exercised; for instance, a time limit for completion was normally included, and both the NAH and LNW had cause to seek extensions of time. Before being passed, the Bill would be referred back to the promoting company to be approved by the board in a so-called Wharncliffe Meeting. This was to avoid Parliament approving Bills for which the promoters had, during the parliamentary process, lost the will to proceed. It also enabled dissenting shareholders to express their views. As we shall see, the Hereford, Hay & Brecon killed a Bill over a Wharncliffe Meeting.

Any substantial amendment or deviation from the original Act had to be referred back to Parliament and, as the process developed, many different projects would be covered in one Bill, a so-called Omnibus Bill; thus by the 1860s the

LNWR was introducing Bills with titles such as LNW (New Lines) or AP (Additional Powers) or NW (New Works), each embracing as many as ten different projects all over their network. Just as with the obtaining of development planning consent today, it was not necessary that the affected company had given prior consent to a project involving its infrastructure even if promoted by a rival company; it was left to the petitioning process in Parliament to resolve any conflict arising. The West Midland tried in this way to obtain control of the Merthyr, Tredegar & Abergavenny.

The process was very typically British: it developed empirically; there were few guiding principles, and the opinion of Parliament on such subjects as monopolies could change without notice. There was no overall plan, no national objective. Bills were the result of local stimuli, often local businesses looking for more economic transportation, and, later, local railway companies seeking to build a network and thereby grow shareholder value, and also national companies seeking to protect their markets from competitors. The iterative process by which the lines around Merthyr and Dowlais were finally resolved was expensive and time-consuming, taking some twenty years and occupying committees, lawyers and executives almost continuously, but the process was open and not noticeably corrupt. Where recourse was made to physical action, as at Hereford, it was normally because of imprecision in the law rather than the flouting of it. Most projects were sufficiently robust to survive for a hundred years; many lasted much longer.

The ravaged landscape at Dowlais as seen from the platform of the High Street Station, looking east; November 1955.

H.F. Wheeler courtesy R.S. Carpenter

An early vignette of the Beaufort viaduct.

Old Bakehouse Publications.

Chapter 2

EARLY SKIRMISHES

In 1850, Shrewsbury was connected to the national network by two lines; one the Shrewsbury & Chester, the other the Shropshire Union, which had a direct line to the LNWR at Stafford. Between Shrewsbury and Wellington this was under joint ownership with the Shrewsbury & Birmingham. Towards the south, under the direction of the versatile engineer and entrepreneur Henry Robertson, who was also engineer for the Shrewsbury & Chester, work was beginning on the Shrewsbury & Hereford (S & H) which had been authorised in 1846. In the same year the Newport, Abergavenny and Hereford (NAH) had been authorised, though this company was slow to undertake any works. The S & H opened as a single track as far as Ludlow in 1852 and reached a station near Barr's Court in Hereford in December 1853. This was shortly before the NAH opened from Barton, on the other side of Hereford, to an end-on junction with the Monmouthshire Railway at Pontypool, thence, by running powers, to the Newport docks. In 1854, a link line across Hereford completed the chain from the Dee to the Bristol Channel.

Shrewsbury was strategically important to the LNWR for its drive into south Wales, but until the opening of the Shrewsbury & Crewe line in 1858, access was only made over the joint line from Wellington; 1913.
Railway Clearing House

Henry Robertson, railway engineer, entrepreneur, facilitator, 1816-88.
Wrexham Library

The old bridge over the Severn which carried the LNWR line from Stafford into Shrewsbury Station. The junction to the right was the point from which LNWR south Wales operations began; *c.* 1875.
Shropshire County Records

Craven Arms Station, point of departure for the LNWR Central Wales Line, was also the junction for the Bishops Castle Railway. This view, taken in about 1910, gives some impression of how busy this place once was. The locomotive is the Bishops Castle's 'Carlisle'.
G.M. Perkins

In 1853 the LNWR's Shrewsbury & Crewe line was authorised; this was a strategic move to create a major link between south Wales and the north of England. In 1846, the Oxford, Worcester & Wolverhampton had been authorised. This was initially a broad gauge line under GWR patronage, but bad management caused it to run short of funds and led it into a dubious courtship with the narrow gauge LNWR. This later provided the LNW with a link between Worcester and London. The last piece of the jigsaw was the proposed Worcester & Hereford (W & H), which would link the midlands directly with south Wales.

In 1851 a key figure in this story and of the LNWR in total joined the LNWR board. He became chairman in 1861 and remained in that position for nearly 40 years, dying in office in 1899. Richard Moon was born the son of a Liverpool merchant in 1814 and lived at a house

The strategic link from Crewe to Shrewsbury opened in 1858. 'Cornwall' heads a LNWR train for Shrewsbury, 1905.
LNWR Soc.

Sir Richard Moon, LNWR chairman and proponent of the policy to drive towards Swansea.
LNWR Soc.

Worcester Foregate Street was eventually built in the centre of the city.
National Monuments Record

called 'Bevere' in Worcester. This may explain why he appears to have taken an early interest in the potential for the LNWR in south Wales, as it was in Worcester that the first rumblings of activity occurred. Worcester had been by-passed by the Birmingham & Gloucester Railway due to jealousy between the two cathedral cities, and had only recently gained access to the railway network through that small part of the Oxford, Worcester & Wolverhampton which had so far been built; this was by means of a branch off the Midland main line from Birmingham to Bristol and was operated by the Midland Railway. For the LNWR, Worcester was quite a step away, access from the south being dependent on the Midland and the OWW. The OWW was critical for the link with south Wales and it was this which lay behind the tug-of-war with the GWR over its control.

In April 1851 the LNWR board were notified by a Mr Hughes of Worcester of local discussions concerning the building of a railway which would link Worcester with Pontypool. The LNWR seem to have reacted quickly because, by mid-August, there were LNWR directors on the board of the projected Worcester & Hereford Railway, and on 15 August the LNWR board, besides noting the formation of the W & H and the existence of the already authorised NAH, determined to act 'so that by this chain when completed the whole system of the LNW and Midland Railways will be brought into direct communication with the important mineral district of south Wales'. The upshot was that the three parties, Midland, LNW, and NAH agreed to promote a W & H Bill in the 1852 session of Parliament, and Charles Liddell, who had recently been engaged as engineer to the NAH, was charged with the job of drawing up plans for the line from Worcester to Hereford.

The route chosen differed from that opened eventually 10 years later; it was designed to be as cheap as possible and was estimated to cost £220,000. From south of the Shrub Hill Station in Worcester on the OWW, a short branch was projected northward into the city centre near the corn market, while the main line skirted the city to the south and then, no doubt in order to keep clear of the Malvern Hills, passed north of both Malvern and Ledbury and over the S & H to enter Hereford by a loop round the north of the town, to an end-on junction with the NAH. Malvern lay at the end of a 1¼ mile branch line, half of which was at a gradient of 1:30. The project had failed to attract much local financial support and was dependent on backing from the LNW and the Midland. The Bill was opposed strenuously by both the GWR and the S & H and, although it was passed in the Commons, was rejected by the Lords.

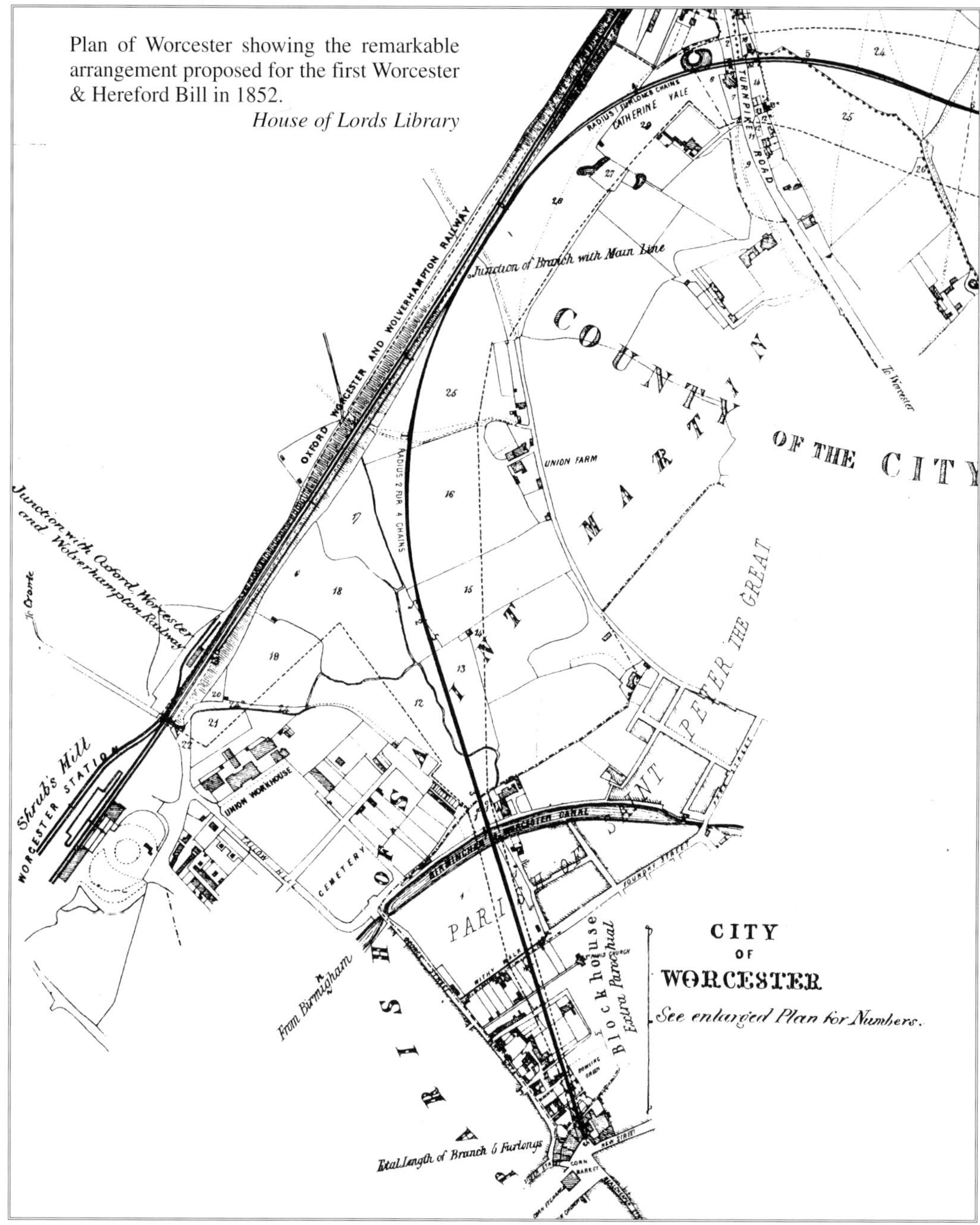

Plan of Worcester showing the remarkable arrangement proposed for the first Worcester & Hereford Bill in 1852.
House of Lords Library

The reports of the committee process cast interesting light on the issues affecting railway development at that time. The witnesses called included such famous names as Robert Stephenson and Brunel, and several important names in the region such as Henry Robertson, Thomas Brown of the Ebbw Vale Iron Co. and W.P. Price, at the time chairman of the Herefordshire & Gloucestershire Canal Co. and later chairman of the NAH, deputy chairman of the West Midland, and then chairman of the Midland. Others were local agents, landowners and businessmen. The project was undoubtedly flawed and T. Heywood, the chairman, had

Great Malvern Station on the W & H on 21 August 1947 with locomotive No. 1418 heading the 5.35 p.m. from Worcester to Colwall and No. 1338 in the bay with the 6.30 p.m. LMS branch train to Ashchurch.

W. A. Camwell

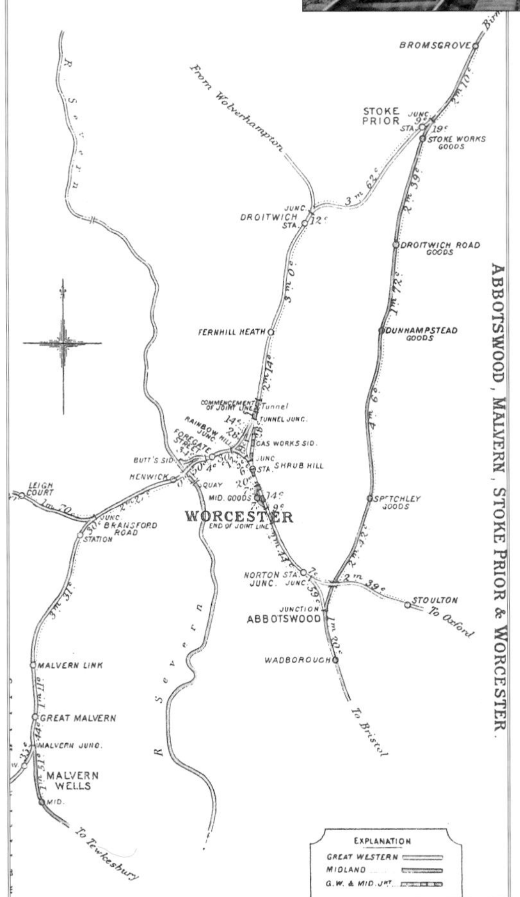

The precarious nature of the Midland's position for its leap into south Wales is clearly shown by this map of the Worcester area in 1913. The loop line from Abbotswood to Stoke Prior was the first stretch of the Oxford, Worcester & Wolverhampton Railway. From Worcester the Midland depended on the GWR (former Worcester & Hereford) line.

Railway Clearing House

clearly not taken the trouble to brief himself; cross-examined on the distance from Shrub Hill Station to the projected station near the corn market at the end of a short branch, he could only rather feebly and off-handedly say, 'Three or four minutes – I only know it by going in a cab at night.' He was challenged that since the project was dependent on LNW and Midland backing due to the small local subscription, the OWW might just as well take over the project, to which he retorted, 'Has it [the OWW] not been lying by with the weeds going [*sic*] over it for years?' A local landowner called Hornyold argued the great economic benefit to be gained from linking Worcester to the mineral wealth of south Wales, and it was he who, in response to a question as to whether there was any advantage in placing Malvern at the end of a short branch line, made the memorable response, 'I do not know that I can see any particular advantage, but it would be a very awkward thing indeed to move Malvern to the main line.' Thomas Brown of Ebbw Vale was a very convincing witness who was able to demonstrate a 4/- per ton saving on the cost of iron delivered to the Birmingham area by means of the W & H, as opposed to shipping via Gloucester. He was also interested in moving iron ore from Northamptonshire to south Wales which could be supplied to his works at 8/- per ton, or half the cost of imported or Cumbrian ore. He was pressed hard on the degree of independence of the NAH after its deal with the LNWR.

This question of big company domination underlay much of the opposition. Robertson, engineer to the S & H, was very critical of the fact that the LNWR was behind the W & H and professed that his company would not have opposed the Bill if the W & H were independent, mainly because of a fear that Mersey-bound traffic from the south would be diverted to Liverpool, rather than travelling to Birkenhead over the S & H.

The following year the parties regrouped and the GWR came forward with a rival, mixed gauge scheme (the Worcester & Hereford Junction). However, it was the revised LNW-backed scheme which won the approval of both houses, perhaps because the city of Worcester gained by revisions to the plan which took the line through the centre of the city, rather than providing a short branch, and then passed through Great Malvern and nearer to Ledbury, this time to join both the NAH and the S & H at Hereford. This improved project was estimated to cost about 50% more than that of the previous year. However, there was a sting in the tail as the Lords made consent conditional on the LNW and Midland having no part in the financing or working of the line. As a result the project collapsed.

At this point we must pause to examine the arrangements at Hereford. This relatively small city in fairly flat open country was to have an undesirably complex railway layout which caused it eventually to become surrounded by lines, with three different stations. The roots of the complexity lay in the NAH planning its route to Barton on the west of the city, and the S & H heading for a site near the canal basin and a house called Barr's Court on the east side. There seems to be no good reason why they had not considered meeting end-on at a joint station from the beginning, but in 1845 promoters were still quite isolationist in their thinking. They woke up to the benefit of through traffic in 1847 when authority was obtained by the NAH to join the S & H, but the junction was to be north of the S & H station and thus two separate stations were still envisaged. Indeed, in 1853, as though to reinforce the point, the NAH obtained authorisation for a deviation from the original 1847 link line still joining the S & H north of Barr's Court, and in 1858 moved their head office from London to their Barton Station.

Part of the complex railway network at Hereford with, in the foreground, the former NAH line from Barton to the Shrewsbury & Hereford line. On the so-called Brecon Curve a former Lancashire & Yorkshire 0-6-0 as BR No. 52525 heads three former GWR coaches *en route* to Brecon; 7 April 1951.

R.J. Doran

A summer Saturday afternoon and the 1.10 p.m. from Brecon arrives at Barr's Court Station hauled by former Midland Railway 3F BR No. 43277; 28 June 1952.

R.J. Doran

Looking north towards Shrewsbury, ex-L & Y No. 42414 leaves the NAH line and moves onto the Barton Curve ('north fork') with the 9.20 a.m. to Brecon; 21 June 1951.

W.A. Camwell, courtesy M. Lloyd

A view northward along the former NAH line with the Brecon Curve bearing away to the right towards Barr's Court; LGRP 8474, probably 1950s. *M. Lloyd Coll.*

Barton Station under flood, looking north; *c.* 1890. *M. Lloyd Coll.*

As noted above, the first plans for the Worcester & Hereford assumed a line meeting the NAH head-on, having crossed 29 ft above the Shrewsbury line with no connection; this was to ensure that traffic to and from south Wales would be routed over the W & H rather than the S & H, a typical monopolistic device of the LNW under the malign influence of the clever Huish. It was, in fact, too clever because the opposition saw through it immediately and it was one of the reasons why the first Bill for the W & H failed. Henry Robertson, engineer to the S & H, told the House of Commons Committee that he knew the NAH had wanted originally to use Barr's Court, but only until they teamed up with the LNW. Robertson's argument was subsequently justified as, once the LNW influence on the W & H was removed, the NAH used the authority of the W & H 1853 Act to make the link.

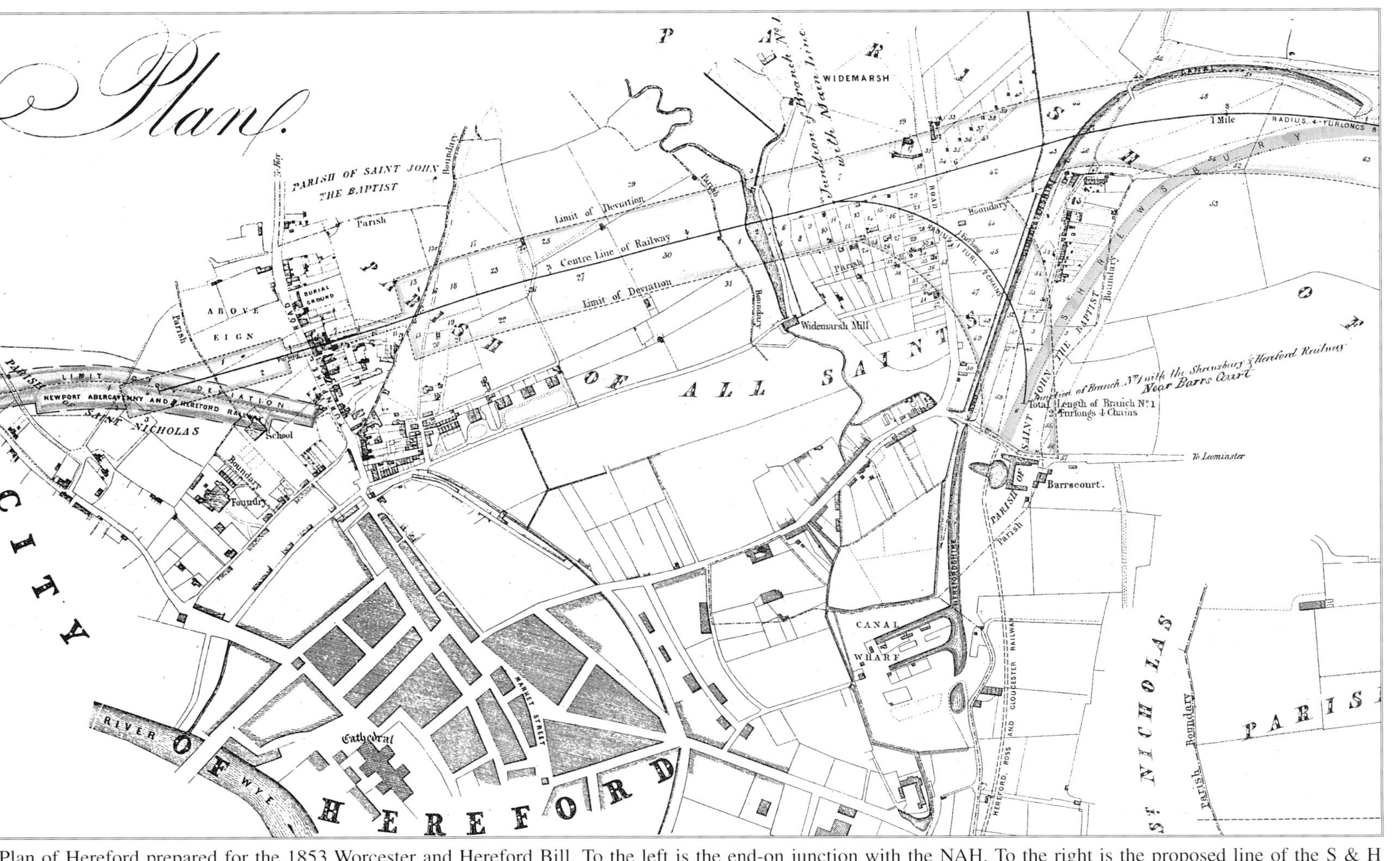

Plan of Hereford prepared for the 1853 Worcester and Hereford Bill. To the left is the end-on junction with the NAH. To the right is the proposed line of the S & H approaching Barr's Court. The Hereford, Ross & Gloucester was already envisaged from the south. The Brecon Curve is shown as part of the W & H proposal though this was not to be effected until 40 years later. The Herefordshire & Gloucestershire Canal is also shown.

House of Lords Record Office

This Act had the W & H join the S & H just north of the city, with a view to sharing the Barr's Court Station, and a further line linking across the north of the town to the NAH. In this respect it was similar to the unsuccessful GW/OWW scheme. Both included the spur (later to be known as the Brecon Curve) which would have enabled trains to run from Barton to Barr's Court without reversing; this was not destined to be built until 1893. Both schemes perpetuated the two separate stations. This was an issue which had concerned the committee

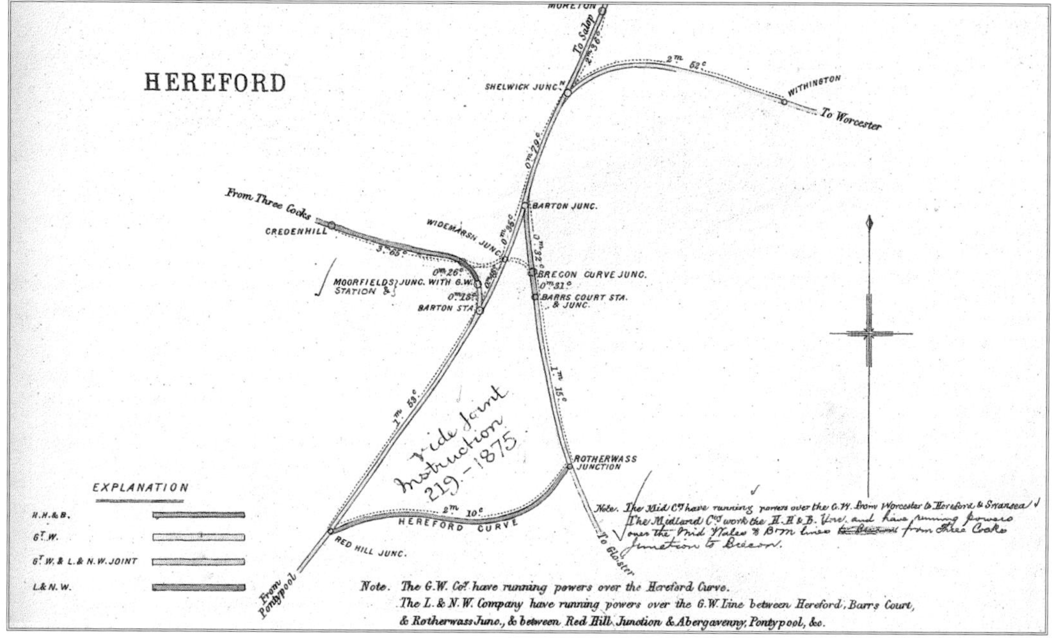

This 1870 Railway Clearing House plan of Hereford has been updated to record the Midland's progress. Both the Brecon and Barton curves are sketched in even though they were not built until 1893.

PRO RAIL 1082/8

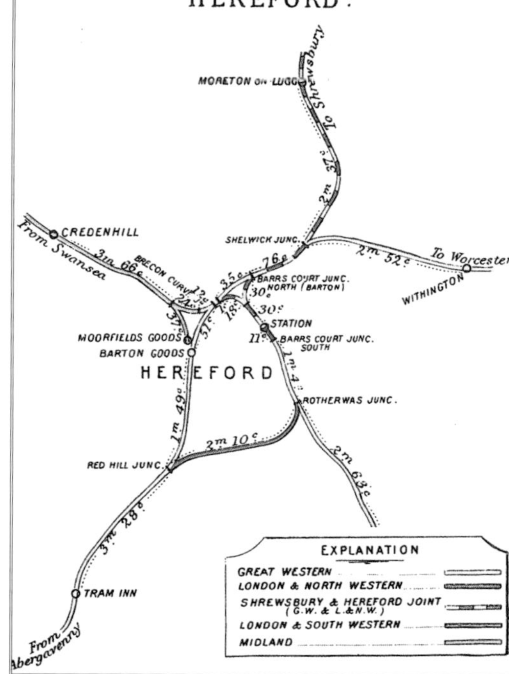

The final solution at Hereford with the 'south fork' cut short at Moorfields, but with both Brecon and Barton curves in place; 1913.

Railway Clearing House

hearing the first W & H case; it was questioned whether it was wise to have more than one railway company sharing a station. The argument ranged from passenger convenience to the disputes and even violence which had clouded shared arrangements elsewhere. Passenger convenience prevailed with the arrival from the south of the broad gauge Hereford, Ross & Gloucester at Barr's Court in 1855, though Barton was not to be totally redundant until 1893.

A further attempt in 1855 to fan the embers of the W & H and to allow LNW participation failed in Parliament. Attempts were then made to find another way of completing a project which was of great importance to the NAH, the Midland and the LNWR (and indeed to the mineral trade generally), and in 1856 the LNW board agreed to sell their remaining 9,645 shares in the W & H provided they could negotiate terms for use of the line when completed. This tactic failed and at this point the LNWR gave up the struggle. In any case, the new OWW management were now steering their company towards an improved relationship with the GWR.

Thus it was with the Midland alone that the NAH and OWW picked up the scheme in 1858 and applied to Parliament for an extension of time and the right to subscribe as companies. This was granted and the project went ahead. When the three companies, OWW, NAH and W & H were merged as the West Midland (West MR) in 1860, the Midland was left with running powers over the W & H line; these were to be the key to its eventual penetration of south Wales, and Hereford was to be its launching pad. The LNW was excluded. In the meantime an important railway connection was not made because of Parliament's distrust of big companies in general and of the LNWR in particular. This was clearly short-sighted, for some railways could only ever be justified as part of a national network. It has to be said that the LNWR's initial handling of the affair lacked sensitivity and professionalism. By the time they had pulled themselves and the project together it was too late.

Looking southward at Barr's Court Junction where, on the left, the S & H line leads to Barr's Court and ahead is the NAH line to Barton; 28 June 1952.

R.J. Doran

A rare occurrence at Barr's Court Junction with 'Hall' Class 6985 hauling a troop special from the NAH line. After the insertion of the Brecon Curve in 1893, passenger trains would not normally have had cause to use this part of the system; 28 June 1952.

R.J. Doran

Two former GWR locomotives Nos. 2287 and 2350 meet on the Barton Curve. In the middle distance is the site of the one time Moorfields Station; 1952.

R.J. Doran

Barr's Court Station with a south-bound train headed by ex-GWR No. 7025 'Sudeley Castle'; 6 August 1962.
Alan Jarvis

It is now time to return to the NAH. Since authorisation of its main line in 1846 and of the Taff Vale Extension (TVE) in 1847, it had done very little to keep its shareholders interested. Three general meetings had had to be abandoned due to the absence of a quorum, shareholders were in arrears, and an extension of two years had been obtained from the Board of Trade in the time allowed for completion of what Parliament had authorised. However, in 1851 it seems that the NAH board had realised that they had to act. According to the NAH board minutes it was they who first approached the LNWR and the Midland in a letter written by Pritchard, the company secretary on 20 March 1851. This letter made strong play of the threat of the broad gauge interests to monopolise south Wales, and proposed joint

On the former NAH line at Abergavenny Junction, ex-LNWR 'Prince of Wales' class No. 5649 arrives with a train from the north; 4 August 1931.
Courtesy J.A. Peden

An ex-LNWR locomotive acting as banker on the former NAH main line awaits its train at Abergavenny; August 1957.
Ian L. Wright

A northbound train on the former NAH at Abergavenny Junction headed by a GWR 'Badminton' class locomotive. Beyond the platform, LNWR carriages can be seen in the sidings; *c.* 1900.

Old Bakehouse Publications

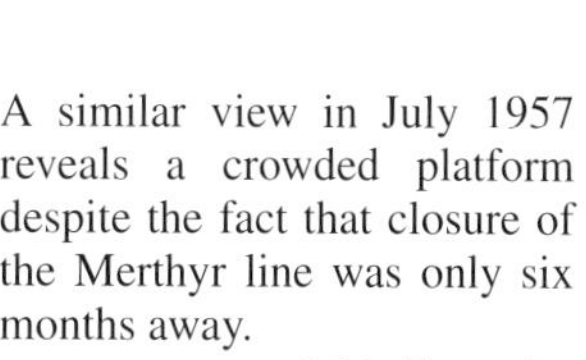

A similar view in July 1957 reveals a crowded platform despite the fact that closure of the Merthyr line was only six months away.

R.M. Casserley

development of the W & H and the payment to the NAH shareholders of 4% on the capital employed up to £500,000; the Midland and LNW were to operate the line and share any surplus profits equally. By April it was a matter of some urgency to the NAH because they had an offer from the Ebbw Vale Iron Company to take up a large block of shares. Pritchard went up to Euston seeking a quick decision, but only Huish was in the office and he offered to take up the shares himself if he could control the nomination of directors.

Negotiations continued and on 16 October 1851 the LNW Special Committee decided to recommend to the board that the NAH be worked by the LNW on the basis of shared gross receipts, the NAH taking any surplus up to 5% after expenses had been shared. This was to take effect on completion of the W & H. A minority of the committee (significant in the light of future events) voted against the proposal arguing that it was 'inexpedient' to take an interest in a railway located 100 miles from the nearest LNW owned line. The board, on this occasion, supported the minority view. However, on 10 January 1852, following a review of south Wales strategy, the board appointed the directors, Captain Carnegie and Messrs Benson and Smith, to negotiate with the NAH 'as may best secure the influence of the LNW in that undertaking'. Captain Carnegie was the leading opponent to engagement with both the W & H and the NAH due to previous bad experience with Scottish mineral railways. Fortuitously, a month later, he was recalled to active service in the Navy, and the two key figures to be involved with the NAH emerged as none other than Richard Moon and another director, Edward Tootal.

As early as the end of January 1852, fresh Heads of Agreement had been drawn up whereby the NAH were to take 4% on the capital employed, plus £1,000 office expenses, but only on completion of the W & H; merger

The NAH main line looking north from Abergavenny Junction towards the summit at Llanfihangel; early 1950s.
John Beardsmore

of the two companies was to follow. The LNW board was motivated by a desire to win favour with the board of the OWW as part of their policy of confounding the efforts of the GWR to monopolise the west midlands and south Wales. As noted earlier, the OWW was also needed to complete the LNWR's link between Worcester and London. On 7 February 1852 the board approved a policy for expansion in south Wales put forward by Moon and Tootal and on 14 February, by a majority of 17:6, approved the W & H and NAH as the vehicles for achieving the objectives and 'determined to pursue Acts and take all steps necessary to carry out the policy'. Accordingly, it agreed to this modification of the NAH deal on 19 February 1852, though not unanimously. The following day the NAH reported the agreement to their shareholders with a slightly different slant, referring to a half yearly payment to the NAH of £10,000 plus the cost of rates, taxes and repairs, the LNW receiving working expenses and interest on working capital. Both were to share the surplus profits.

The steps taken by the LNW in pursuit of the strategy were coherent and forceful:

The NAH main line at Pontrilas, junction for the Golden Valley Line to Hay, seen on a summer's afternoon early this century.
Courtesy J.A. Peden

1. We have already noted the agreement associated with the promotion of the W & H.
2. The LNWR bought 1,940 shares in the NAH representing about 8%. These were in the names of various LNW executives.
3. In the restructured NAH board, three LNW-nominated directors were appointed, initially Captain Carnegie, Richard Moon and Blake, but after Carnegie's return to the Navy, Edward Tootal took his place and remained on the board until the demise of the NAH in 1860.
4. During the summer of 1852 the LNWR directors encouraged the NAH to look further west than the Taff.

This was the objective of the Taff Vale Extension (TVE) which had been authorised in 1847. It was now proposed that the NAH build what was called the Swansea Junction Extension Railway; this was to be a line westward over the Taff at Quakers Yard, and through the mountain barrier into the Cynon valley below Aberdare. There a branch was to link with the Taff Vale Railway's Aberdare branch while the main line headed up the valley, and then, in a broad arc over the high ground, cross the Mellte river on a 410 yd long and 307 ft long viaduct similar to that destined to be built at Crumlin. The abutments were to be 55 ft and 19 ft, indicating the steepness of the valley side. A second viaduct over the Neath was to be 267 ft high and 400 yds long but with 60 ft abutments. The line reached the Tawe valley near Colbren, and then descended to Swansea. This project was actively pursued both in Parliament and locally. J. Palmer Budd, having offered his services with characteristic self-assurance, was now a member of the NAH Board, as he said, 'to put new vitality into the company'. He represented the company at a public meeting in Swansea held in April 1853. He was particularly interested in the project because a short branch line was included up to Ystalyfera, where his works were located.

In October 1852, Moon and Tootal conducted a survey of the opportunities for the LNW in south Wales. Because it throws interesting light on the way managements thought at that time, their report is worth reproducing (with original punctuation and spelling):

We have to report that the arrangements for the prosecution of the Swansea Junction Railway, on the direction of which we were placed by a vote of last Board, are proceeding and that, with some assistance the project will be in a position for Parliament in the ensuing session.

We assume that, with Broad Gauge Lines open to Birmingham and with the avowed determination of the Great Western company to apply for powers to lay down that Gauge to Birkenhead and into Lancashire: the Board will become all the more earnest in its determination to prosecute and encourage Narrow Gauge lines throughout South Wales:– the chief source of the 'Thro Traffic' of the Great Western Company which notoriously is, though heretofore ending at Bristol, South Wales Traffic.

In this state of affairs it may be opportune to recapitulate the position of Narrow Gauge Interests in South Wales.

In the first place, the Newport and Abergavenny Lines (now under Traffic Agreements with this Company) are rapidly proceeding.

The Main Line (Hereford to Pontypool) will be completed by August next year.

The land for the Quaker's Yard Branch is bought from end to end, and the Works have just been let & if the Funds can be raised with sufficient rapidity that Extension will be completed by June 1854, if not earlier.

The Newport & Pontypool Line of the Monmouthshire Co. is opened for Traffic & connects the Newport, Abergavenny & Hereford Company Line with Newport.

The 'Western Valley Lines' are also working and give communications up the Vallies from Newport, to Ebbw Vale Rhymney & other seats of the Iron Manufacture.

The 'Taff Vale Co.'s' Lines from Cardiff to Merthyr Tydvil and from the Junction near Quakers Yard to Aberdare and Hirwan, have long been at Work.

The Swansea Valley Railway runs from the Southern side of the Town of Swansea up the Western Slope of the Swansea Valley: and is opened for a distance of above 9 Miles.

This Company had a Treaty with the Broad Gauge Interests which has since been repudiated: but the discussion of which has recently & since the proposition of the Swansea Junction been renewed.

The 'Llanelly Railway' runs from the Port of Llanelly to the head of the Llanelly Valley.

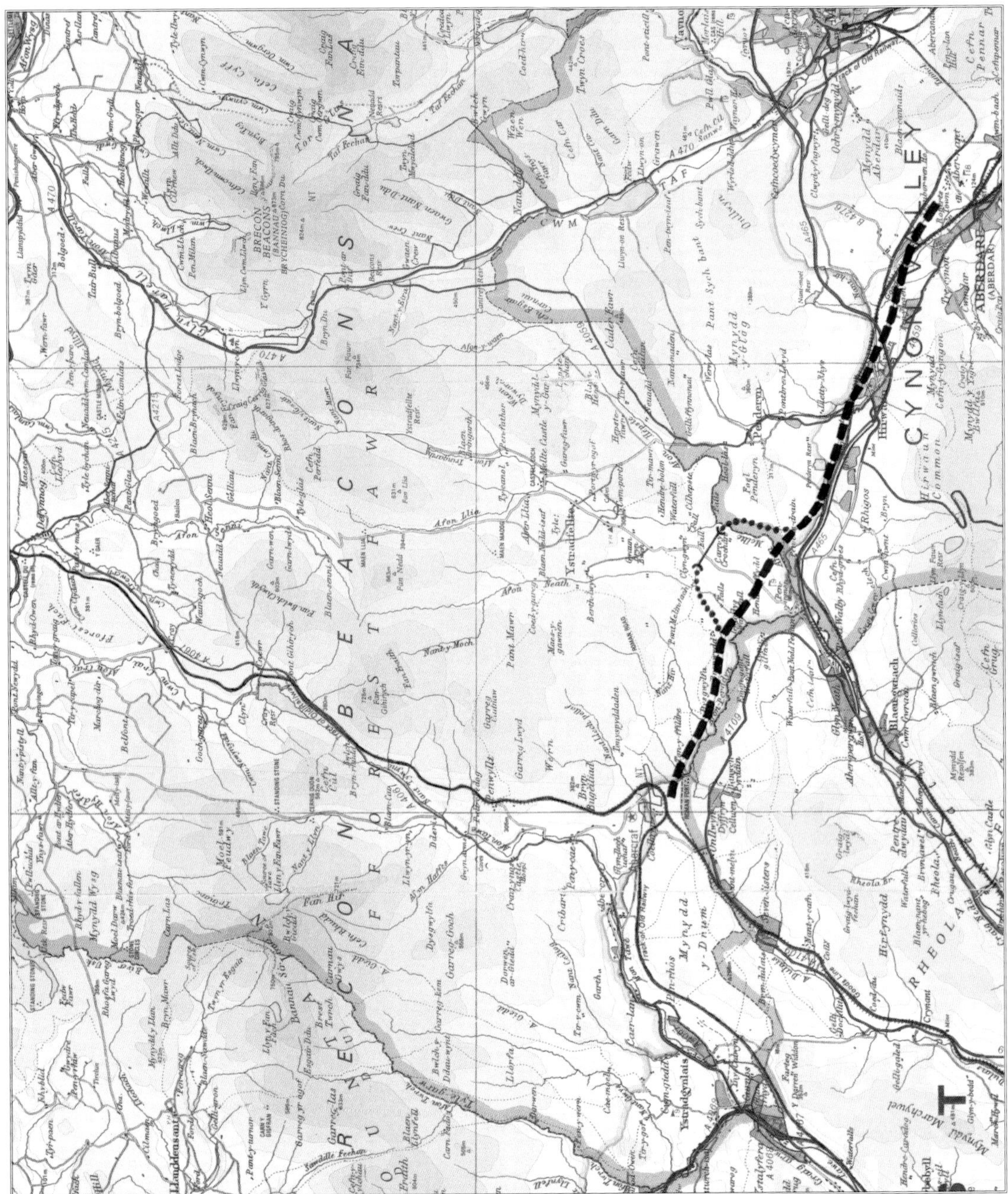

Part of the route of the Swansea Junction Extension Railway is indicated on this map of Fforest Fawr and the Brecon Beacons. The heavy broken line indicates the path proposed in 1853; this was amended in 1854 as indicated by the row of dots in order to reduce the height of the crossing of the Neath and Mellte valleys. The route of the later Neath & Brecon is in black.

John Bartholomew and GBJ

The Board will bear in mind that at the back of all the South Wales Ports, are Vallies running right up the Country, in which Vallies the principal Works Iron, Copper, and Tin Works are situated.

This being therefore the actual position of the Narrow Gauge in South Wales, & the situation of the Manufacturing Establishments, – it is proposed by Means of the 'Swansea Junction

Railway' to connect together the whole of the Narrow Gauge Lines, and to bring them by means of the Worcester & Hereford Line into direct and continuous communication with the Midland and London and North Western Railways system.

The 'Swansea Junction Line' will therefore commence at the new 'Swansea Docks' now in course of construction (and which will cover 18 Acres of Ground) & will go up the East side of the Swansea Valley passing several very important Works, crossing & joining the Swansea Valley Railway to the summit.

From this point a Branch of 5 Miles will connect it with the Llanelly Railway, to the Westward.

It will proceed onwards round the head of the Vallies to Abcrdare & thence to the Quakers Yard Extension of the 'Newport, Abergavenny and Hereford Co.' the whole length will be 43 Miles

Typical Midland activity forms the backcloth to the filling in of the Swansea North Dock in 1930.
GW/WIMM

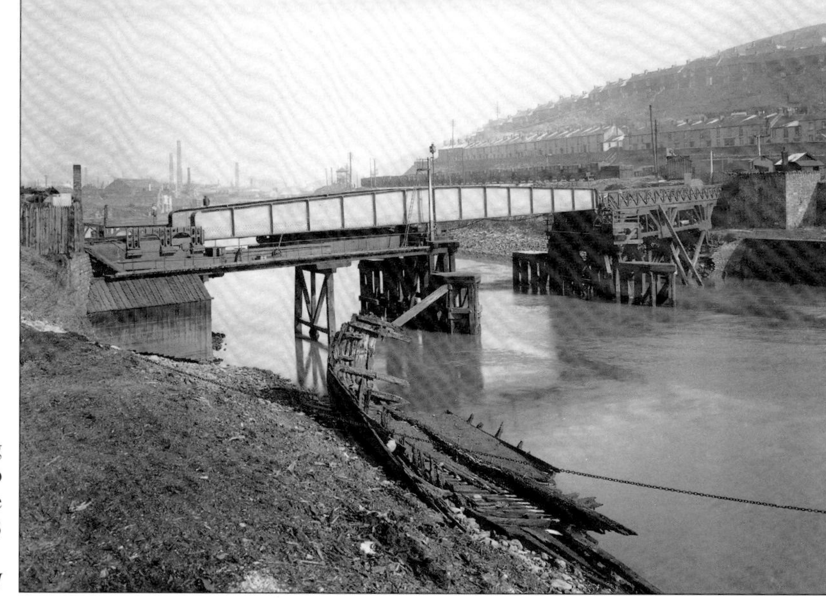

The Midland's swing bridge connection to the west bank of the Tawe in Swansea; 13 March 1928.
GW/WIMM

Midland Railway Dock shunting engine No. 1523, built in 1903 to a design by Johnson. Compare the location with that of the previous two photographs; *c.* 1908.
E. Pouteau, courtesy R.H. Marrows

Provided proper arrangements can be made with the Taff Vale & Swansea Valley Co.s the length of Line to be applied for may probably be reduced to about 29 or 30 Miles.

The Estimate for the whole 43 Miles, double Line is about £400,000: the Engineer applying his actual experience in the Construction of the Newport, Abergavenny & Hereford Line, reports that the Line can be made without doubt for an Average Cost of £10,000 per Mile.

Supposing it made, all the important Mineral Ports of South Wales except Neath: viz Llanelly, Swansea, Cardiff, & Newport, with the Districts with which they are connected could be joined to our system; and would feed the 1200 Miles of Line, of which the London & North Western & Midland Systems consist.

That all this can be effected at so small an Outlay of Capital is unprecedented –

That it can be so done is the result of a combination of circumstances of which the London & North Western Co. should profit; and which may not, indeed cannot, exist a Year hence.

For in the first place, all the Narrow Gauge Lines of South Wales are at present detached: & divided into separate & small Interests:- Again they are at present at War with the Broad Gauge.

The Public of Swansea are strongly in favour of the 'Swansea Junction' project as now proposed.

The Great Landed Proprietors of South Wales– the Duke of Beaufort and the Marquis of Bute, tho' hitherto supporting Great Western interests, have so strong a desire for a connection with the narrow gauge system that they are disposed warmly to support the project the former amongst other reasons in development of the Swansea Docks.–

Then the landowners are just now generally speaking disposed to sell their land at agricultural value.–

If the 'Swansea Junction' project goes on it will be this Session in Parliament without any competing or counter schemes in opposition.– But the state of things may be riversed, if the breathing time of another session be given to the Great Western: & its allies.– The 'Swansea Valley' Compy may be arranged with – that line may pass over to the Great Western; Landowners may be bought off; & even the project now proposed may become a Broad Gauge project & be successful, in which case the country would be closed to us finally.–

Already renewed overtures have been made to the Swansea Valley Company thro' the Vale of Neath (broad gauge) Co. but the parties in our interest at Swansea one of whom is a Director of the 'Swansea Valley' Line are confident of being able to keep the discussion pending long enough to prevent any hostile project being in time for Parliament in the coming session.

With Broad Gauge Lines from Birkenhead & Manchester to Shrewsbury, with the Shrewsbury and Hereford Line also turned into Broad Gauge, (which its Engineer has publicly stated it is to be, if Parliament assents next Session) with the Broad Gauge Hereford, Ross & Gloucester (now constructing) & the extensions of that line proposed to be made so as to afford, a communication with the mixed gauge Oxford, Worcester & Wolverhampton at Worcester on the one hand, and the Vale of Neath Broad Gauge line at Merthyr on the other,– there would only want this extension to complete the Broad Gauge possession of South Wales, in such event the narrow gauge lines must become Broad, or be seriously jeopardised.–

This is a subject which should be fully discussed; & considered; & we beg to recommend that, next week, if the Midland Joint Committee meet in London a Sub Committee from the Boards of the London & North Western & Midland Companies (the former to be now nominated) should meet the Chairman & a deputation from the Newport, Abergavenny & Hereford Company to confer upon the position of affairs and report to the next Board.–

In the meantime, we would recommend that the expenses of placing the Swansea Junction project in Parliament –i.e. all expenses up to 31 December– plans, references, notices etc. should be provided for by subscription, the amounts being repaid if the scheme proceeds either independently or as an extension of the Newport, Abergavenny & Hereford.–

The Engineer, Mr Liddell, and the Solicitor of the Newport, Abergavenny & Hereford Company Mr Farquhar have agreed to undertake, under the circumstances that, these expenses shall not exceed £3000 for the whole 43 miles– of this sum £2300 has been already raised by subscription.–

We recommend the Board to subscribe a sum not exceeding £350 towards the Balance & suggesting to the Board of the Midland Company to do the same.–

Before concluding this report we would draw attention to the position of the London & North Western Company consequent upon the opening of the Birmingham & Oxford Line;

The argument of the Chairman of the Great Western before his Proprietors was the very simple one– 'We can compete for London & North Western Traffic in their best districts– they cannot compete for ours– & therefore a settlement with them must involve a complete recognition of our position– must give us the share of Traffic which that position commands–- without abatement for any chance of counter competition– & must be simply an arrangement securing to both parties the amount of Extra loss resulting from a great reduction of Prices, or in other words from ' injurious competition.'–

Had this Company had the uninterrupted and absolute possession of a Road into South Wales, namely, Worcester & Hereford,– how greatly altered would have been these premises!!

Indeed let us not forget that the Great Western Management shewed by their desperate Opposition to the Worcester & Hereford Scheme, their full recognition of the extreme damage to their position which the passing of that scheme would effect.

We are convinced that the more the Board investigate the subject, the more will they see the advantage– the sound policy and necessity of a complete connection with the vast Mineral & Manufacturing Districts of South Wales.

A portion of the Empire which already consumes, – 4,000,000 Tons per Annum of raw Minerals in producing its 750,000 Tons per Annum of Manufactured Iron; which possesses the largest portion of the Copper Trade of Britain; which exports already more than 3,000,000 Tons of Coal; the Population of which increases in a more rapid ratio than that of any other District and the Mineral resources of which are boundless!!!

Richard Moon

Edward Tootal

Such was the enthusiasm for south Wales of the man who was to become chairman of the LNW in 1861.

During 1853, as the day for opening the NAH from Hereford to Pontypool approached, the attraction increased of having the LNW work the line immediately, rather than wait for the uncertain completion date of the W & H. On 28 July a sub-committee of the NAH board was appointed to take up again the terms of the traffic agreement with the LNW; they were thinking in terms of 3½% in Year 1, rising to 4% in Year 2; the terms of the original agreement would apply once the W & H was open, but significantly they were already wanting to delay the opening of the Crumlin viaduct from July to September 1854. On 31 August the so-called Supplemental Agreement was made and a second such agreement covered the TVE, the whole dependent on completing the Crumlin viaduct by September 1854. Moon and Tootal both took part in the negotiations. In October 1853, when the line from Pontypool to Hereford was nearly ready, Huish travelled by train all the way from Newport to Hereford and reported, 'the line appears admirably constructed'.

The NAH committee of the LNW, on which Moon, Benson and Admiral Moorsom sat, was

Passenger Receipts
to 30 June 1854.—

Capt Huish laid on the Table the following return showing the earnings of the Passenger Trains for the halfyear ending 30 June 1854

Name of Station	Classes 1st	2nd	3rd	Day 1st	Day 2nd	Total No of Passengers	Total amount £	s	d
Hereford	645	2,306	7,423	171	1256	11,801	1,403	10	8
Tram Inn	59	472	1525	7	431	2494	123	19	7
St Devereux	57	380	1491	28	577	2,533	121	7	5
Pontrilas	122	873	2605	107	1861	5,508	417	11	10
Pandy	28	271	2142	13	412	2,861	128	1	—
Llanfihangel	31	264	1804	31	241	2,371	96	0	7½
Abergavenny	1392	5631	12873	241	1654	21,791	2,506	13	2½
Penpergwm	279	797	1777	61	394	3,308	147	17	2
Llanvair	87	320	1073	36	310	1,826	101	14	2½
Nantyderry	219	251	1198	89	146	1,903	91	6	4
Little Mill	159	891	2846	28	390	4,314	214	12	10
Pontypool Road	257	2362	5031	46	1071	8,767	739	4	10
Pontnewydd	54	351	359	10	84	858	43	12	8½
Newport	1397	4789	6316	132	616	13,250	2420	18	4½
Total —						83,585	£8,556	10	10

Statement of passenger receipts for the first half year of NAH operations presented to the LNWR's NAH Committee in July 1854.
PRO RAIL 410/505

Proposed Staff of the Newport, Abergavenny and Hereford Railway

Description of Situation	Hereford (Passenger 1st Class Goods)	Tram Inn	St Devereux	Pontrilas (Passenger 2nd Class Goods)	Pandy	Llanvihangel	Abergavenny (Passenger 1st Class Goods)	Llangattock	Llanfair	Little Mill	Pontypool (Passenger 1st Class Goods)	Newport	Total Per annum £	s.	d.
General Traffic Superintendent	Mr Leyland Warrington £250 ✓	–	–	–	–	–	–	–	–	–	–	By Ordinary appt	£250	0	0
Station Master	1. Baker £130 ✓	–	–	1 @ £90 ✓	–	–	1. Feake @ £120 ✓	–	–	–	1 @ £120	1 @ £120	✓ 580	0	0
Booking Clerks	1 Youth 10/- per Week ✓	–	–	Youth 10/- p. wk		–	1. Youth 10/- per Week	–	–	–	1. Youth 10/- p. Week	–	78	0	0
Goods Clerks	1 Experienced Man £100	–	–	–	–	–	1. Assist £70	–	–	–	1. Assist £70	–	240	0	0
Porters	1. Parcel porter (Boy) 21/- per Week; 4. other porters 16/- per Week	–	–	–	–	–	–	–	–	–	–	–	–	–	–
Police booking		1 – 20/-	1 – 20/-	2 @ 16/-	1 – 20/-	1 – 20/-	3 @ 16/-	1 – 20/-	1 – 20/-	1 – 20/-	3 @ 16/-	–	700 / 364	0 / 0	0 / 0
Police	2 @ 17/6	–	–	1 @ 17/6	–	–	2 @ 17/6	–	–	–	2 @ 17/6	–	308	0	0
Guards	2 @ 23/-	–	–	–	–	–	–	–	–	–	–	–	120	0	0
Breaksman	4 @ 20/-	–	–	–	–	–	–	–	–	–	–	–	208	0	0
													£2,848	0	0

The LNW's close attention to NAH affairs is demonstrated by this draft staff plan prepared in 1853.
PRO RAIL 410/504

LNWR penetration of south Wales in the early 1860s.

A Newport train, hauled by a Crewe-type 2-4-0 locomotive, is portrayed at the old station, Pontypool Road. A former 0-6-0 locomotive passes with a freight train from the Taff Vale Extension. [*GBJ*]

LNWR penetration of south Wales in the early 1920s.
A Beames 0-8-4T hauls a coal train from the Sirhowy valley on to the TVE at Bird-in-hand, bound for the Rhymney valley. The GW 2-6-0 heads towards Pontypool Road. [*GBJ*]

at this time considering urgently the vehicle requirements. For four passenger trains a day they estimated that two sets of carriages would be sufficient between Newport and Hereford. For the goods traffic they decided to order initially 1,000 wagons. Cunard had indicated a requirement for steam coal of 100,000 tons p.a. at Birkenhead and 300,000 at Liverpool, and they seem, by a rough calculation, to have estimated that they would need 600 wagons for every 100,000 tons in a year. They foresaw demand reaching 1,500,000 tons.

But in the same year, 1853, the LNW suffered three rebuffs from Parliament:

1. The banning of the LNWR and Midland from financial involvement in the Worcester & Hereford.
2. Advice from the Cardwell Committee against merging with the NAH.
3. The rejection of the first Swansea Junction Extension Bill.

It is not clear why this scheme failed, though the committee proceedings hint at some suspicion as to the financial capacity and management capability of the NAH who had taken a long time to implement their 1846 enabling Act. There was also some determined opposition by the Vale of Neath and Swansea Vale. The arguments of Benjamin Hall Blyth, engineer to the Glasgow & South Western and Great North of Scotland Railways may have carried weight; he succinctly expressed his objections as 'viaducts, gradients and duplication'. Liddell, the highly competent NAH engineer, gave a convincing rebuttal of the argument about the viaducts being too high, but the line did duplicate much of the Vale of Neath which was only just in the process of opening. Thomas Brown of Ebbw Vale emphasised the importance of access to the sea at Mumbles for workmen engaged in the ironworks and mines to go bathing, but, as this had also been argued in the case for the Vale of Neath, it perhaps heightened the sense of duplication. In 1854 a further attempt was made to get parliamentary approval. In order to reduce the height of the viaducts, Liddell took the line further up the Mellte and Neath valleys which necessitated a tunnel 1,300 yds long, but in spite of the Mellte viaduct being reduced to 264 yds 226 ft high and the Neath to only 88 yds long and 100 ft high, this was to no avail. An interesting addition was made by extending the Ystalyfera branch to Brynamman; this forshadowed the line later built by the Swansea Vale but which was not to be completed for another ten years.

After the opening of the NAH in January 1854, the relationship between the LNW and NAH soon became uneasy. The NAH complained at the manner in which the LNW were managing their railway; receipts at £10 per mile per week were, for example, half those on the neighbouring Monmouthshire Railway, due partly to inadequate locomotive capacity. In what smacks strongly of the scheming Huish, the LNW were also refusing to allow the NAH to route traffic over the Shrewsbury & Chester. When the NAH suggested a joint committee to improve matters, it was reluctantly conceded in March 1854, to the extent that the NAH representatives were to be invited to attend the meetings of the LNW's NAH committee. On 9 June the chairman of the NAH, Captain Fitzmaurice, wrote to the LNW chairman, Lord Chandos, to complain at the management of the line; he sought an assurance that the LNW were still serious about working with the NAH, and stressed that if the LNW wished to treat the NAH as what he termed a 'fighting line', then it would be better to be open about it and terminate. Alternatively, a Joint Management Committee should be established. On 17 June Chandos replied assuring Fitzmaurice of the LNW's good intentions; he was against joint committees as he believed in responsibilities being clear and unambiguous, but agreed to a trial, with either side having the right to terminate any aspect of the agreement by three or six month's notice. The committee was to meet fortnightly on dates which fitted with Huish's busy diary, so that he could attend. On 4 July the committee asked to see a return showing the plant in use on the railway and this was produced on 10 July. It revealed :

8 1st Class carriages
8 2nd " "
8 3rd " "
5 passenger brake-vans
6 horse boxes
6 carriage trucks
350 goods waggons (rather less than earlier proposed)
3 brake-vans
25 cattle trucks
8 timber trucks
4 passenger locomotives
3 goods "

When Fitzmaurice in August requested Chandos' intervention to subsidise the NAH costs incurred in connection with the unsuccessful parliamentary efforts to get the Swansea Junction Bill passed, Chandos replied that perhaps the agreement should be terminated.

It will be recalled that it was a condition of the agreement to include the TVE in the deal with the LNW that it was dependent upon the line being open as far as Crumlin by September 1854. Unfortunately, due to financial constraints, this condition was not to be fulfilled and on 8 August 1854 the LNW's Special Affairs Committee seem to have taken this as an opportunity to withdraw from all agreements between the two companies. No doubt they had recently been informed of the failure of the second Swansea Junction Bill.

This second defeat of the Swansea project was a serious matter for the LNWR, coming one year after exclusion from the W & H, and it caused J. Palmer Budd to turn to the Swansea Vale to achieve the improvement in communication he was seeking (see Chapter 6). On 11 August the LNW shareholders were told 'circumstances have arisen which have compelled the directors to decline proceeding with the working arrangements on the terms now proposed'; the LNW would, however, 'willingly assist by friendly cooperation in developing the traffic of that line'. In the same month Richard Moon resigned from the NAH board. The only sign of sustained interest in the NAH was that Edward Tootal remained on the board; not only did he continue to attend meetings, but he also took an active part in committees. With a feeling of intense frustration, from October 1854 the NAH took over operation of their line. For a time the LNW continued to loan vehicles, but these were summarily withdrawn on 1 April 1855.

This change in attitude by the LNWR is not immediately understandable. On the one hand, the NAH was isolated from the rest of the LNW system. At that time the nearest points were Shrewsbury and just north of Oxford, so even Worcester was only accessible by running powers over the OWW and the Midland. This had not, however, prevented the LNWR from initiating a somewhat circuitous service between Worcester and Euston. In 1854 Parliament barred the merger of the LNWR with the Midland against a background of a fairly general distrust of LNWR methods and a fear of monopolies. Captain Mark Huish, while dynamic and clever, had created many enemies and was to retire early from the position of General Manager in 1858.

On the other hand, the possibility of running powers over the S & H from Shrewsbury must have been within contemplation. As early as the spring of 1854, the LNW had been checking on the terms of Brassey's lease. A working arrangement with the NAH could well have been maintained within the requirements of Parliament; positive cooperation and active support could have avoided the NAH slipping into the hands of the GW. The desire to continue the strategy is demonstrated by the retention of Tootal on the NAH board; this can hardly have been an oversight. The NAH had serious financial difficulties in building the TVE which kept on causing delays in work on the Crumlin viaduct, and this no doubt heightened the concerns of the minority on the board about possible financial exposure arising from an agreement to work with the NAH. But to give up completely, for probably little cost, an opportunity to control an important route into the valleys of south Wales does seem short-sighted. More so because this was part of a clearly identified and articulated strategy. Within six years, Moon himself was actively involved in gaining control of an alternative and much less attractive vehicle in the form of the Merthyr

Tredegar & Abergavenny Railway, though admittedly by then progress was being made in building the relationship with the S & H.

Something more must have happened to cause such a reversal. The passing of the Bill for the Shrewsbury & Crewe line had no doubt turned attention to the possibility of reaching Swansea through central Wales. There is no evidence but perhaps in the corridors at Westminster, Chandos was given a strong hint that the LNW should slow down. No doubt, now that merger with the Midland had been stopped by Parliament, the minority on the board, who had been opposed to involvement with the NAH at the outset, were able to highlight the LNWR's exposure. Perhaps Chandos hoped that Tootal would be able to keep a sufficient eye on events to avoid disaster and keep the options open. Whatever the truth of the matter, from this distance it looks like a lost opportunity.

Then after 1860 the mood changed. At the LNWR the virtuous Moon was pre-eminent and the pirate, Huish, had gone; the GWR which had, at least in its own eyes, occupied the moral high ground, revealed to universal astonishment that it had decided to sup with the devil and create a merger with the West Midland. This had been prompted by a threat by the West Midland to create another approach to north-west London from the west midlands which had united even the GWR and LNW in opposition. From 1 July 1861, the GWR leased the West Midland.

This new alliance alarmed the Shrewsbury & Hereford which after a shakey start had become a very successful small railway. It was producing 6% dividends and earning £40 per mile per week which was nearly as good as the Taff Vale Railway. Its success was due to competent management by Brassey of his operating contract, and in particular to the skill of the young man he had been clever enough to identify and had appointed as his general manager, while still in his early twenties. This young man, George Findlay, who later became General Manager of the LNWR, was the son of a railwayman; he had left school at 14 and become a stone mason. In later life he was able

Sir George Findlay, the stone mason who became general manager of the largest corporation in the world, the LNWR. As such he contributed to the building of that railway's great reputation.
Courtesy of Jack Simmons

to point to the stones in the walls of the engine shed at Camden Town which he himself had shaped. He was a quietly able man and was to contribute greatly to the high reputation acquired by the LNWR by the end of the century.

In July 1860 the S & H was involved in a meeting with the LNW about the Central Wales Line and Swansea (see Chapter 5). On 9 October an agreement was made between the LNW, the S & H, the Knighton, and the Central Wales by which running powers were exchanged and the LNW guaranteed a return to the Knighton shareholders by undertaking to give a rebate on their rates sufficient to ensure a 5% return; the S & H undertook to double their line between Shrewsbury and Craven Arms, once the Central Wales Line was complete. The S & H board expressly welcomed their contact with the LNW directors. When in 1861 they began to feel uncomfortable at being surrounded by the combination of the GWR and the West Midland and by the impending opening of the W & H, it was not altogether surprising that they looked with favour on this new grouping.

At the former LNWR shed at Hereford, a trio of pre-grouping locomotives with, to the left, a 'Prince of Wales' with Walschaert's valve gear No. 25726, and, on the right, a former L & Y 0-6-0.

W. A. Camwell/ M. Lloyd Collection

Brassey's contract was due to expire in 1862, and on 2 May 1861 the LNW made an offer to lease the S & H, but in statesmanlike manner proposed that the GW be a joint lessee. The S & H were quick to accept the proposed 6% return. They, who in 1852 and 1853 had argued before parliamentary committees against the malign and dominating influence of the LNW, now offered their company to it in perpetuity. Times had certainly changed. Even more remarkable is the attitude of the LNW in offering a share in it to the GWR and West Midland. This was churlishly rejected by the GWR who proceeded to oppose the Bill to authorise the lease in Parliament. This opposition was to no avail. Parliament had now realised that railway amalgamations were inevitable and that even the LNW should participate. What is even more surprising is the magnanimity with which the LNW again offered to share the S & H lease with the GWR and its partner. This time they grudgingly accepted and the joint lease took effect from 1 July 1862. The GWR then set about a further series of mergers involving the South Wales Railway and the Vale of Neath, and in the process became virtually bankrupt. By the middle of the decade, it was therefore inclined to become more co-operative. With the death of Brunel in 1859 and its success in acquiring the standard gauge 'fighting Shrewsbury's', it began to appear that the days of the broad gauge might be numbered.

One of the benefits to the LNW of this round of bargaining was that they obtained the services of George Findlay as their Shropshire and South Wales representative. Simultaneously, with LNW connivance, Savin appointed Findlay as manager of the line between Oswestry and Llanidloes, the HHB, the B & M, and the 'Old Rumney'. This only ended when Findlay got cold feet about some of the companies for which he had become responsible. On mentioning his worries to Richard Moon, he was transferred to Euston to become General Goods Manager of the LNW in 1865. He got out in time as Savin was bankrupt by 1866.

There was another and more profound benefit from the lease of the S & H; this arose from the bargaining over the GWR lease of the West Midland. For the price of not opposing the lease, the S & H had been granted running powers over the NAH in 1860. These powers the LNWR inherited, thereby gaining access not only to the NAH but also to its Taff Vale Extension and, thence, to Swansea over the Vale of Neath. This, by 1864, had become a mixed gauge railway. Indeed, it was in an endeavour to unscramble this penetration by the LNW into south Wales that the GWR had sought in vain to get Parliament to ban the whole deal. The acquisition of a share in the S & H was a major breakthrough for the LNW; the loss of involvement in the W & H had been a set-back, but the S & H unlocked the door to south Wales, as the GWR were only too painfully aware. By a further arrangement with the Monmouthshire

Railway in 1863, the LNWR obtained running powers from Pontypool to Newport. In some respects it recovered much of what it had lost in the NAH. In addition, in 1862, it obtained the lease of the Merthyr, Tredegar & Abergavenny, its first sole operation in south Wales. In any case, by 1858 the Central Wales Line was beginning to be manifest (see Chapter 5).

While the LNW had been caught up in this frenzy of activity the Midland had been thinking of other things, in particular its London extension, and the LNW was to make some further significant strides in south Wales before the Midland found an attractive opportunity.

16

L. & N. W. GOODS TRAINS,

BETWEEN

Swansea, Merthyr, and Abergavenny Junction.

APRIL, 1868.

UP.—WEEK DAYS.

Dist.	STATIONS.	1 arr.	1 dep.	2 arr.	2 dep.
		p.m.	p.m.	p.m.	p.m.
...	SWANSEA	...	...	...	2 0
...	New Neath	...	...	...	2 20
...	Old Neath	...	...	...	2 25
7¾	Neath Junction	...	..	...	2 35
9	Aberdylais	...	...	...	2 45
16¼	Glyn Neath	...	...	...	3 15
22¾	Hirwain	...	...	3 50	4 25
26	Aberdare	...	..	4 40	4 55
29	Middle Duffryn	...	...	...	5 5
30¼	Mountain Ash	...	...	5 10	5 15
...	Merthyr Tydvil	...	12 30	...	...
...	Dowlais Branch Junc.	12 33	12 37	...	...
...	Plymouth Siding	12 46	12 50	...	...
33½	Quaker's Yard	1 10	1 15	...	5 30
38½	Rhymney Junction	1 35	2 0	5 50	5 55
40½	Tredegar Junction	...	2 10	...	...
43	Crumlin	...	2 20	...	...
43¾	Crumlin Junction	...	...	..	6 15
...	Blaendare	...	2 40	...	6 30
49	Pontypool Road	2 55	3 5	6 50	6 55
59½	ABERGAVENNY JUNC.	3 45	3 55	7 40	7 50
80¾	HEREFORD	5 20	5 50	9 20	..

No. 1 Up Train to Shunt at Pontypool Road to allow Great Western Passenger Train to pass.
No. 2 Up Train to Shunt at Hirwain, to allow Great Western Passenger Train to pass.

DOWN.—WEEK DAYS.

Dist.	STATIONS.	1 arr.	1 dep.	2 arr.	2 dep.
		p.m.	p.m.	p.m.	p.m.
...	HEREFORD	...	5 15	...	12 50
21½	ABERGAVENNY JUNC.	6 35	6 45	2 20	2 40
32	Pontypool Road	7 25	7 30	3 30	3 35
38	Crumlin Junction	8 0	8 2	...	4 5
38¾	Crumlin	...	8 5	...	...
41½	Tredegar Junction	8 15	8 20	...	...
42½	Rhymney Junction	8 35	8 45	4 25	4 35
47¾	Quaker's Yard	9 5	9 10	...	4 55
54½	Merthyr Tydvil	9 50	...	...	...
...	Mountain Ash		...	5 10	5 15
52	Middle Duffryn	...	...	...	5 25
54¾	Aberdare	...	...	5 40	5 45
58	Hirwain	...	...	...	6 0
...	Hirwain Pond	...	...	6 5	6 15
64½	Glyn Neath	...	...	...	6 45
71¾	Aberdylais	...	...	...	*
73	Neath Junction	...	...	...	7 10
...	Old Neath	...	...	...	*
...	New Neath	...	...	7 15	7 20
...	Neath Abbey	...	...	...	*
80¾	SWANSEA	...	...	7 50	...

* **Calls when required.**

No. 2 Down Train to Shunt at Hirwain Pond on Neath Junction for Great Western Train if required

N.B.—The times of running these Trains are shown for the information of the Company's servants; but the Engine-drivers and Guards running through to Swansea, must be supplied with the Great Western and Vale of Neath Working Time Bills, and the Special Regulations relating to the working of those Lines.

LNWR Working Timetable in the last year of freight trains for Swansea over the Vale of Neath line. The completion of the Central Wales Line in 1868 enabled such trains to be diverted over a mainly LNWR route.
PRO RAIL 946/5

Deep in the heart of Wales: Cynghordy viaduct on the Central Wales Line with LNWR train bound for Shrewsbury.
John Miles Coll.

Tickets I: The tickets mainly speak for themselves, but ticket No. 061 is of special interest, reflecting as it does the effect of the elimination of 2nd class travel on the Midland from 1875; the appropriate class on the Midland for a mainly 2nd class journey on the GW was First. Ticket No. 150 is unusual as the Mid Wales operated the HHB for only one year. Ticket No. 733 could have required changes at Llandilo, Shrewsbury, Stafford and Rugby. The circuitous routing of No. 043 avoided a taxi ride across Swansea from St. Thomas to Victoria or High Street. Ticket No. 487 offered a mainly LMS route; an alternative via Pontypool Road might have been quicker though an extra change at Abergavenny Junction would have been required.

Chris Green and Trefor David

Tickets II: Ticket No. 157 enables the holder to avoid changing stations at Gowerton, but at the expense of a longer journey, changing at Pontardulais.

Chris Green and Trefor David

Tickets III. *Malcolm James Coll.*

Chapter 3

OVER THE TOP TO CARDIFF AND NEWPORT

Up to Brynmawr

Abergavenny occupies a controlling position where the Usk river emerges from its passage between the Black Mountains to the north and the Brecon Beacons and associated mountains to the south. A Roman site, Gobannium, it was the scene of bitter fighting in the Middle Ages and in 1404 Owain Glyndŵr seized the castle and reduced the town to ashes. Since then it had settled down to life as a small market and manufacturing town, wool from the sheep in the surrounding hills being the main raw material; it gained a reputation for its Welsh flannel and goats' hair periwigs. Before the arrival of the railway, manifest by the Newport, Abergavenny and Hereford, on 2 January 1854, Abergavenny had been served by turnpike roads: from Hereford to Newport; from Brecon along the Usk valley; and to Merthyr by a rough road up the Clydach gorge and over the top of the mountains at over 1,000 ft, a road described by a witness to a parliamentary committee as 'the worst even in Wales'. Abergavenny was also served by the Brecknock & Abergavenny Canal which went up the Usk valley, linking the Monmouthshire Canal near Pontypool to Brecon, and by tramroads in disconnected stretches from the area of Brynmawr to Hereford. In 1858, when this chapter opens, the town was in a poor state with the economy suffering and much unemployment. Within ten years it was to become a railway centre with three stations.

From Abergavenny to Hereford three old tramroads had been used by the NAH as the basis for their railway, but a stretch of one of these, the Llanvihangel Railway, from Abergavenny to Govilon had not been required. This 3 ft gauge tramroad had an end-on connection at Govilon with another tramroad with a gauge of some 4 ft 4 ins known as Bailey's Tramroad. This had been constructed in the 1820s to carry the products of Bailey's Nantyglo ironworks down the side of the Clydach Gorge to the Brecknock & Abergavenny Canal.

From the valley of the Usk the mountains to the south appear to present a continuous barrier of steep bracken-clad slopes with rocky

Railway, river and mountain setting in Abergavenny. A coal tank passes Brecon Road engine sheds on the approach to the Usk Bridge.

Nigel Lewis Coll.

outcrops and crags. However, some four miles west of Abergavenny there is a break in this mountain wall where the Clydach river has carved a narrow defile in the limestone mountain mass and, in a distance of only three miles, tumbles through a steep-sided gorge to the Usk valley nearly 800 ft below. It is spectacular country, presenting magnificently picturesque views of rock, woodland and river. However, in the eighteenth and early nineteenth centuries this idyllic scene was alive with the 'groaning of engines and beating of hammers' associated with the extraction of coal, limestone and iron-ore and their tempering in furnaces, forges and rolling mills. For beneath the beautiful landscape lay the three vital components of the iron industry, while on the surface was a plentiful supply of timber and water power. To bring these components together and to move the finished products called for an intricate network of tramroads, along, around, down and up the mountains.

The exploitation of iron in this part of Wales was led by members of the Bailey family who came originally from Yorkshire. Richard Bailey built up the massive Cyfarthfa ironworks at Merthyr and his nephews, Joseph and Crawshay, were responsible for developing the works at Nantyglo of J. & C. Bailey, for a time, the greatest ironworks in the world. Crawshay Bailey was a tough character, a man of great determination, of little formal education, but immensely practical and with plenty of common sense. As a result he was rich; he admitted in parliamentary committee that he earned over £20,000 a year. This was more than 20 times a normal executive salary, and 100 times the wage of a skilled workman. In the same committee, when asked whether the large number of employees he had all earned good wages, he replied with characteristic vigour, 'They may not think so, but we consider they have very good wages.' He went on to remind the committee that he could remember Brynmawr

The Brecon & Abergavenny Canal at Govilon with the MTA crossing in the distance. At this point there were a dock and sidings for transshipment between canal and rail, which appear to be out of use at the time when the photograph was taken, probably about the late 1930s.

GW/WIMM

Crawshay Bailey, ironmaster, politician and creator of the MTA.

National Museum of Wales

when it was only one house; there were now over 7,000. He was M.P. for Monmouth between 1852 and 1868 and lived in the later part of his life at Tŷ Mawr (the Great House) in Llanfoist. In the summer of 1858 he appears to have instigated an examination of the possibility of converting the tramroads leading from the NAH at Abergavenny to Brynmawr into a railway and then extending the line across the top of the mountains, linking with the Sirhowy valley, the Ebbw, the Rhymney and finally the Taff at Merthyr.

The first meeting of the provisional directors and promoters was held on 15 November 1858 under Crawshay Bailey's chairmanship in Abergavenny Town Hall. This led to an application to Parliament for authorisation to construct such a railway line. It is not altogether surprising that the name of the NAH appeared among the 12 petitioners against the Bill. The NAH had been trying to get a project off the ground to build a railway from Govilon to Brecon along the route of the canal, and accordingly sought running powers as far as Govilon. Charles Liddell, the engineer, was their chief witness. Thomas Brown also gave evidence and admitted that, as a NAH director, he could not see the NAH ever converting the tramroad to Govilon into a railway and thought the MTA would in fact serve to boost traffic on the NAH rather than detract from it. In the Act the NAH was granted the right to running powers for five years, provided it built the line to Brecon. This it never managed to do.

Road entrance to Brecon Road Station, Abergavenny, *c.* 1950. *Nigel Lewis Coll.*

Brecon Road Station, looking west. Date unknown.
Nigel Lewis Coll.

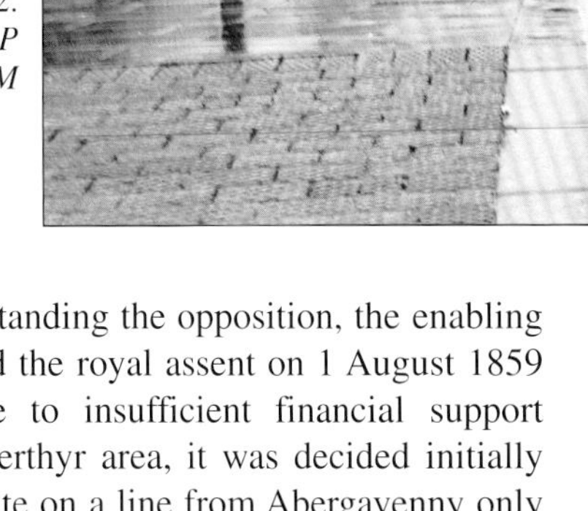

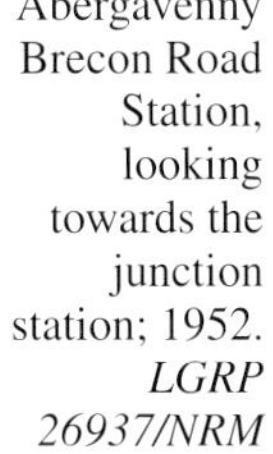

Abergavenny Brecon Road Station, looking towards the junction station; 1952.
LGRP 26937/NRM

Notwithstanding the opposition, the enabling Act received the royal assent on 1 August 1859 though, due to insufficient financial support from the Merthyr area, it was decided initially to concentrate on a line from Abergavenny only as far as Nantybwch, a small settlement near Tredegar at the head of the Sirhowy valley.

The first general meeting of shareholders in what was called the Merthyr, Tredegar and Abergavenny Railway was called on 29 August by the company's solicitor, W.F. Batt, who practised in Monk Street, Abergavenny; this was conveniently close to the Angel Hotel where the meeting was due to take place. Unfortunately, the accounts were not quite ready for presentation and, since Crawshay Bailey was not available either, the meeting was adjourned until 6 September. The records in the minute books of this company are particularly full and provide a fascinating insight into the development of a railway and the relationships between a local company and the national LNW.

On the morning of that day four directors met in the Monk Street offices of Mr Batt. Crawshay Bailey was there and was elected chairman; the others were Captain James Charles Hill and coalowner James Jayne, both of whom were local residents, and Edward Charles Chetham Strode from Somerset. James Hill, who became Deputy Chairman and in that capacity chaired most of the subsequent board meetings, owned the ironworks at Govilon from which, according to Bradney, he made a fortune enabling him to retire in 1870 to live in comfort at a house called 'The Brooks' near Abergavenny. Govilon may be interpreted as meaning, appropriately enough, 'the forges'.

At the First General Meeting attended by 72 shareholders out of 654, it was reported that it had cost £7,000 to obtain the Act. (A not unreasonable figure: the NAH had cost £12,000, the HHB £13,000.) It was also pointed out that the cost of promoting the line and canvassing for shareholders had been borne by the engineers and solicitors engaged at various places along the line. Consequently, all shareholders were required to pay up not only their deposits but also a call of £2; out of the 654 shareholders holding 3,293 shares of £20 each, only £4,664 in deposits had so far been paid. This was an indicator of how the company was going to struggle.

At the resumption of the adjourned board meeting back in Mr Batt's offices, it was decided to ask Thomas Brown of the Ebbw Vale Iron Company to become a director, but he declined. This may have been because he was still a director of the NAH, though this had not prevented him from becoming a shareholder in the new company. This surmise is supported by the fact that he changed his mind on 2 April 1860 by which time he would almost certainly have known that the NAH was about to merge in the West Midland. The board meeting also appointed John Gardner engineer to the line. He had previous railway experience and had been involved in initial surveys and discussions about the gradient of the proposed line. It was Crawshay Bailey who finally decreed that the intended gradient of 1:40 was unlikely to be beyond the capacity of a steam locomotive. Gardner was reputed to have been a capable engineer, conscientious and careful, and certainly the LNWR later found the line to have been very soundly built, but he was, as we shall see, an incorrigible optimist. Gardner was to be paid £200 per mile of line completed for traffic, one quarter of which was to be paid in shares. At a board meeting on 11 December he produced plans for the line as far as a place called Llanelly, about one mile short of Brynmawr, 8½ miles in all, and promised to produce estimated costs for both double and single track in early January. This must have caused some concern as, at the next general meeting on 29 February with 44 shareholders present, J.C. Hill went out of his way to explain to the meeting why they should not be surprised

The massive proportions of Beames' 0-8-4 tank engines are displayed by the proud driver of No. 7936 at Abergavenny shed. No date.

V.R. Webster/WIMM

at the engineer's estimates being different from the preliminary forecast made for the purpose of gaining authorisation from Parliament. In any case it was decided to lay a single line only. He then went on to complain that of the £20,000 due from shareholders (£2 deposit and 2 calls of £2), so far only £12,752 had been paid and that the £7,798 in arrears was mainly due from 'persons whose ability to pay is unquestionable'.

At about this time the company bought the tramroad from Brynmawr to Govilon from Baileys for £20,000, paid in shares. This was to form the basis for the railway down the side of the Clydach gorge, whereas beyond Brynmawr entirely new construction would be required. Baileys had been acting as bankers to the company and owned a bank in Abergavenny. In November the board repaid £7,000 to Baileys and made a further £2 call payable by 11 January 1860. In May 1860 the purchase of the remnant of the Llanvihangel Railway from Abergavenny to Govilon was completed.

Abergavenny Brecon Road shed on 16 August 1963. *Brian Hilton, courtesy Nigel Lewis.*

Abergavenny shed beneath the hazy backdrop of Blorenge Mountain; 7 July 1938. *H.C. Casserley*

In April Mr Batt was engaged as secretary to the company; for £210 he agreed to provide accommodation for board and general meetings as well as acting as secretary; any activity in his capacity as solicitor was to be extra. At this time, as already noted, Brown became a director, together with Isaac Isaacs of Abergavenny. As a result of an invitation to tender for the construction of the first 9½ miles to Brynmawr, a contract was awarded to one Eckersley whose bid at £6,000 per mile payable 50% in cash, the rest in paper, was by far the lowest. There must have been something seriously wrong with the bid because one month later the job was given to McCormick & Co for £84,000, to include the section from Brynmawr to Nantybwch. He must have got on with the job because by the 3rd General Meeting in August 1860 he was able to report that eight bridges were under construction, that the old tramroad bridge over the Usk at Abergavenny had been pulled down, and the foundations begun for the new bridge. Gardner, on the other hand, must have had some distraction at this time; he stated that the drawings for the line from Brynmawr to Nantybwch were complete in August, but they were still not available in October, at which time he promised them in six weeks. We shall see other instances of Gardner's tendency to be over-optimistic about time and cost.

Most board meetings were chaired by J.C. Hill and it was only for special issues that Crawshay Bailey appeared. One such was the question of the type of rail to be used. The original specification had been for 74 lb rail, but Bailey, with Brown also called in specially, decided to raise it to 80lbs. At this time it was also decided to provide for double track at the bridge over the Brecon Road in Abergavenny. Work was proceeding well with 14 out of 27 bridges complete and the major culvert and embankment at Llanelly nearly finished. In an atmosphere of confidence, it was decided to apply to Parliament for authority to extend the line from Nantybwch to Merthyr. In spite of a very severe winter it was also decided to start extending the works beyond Brynmawr. This was no mean task as the route lay across open windswept moorland, where snow in winter is assumed, and where even today, in spite of the pylons and road traffic, there is a certain exhilaration about travelling what is now the Heads of the Valleys road.

Then the mood changed. In April 1861 the board was informed that there was an overdraft at Bailey's Bank in Abergavenny and it was resolved to pay the bank the parliamentary deposit of £9,920 plus interest as soon as it was repaid; this would be due once half the share capital in the Act was paid up. This amounted to £10,228 in all and was not repaid until early in 1862. It would have been repaid earlier if Brown had been more cooperative; in July, in what was clearly a matter of intense

An impressive collection of fire-irons, as though prepared for exhibition at the Tate Gallery, stand alongside coal tank No. 58888 at Abergavenny shed; 16 August 1963.
Brian Hilton, courtesy Nigel Lewis

Webb coal tank No. 7782 stands with a Merthyr train at Brecon Road Station; 4 August 1936.

L. Hanson, courtesy N.T. Wassell

An ex-LNWR 0-8-0 catches the evening light as it heads for Merthyr from Abergavenny Junction; July 1953.

John Beardsmore

With equipment resembling medieval armour, coal tank No. 58926 stands inside Brecon Road shed awaiting snowplough duties; date uncertain.

R.W.A. Jones

embarrassment, Jayne and Batt were asked to call on him to seek the payment overdue on his shares. In May, Bailey had intervened and instructed McCormick to stop work beyond Brynmawr. At the 5th General Meeting in August authority was obtained to borrow up to £49,000 and to forfeit unpaid shares, many of which were still in arrears. The financial statement on 4 February 1862 showed:

Shares paid up	£ 72,777
Returned deposit	10,228
Debentures, loans	24,225
Total receipts	107,260

In spite of the delicate financial position, work was proceeding; by August 1861, 27 out of now 30 bridges were nearly finished, plans for stations at Abergavenny and Brynmawr were almost ready and the line was expected to be completed in about March 1862.

During this period Bailey must have been having thoughts about the future of the railway, leading to secret discussions with one or more intermediaries of the LNWR. On 5 January 1861 Moon had become deputy chairman. As early as May, the LNW was making the approach to the Shrewsbury & Hereford noted in the previous chapter, which was to prove so critical to the south Wales strategic development. On 19 October 1861 the chairman's sub-committee noted a letter from Henry Robertson with a 'proposed arrangement' with the MTA and by the 30th of the same month the MTA board had received a copy of a memo between Moon and Bailey proposing that the MTA be leased to the LNWR. There is no evidence as to what had been discussed, nor whether it was conducted purely through Robertson or in person; as an M.P. Bailey would have had plenty of opportunities to meet Moon

A Beames 0-8-4T on the MTA just west of Govilon climbs towards Brynmawr with a mixed freight, probably in the 1930s.
GBJ Coll.

A Webb Compound 0-8-0 No. 2525 forms the background to a smartly turned out group of LNWR employees at Brecon Road shed; late nineteenth century.
Nigel Lewis Coll.

in London, for he had a house at 16 Spring Gardens, just behind Trafalgar Square. By whatever means the proposal was generated, it received a cool reaction from the rest of the MTA board. They were not opposed to the idea of a lease, but wanted payment to include all debenture interest due, all liabilities in respect of rent charges and interest on the expended share capital of 5%, plus 50% on surplus profits. This must have caused a flurry of activity at Euston as negotiations were continuing in February 1862 and the deal was eventually done and ready for approval by a Special General Meeting called for the purpose on 23 June. At the 7th General Meeting on 30 August it was reported that the enabling Act had been passed; the MTA was to be leased to the LNWR for a period of 1,000 years at 5% on the capital half yearly, plus 50% of surplus profits. The 1862 MTA (Lease) Act required doubling of the track by 1864 from which time running powers were to be available to the West Midland.

The view towards Brynmawr through a cab window of what was probably an 0-8-4T locomotive at Govilon. Brynmawr is at the height of the distant mountain only six miles away; early 1920s.
J.M. Dunn/W. Rear Coll.

Meanwhile work on the line to Brynmawr continued. In December station plans for Abergavenny (Brecon Road), Brynmawr and Llanwenarth were approved; the latter was later called Govilon which, as a modern parish, was carved out of the ancient parish of Llanwenarth (where J.C. Hill lived). By April 1862 there were 32 bridges, the Usk viaduct was complete and the Gelli-felen tunnel, which nearly described a semi-circle underground, was almost finished; the junction of the headings had been, according to the report, 'most perfect'.

While progress was being made up the Clydach gorge, competitors had not been standing idle. Further ahead across the mountains the Brecon & Merthyr Railway (B & M) had applied for authority to build an extension from its line at Dowlais, east of Merthyr, along the proposed line of the MTA to Nantybwch, while the West Midland, successor to the NAH, was proposing a line from Nantybwch to near Dowlais. This was manifest in an audacious piece of hustling in which a Bill was submitted without the MTA agreement not only to allow the West Midland to extend the MTA but actually to take it over. The MTA board clearly had to oppose both these ventures and for the first time acted in concert with the LNWR. The West Midland Bill was withdrawn.

At the same meeting, held on 14 February 1862, the MTA awarded McCormick the contract to build the line to Nantybwch and accepted Eassie's bid to build the stations as far as Brynmawr; it was he who had built the stations on the Vale of Neath Railway. The single line from Abergavenny to Brynmawr was opened eventually on 1 October 1862, having been promised by Gardner for early September; the LNWR had been waiting 'at one day's notice'. The formalities associated with opening railways at that time were conducted on 29 September with Mrs Hill, described by *The Hereford Times* as the 'amiable wife' of Captain Hill, driving the locomotive of the ceremonial train under John Gardner's supervision. The total cost of the first section was £101,000, compared with an estimate in the original Act of £124,000 all the way to Nantybwch.

The perspective of the station building at Gilwern illustrates the steepness of the gradient down from Brynmawr whence the approaching 'coal tank' is descending; *c.* 1910.
Old Bakehouse Publications

At this stage, among the disputes with landowners whose land was required for the railway was a case involving none other than J. Palmer Budd, the owner of the ironworks at Ystalyfera. A house which he owned at Beaufort lay in the path of a cutting for the extension to Nantybwch. He proposed that the railway should take down his house and move it, and in addition pay him £200. In response the MTA stated that there was no room to re-erect the house but offered him £400 and the opportunity to salvage the materials. He accepted.

The viaduct at Beaufort in the 1920s with an Abergavenny train consisting of former LNWR carriages.
National Tramway Museum

From this time onward, life was never to be the same again for the MTA directors. Henceforth the courtesy of the language in the remaining records veils the irritation which can be sensed on the part of these tough local businessmen; even the diplomatic George Findlay, who was the superintendent for Shropshire and South Wales, was a problem to them. The relation of owners to leaseholder and operator must inevitably be delicate (though the Act was very specific and granted wide powers to the LNWR) and as far as can be seen the LNWR sought to do nothing beyond its rights, but, to anyone familiar with dealing with a distant head office, the LNWR questions, requests and rules have a familiar ring. Behind

The last stop before Brynmawr was Gellifelen Halt from which there was an outstanding view down the Clydach gorge towards Abergavenny and the distant Skirrid Mountain. This photograph was taken after the track had been removed in the early 1960s.

Nigel Lewis

them the cold probing of the distant and chilly Richard Moon can be detected, notwithstanding his enthusiasm for the south Wales strategy. Nevertheless, the MTA directors towed the line, realists to a man.

The importance the LNWR attached to the south Wales venture can be gauged from the fact that both Moon and the then general manager, Cawkwell, attended the 22 October board meeting, at their own request. A number of requirements were placed on the MTA:

1. The proposed north-facing junction at Abergavenny would not be built, though land acquisition would be pursued.
2. Work on the engine shed which the MTA had recently decided to build at Abergavenny Junction was to be suspended, but the West Midland were to be asked for a platform for passengers, to be built by either the West Midland or the MTA.
3. The LNWR wished to see all plans for doubling the line to Brynmawr and any other plans for new work before any work was begun.
4. Parliamentary permission to raise £100,000 extra capital for doubling the line was to be sought.
5. Copies of all board meeting minutes were to be sent to Stewart, the LNWR secretary.
6. The LNWR wished to know when it was proposed to build intermediate stations between Govilon and Brynmawr, and to see the plans.
7. Batt was requested to visit Euston to receive instructions and to discuss the terms of the projected Bill.

Attention was then turned towards the Sirhowy Railway. On 16 April 1860 an Extraordinary General Meeting of the MTA had supported the Bill to transform the Sirhowy Tramway into a railway. This line ran down the Sirhowy valley from Tredegar, a fast growing coal and iron town, to a junction with the NAH at Pontllanfraith known as Tredegar Junction. It then ran further down the valley to an end-on junction with the Monmouthshire Railway; this gave an outlet to the docks at Newport. It was important for the MTA that a link be made to the growing economic activity of Tredegar, whose name was in any case part of the company's title, and it was for this reason that the extension to Nantybwch was under way. What was needed was a link between Nantybwch and Tredegar.

At the board meeting held on Boxing Day 1862, Batt was asked to contact the Sirhowy Railway, urging them to complete a line to Nantybwch in time for the MTA opening and proposing a joint meeting, with the LNWR present as well. It was clearly felt that some heavy breathing from Euston could re-focus the attention of the Sirhowy Railway. Accordingly, on 4 February 1863, the MTA board met with the Sirhowy directors at the Westgate Hotel in

General view of Nantybwch Station during the 1950s, with a former GWR auto-train in the branch platform. Part of the extensive sidings is visible in the distance.

National Monuments Record of Wales

The bleak nature of the location of Nantybwch Station is revealed in this photograph of the branch platforms after closure.

National Monuments Record of Wales

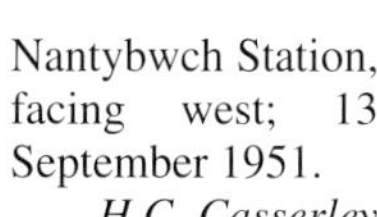

Nantybwch Station, facing west; 13 September 1951.

H.C. Casserley

Weak spring sunshine does little to relieve the bleakness of Nantybwch Station in May 1954. Locomotive No. 40097 is about to depart for Tredegar.

R.S. Carpenter

Newport. They were assured that work would proceed without delay. In March, Gardner and Yockney, the engineer and general manager of the Sirhowy, met at Nantybwch but Yockney complained to his board that Gardner had failed to bring any plans. In April, Yockney produced some plans himself. In July, in reply to a letter from Batt, it was agreed that the MTA would be assured that the extension line was being prepared; an ink note in the margin in the Sirhowy minute book says: 'not done'. In the absence of any progress on the part of the Sirhowy throughout the summer, Findlay wrote in September and the Sirhowy sent a holding reply asking him to specify exactly what he wanted. When he attended the MTA board meeting on 5 November he was clearly in a mood to increase the pressure; the might of the LNWR was being frustrated by an upstart little line which was failing to grasp the economic opportunities falling into its lap. Batt was to write to the Sirhowy again, asking what they were proposing to do 'so that the LNWR might determine what course should be adopted'.

Findlay's frustration was no doubt increased by the MTA itself experiencing delays in reaching Nantybwch due to a landslip at Beaufort. He asked them to build a temporary goods station at Nantybwch in the absence of the link to Tredegar, and asked specifically that, at the next board meeting, a firm date for opening be given, so that the Board of Trade could be given the required one month's notice. Accordingly, at the next meeting on 19 November, Gardner gave an opening date of 1 January 1864. This seems to have been too optimistic as it was at the next meeting on 31 December that the board fixed 1 February for opening to Nantybwch. In fact, it was inspected on 11 February and eventually opened on 1 March 1864, shortly after the branch from Ebbw Vale up to Beaufort.

The LNWR station at Ebbw Vale on 27 July 1957. It had been closed to passengers since 5 February 1951 and was to close completely on 6 November 1959.

R.M. Casserley

The approach to Ebbw Vale seen from the special SLS train on 5 January 1958. The line converging on the right is from local mineral workings.

John Beardsmore

At the 31 December board meeting it was reported that the Sirhowy still had no intention of abandoning their plans to make the link to Nantybwch, but their first priority was to upgrade the line as far as Sirhowy for passenger trains, which was proving to be less than straightforward. Accordingly, the LNWR solicitor suggested to the MTA that once they had opened to Nantybwch, they should notify the Sirhowy and call on them to complete their extension and, if they failed to do so in the time allowed by the enabling Act, they should threaten to apply for an injunction, putting a stop on the payment of dividends until the line was completed. During 1864 Findlay did what he could to alleviate the problems caused by the Sirhowy; first he obtained running powers over the Ebbw Vale Co's junction at Sirhowy; he then got the agreement of the Sirhowy to direct coal for Staffordshire northward, instead of to the GWR at Tredegar Junction. In September he made an unrecorded proposal which was rejected but which was probably a request to allow the LNW to build the line to Nantybwch, because, immediately after the proposal was rejected, Yockney was told to get on with the surveys with all despatch and a letter was written to the LNW to the effect that the Sirhowy would build the line themselves.

Meanwhile, the LNWR had been thinking about the Bill to increase the MTA authorised capital; this was prompted by three distinct issues:

1. The doubling of the line from Abergavenny to Nantybwch.
2. Improvements to the line by way of a station at Gilwern (opened April 1863), a siding for limestone workings at Cuckoo's Nest, just below Clydach, a station at Clydach (opened December 1863) together with a siding for the limestone works in which Moon himself had become involved, a check rail on the Clydach viaduct, passenger platforms at Trevil and Nantybwch, and a waiting shed at Abergavenny Junction.
3. An extension from Nantybwch to the Rhymney Railway at Rhymney Bridge.

This view of the Blaen-y-cwm viaduct, which carried the MTA over the Sirhowy river, shows the viaduct in its setting in the early 1930s. The Sirhowy branch crossed the road behind the photographer on its way up to Nantybwch Station, which was in the distance, just to the left of the picture.

Old Bakehouse Publications

A crowd of spectators, all female, turned out to watch the last train on the MTA as it climbed into the tunnel at Clydach; 5 January 1958.

John Beardsmore

Clydach Halt on11 June 1957.
O. H. Prosser/Ian L. Wright Coll.

The LNWR were opposed to doubling below Brynmawr and believed they could possibly avoid it. No doubt they were deterred by the thought of two new tunnel bores and a difficult widening requiring a girder bridge over a tramroad at Llanelly. The MTA board took the line that they were keen to fulfil the obligations of the original authorisation which was for double track, but ended with the emollient qualification 'without prejudicing shareholder interest, they were anxious as far as possible to comply with LNWR wishes'. A decision was postponed.

The original authorised capital of the MTA was £150,000 in 7,500 £20 shares. It was now proposed to raise a further £100,000. This was endorsed by a Special General Meeting held on 1 June 1863. On 27 August shareholders were alarmed when told that, in the 1863 MTA Act, Parliament had refused consent for the extension to Rhymney Bridge. This was in fact no surprise to the LNW management as they were now discussing with the Rhymney joint construction of the line from Rhymney Bridge to Nantybwch. This had emerged as the best solution as the Rhymney had managed to neutralise the B & M who had been thwarting LNW progress. Parliament had extended the date for doubling the existing line to 1866 (subsequently extended further to 1868), and had absolved the railway from doubling the two tunnels. Accordingly, the additional capital had

A train on the Sirhowy line leaves Sirhowy Station heading north in wintry conditions in January 1960. The line here was single track and the second line is a siding.

Alan Jarvis

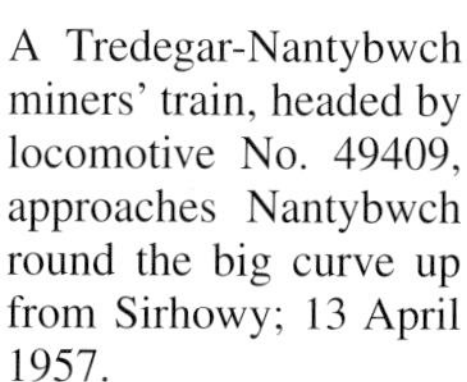

A Tredegar-Nantybwch miners' train, headed by locomotive No. 49409, approaches Nantybwch round the big curve up from Sirhowy; 13 April 1957.

Ian L. Wright

been limited to £70,000. The MTA board got an undertaking from Findlay on behalf of the LNWR that, if costs exceeded the available capital, the LNWR would jointly approach Parliament for more. The board minute bears the handwritten marginal note 'sent to LNWR Co. 31 Aug 1863'. Great importance was clearly attached to this undertaking; indeed it had been requested that Moon himself attend the previous board meeting to discuss it, and regret that no LNWR representative attended was recorded in the minutes.

There was then a difference of opinion on how the new shares should be allocated. The MTA wanted to allocate them pro-rata to existing shareholders, while the LNWR preferred that they be offered generally. There must have been a feeling of triumph in the Monk Street office at the 24 September board meeting when, as a result of the poor response to the offer, it was felt that the MTA preferred route of offering pro-rata could now be pursued. The LNWR subsequently objected to this decision, but there was little they could do about it. This followed another sign of rancour when, at the 1 June board meeting, Findlay asked with great courtesy that in future the LNWR be given notice of all board meetings, in case the MTA board wished him to attend 'to give any information'. The board agreed but made a point that they considered he could not attend as a matter of course. The LNWR did, however, have its uses; when local residents asked for a screen between the Usk bridge and the road because of the noise of the trains, the matter was referred to the LNWR, no doubt with a chuckle.

At this time there were also disagreements between the LNW and the MTA over responsibility for capital investment. Stewart, the LNW secretary wrote asking the MTA to build a water tank at Clydach for £110. The board reacted on 18 April 1864 by suggesting that this type of additional work was for the LNW's account, arguing that thereby the LNW would be able to ensure it met with their requirements. The LNW were not moved from their insistence that it was a job for the MTA. Then on 11 August Findlay wrote asking the MTA to build some cottages at Abergavenny Junction for LNWR workers; the MTA replied that they had

A view up the southern side of the Clydach gorge with Clydach Station and tunnels; date uncertain.
Old Bakehouse Publications

Brynmawr Station with an Abergavenny-bound mixed freight. Some of the Webb 0-8-0 locomotives which worked the line were fitted with tender cabs to allow for the harsh weather and the need for extensive tender-first running; date unknown.

R.C. Riley

An overall view of Brynmawr Station which demonstrates the general layout and setting on the occasion of the Last Train on 5 January 1958.

R.W.A. Jones

This postcard shows a rare view of the south fork at Abergavenny Junction in use as sidings for some elderly LNWR carriages. Although the southward connection was retained after the main north fork was inserted in 1869-70, it was only occasionally used. In the distance can be seen the north fork and the carriage sheds at the junction station; *c.* 1923.

Old Bakehouse Publications

no funds for this kind of investment, adding that this was clearly a job for the LNW. The MTA were probably inclined to be obstructive on these minor investments as it appears that they were still keen to see the whole line doubled, and also wanted a north-facing spur (a so-called 'north fork') put in at Abergavenny Junction. One can only presume that this was less motivated by a corporate desire to act conscientiously in accordance with the will of Parliament than by a desire as producers of minerals to speed the path of their products to markets in the north.

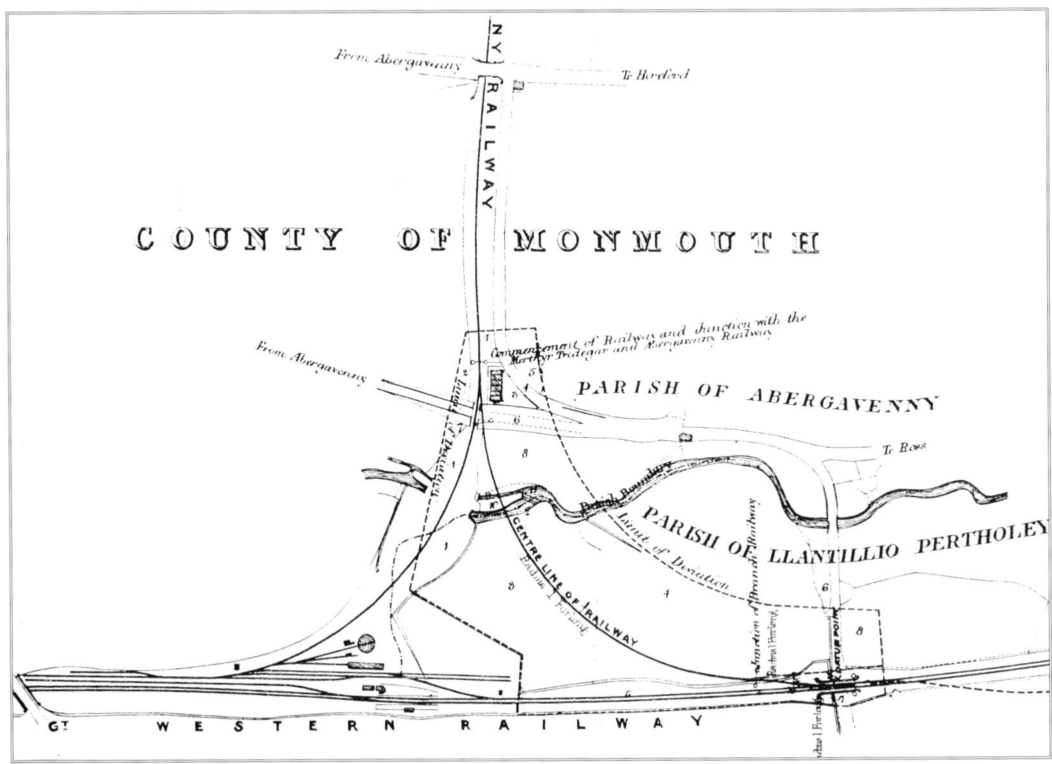

This plan of the north fork at Abergavenny Junction included in the LNWR (New Lines) Bill of 1867 shows the layout of the first station at the junction, which was inconveniently located on the south fork.
House of Lords Library

It is not clear whether these disagreements led directly to the next and final step in the relationship between the two companies, but on 12 July in the following year (1865), Moon and Findlay met Hill and Isaacs and agreed to recommend to Crawshay Bailey and Thomas Brown that they meet the LNW to agree the sale of the line. The terms proposed were that the MTA should give up the annual £500 management fee and share of profits and receive 5% for four years, 5½% for the next four, and then 6% in perpetuity. There must have been some internal disagreement on this proposition as by 31 August no such meeting had been held. Instead, the directors seem still to have been keener on getting the line doubled and the north fork installed, to the extent that they decided only to agree to the LNW terms provided both these measures were taken; if the LNW refused, they would go to Parliament and raise additional capital to do the work themselves. This attitude seems to have compelled the LNW to acceed because on 17 January 1866 a meeting between Moon, Bailey, Brown and Hill reached agreement on the following:

> The LNW accepted the MTA accounts.
> The MTA would sell at par the unallocated shares.
> The MTA shares would be converted into LNW 5% preference stock.
> The MTA would give up their share of profits and fee.
> The LNW would double the whole line and make the north fork.

The whole was authorised by an Act of Parliament later that year. Thereafter the MTA became an integral part of the LNWR. Abergavenny became headquarters of the District, Brecon Road Station housing the office of the district manager, at one time James Findlay's son, and here the engine shed was built in 1867. Subsequently extended, at one time it accommodated as many as 100 locomotives. In the same year the doubling, except in the two tunnels, was completed. Gardner had recommended using steel rails on the steepest parts of the downward line due to the serious problem of wear. Ten years later the tunnels were doubled. This was hardly too soon

The smoke from a Brynmawr-bound train creates a ghost-like spectre at the western end of the Gelli-felen tunnel; 13 September 1951.

H.C. Casserley

as by 1882 some 50 trains a day were operating in each direction between Brynmawr and Abergavenny. In November 1869 Joshua Williams, the former hero of the Vale of Neath Railway and now district supervisor for the GWR, met Bishop, the Abergavenny manager, at the site of the projected north fork at Abergavenny Junction and agreed that the LNW could build the platform and waiting-room on the down side, even though on GW land. In 1870 the north fork was built and a new Abergavenny Junction Station just to the north of it. It was a rare example of a station of one company on the tracks of another.

The MTA was becoming exposed to the meticulous style of Moon's management. Among the multitude of issues with which it dealt under Moon's chairmanship, the Shrewsbury and South Wales Committee agreed to the furnishing of the station; the ladies' waiting-room was to have :

one set of fire irons
one fender 3' 10" wide
six chairs
one small round table
one hearth rug
two door mats
an oil cloth for the floor 12' by 11' 11"
one small lamp for the mantlepiece.

In 1867 Bishop had been asked by the committee to look into the question of the winding of clocks at stations in his district. It was currently costing four guineas a year for a clock maker to do it and it was subsequently decided to get the company's staff to do it. Such was the attention to detail and cost control instilled in his staff by the painstaking Moon.

ERTHYR, TREDEGAR, & ABERGAVENNY BRANCH. 1

JANUARY, 1867.

Distance.	DOWN. Stations.	1 Passenger. 1, 2, P.	2 Goods. arr.	2 Goods. dep.	3 Goods. arr.	3 Goods. dep.	4 Passenger. 1, 2, 3	5 Goods. arr.	5 Goods. dep.	6 Passenger. 1, 2, 3	7 Goods. arr.	7 Goods. dep.	8 Goods. arr.	8 Goods. dep.
		a.m.	a.m.	a.m.	a.m.	a.m.	p.m.	p.m.	p.m.	p.m.	p.m.	p.m.	p.m.	p.m.
..	TREDEGAR ...	7 0	...	...	...	11 0	12 50	...	4 0	5 25	...	6 15	...	...
1¼	Trevil Junction...	7 6	...	...	11 10	11 20	12 56	4 10	4 20	5 31	6 25	6 40	...	...
2¼	Beaufort	7 12	...	...	...	...	1 4	...	...	5 37	...	...	...	...
4	* Brynmawr	7 17	...	7 45	11 49	11 50	1 10	4 40	5 20	5 42	7 0	7 45	...	8 4
4¼	Bailey's Siding...	...	7 50	8 0	...	...	...	...	...	...	7 48	7 58	...	*
4½	Brecon Bt. Siding	...	8 5	8 10	...	...	...	...	...	...	8 2	8 7	...	...
4¾	Ellwood's Siding	...	...	...	...	...	...	...	...	...	8 10	8 15	...	...
5½	Gellavalln	...	...	...	...	...	...	...	...	...	...	...	...	...
6¾	Llanelly Siding...	...	8 20	8 50	...	...	...	...	...	...	8 25	8 35	...	...
7	Clydach	7 31	...	...	...	...	1 23	...	...	5 57	8 40	8 45	*	9 1
8¼	Cuckoo's N. Sid.	...	...	...	...	...	...	...	...	...	...	...	...	...
9¾	Gilwern	7 36	...	...	...	...	1 30	...	...	6 3	...	...	...	...
10¼	Gilwern St. Q'rry	...	...	...	...	...	...	...	...	...	...	...	...	...
	Govilan	7 41	8 50	8 55	...	...	1 34	...	...	6 8	9 0	9 10	...	9 3
11¾	Govilan Wharf...	...	...	...	...	...	...	...	...	...	†	...	...	...
	Llanfoist	...	...	...	...	...	...	...	...	...	†	...	...	...
12	Gas Works Siding	...	...	...	...	...	...	...	...	...	†	...	...	...
12½	* Abergavenny (Brecon Road)	7 54	9 20	...	12 50	1 0	1 45	6 5	6 31	6 21	9 30	9 35	9 45	9 5
13½	* WEST MIDLAND JUNC.	8 0	...	...	1 10	...	1 55	6 36	...	6 26	9 40	...	9 55	...

No. 2 Down, on Tuesdays, starts from Tredegar at 8.30 a.m., and runs as a Market Passenger Train.

No. 8 Down to run when required only, and to stop at Stations marked thus (*) when necessary.
*** Stations marked thus (*) are Staff or Crossing Stations.**
† To stop when required.
═ Lines across the columns denote the Stations appointed for Trains to meet and pass each other.

Note.—The greatest caution and vigilance must be observed by the Engine Drivers and Guards in working down the incline from Brynmawr to Llanfoist; and the following special instructions must be attended to:—

AS TO SPEED OF TRAINS:—

Down.	Goods Trains, Maximum Speed.	Passenger Trains, Maximum Speed.
From Brynmawr to Llanfoist	**10 Miles Per hour.**	**15 Miles Per hour.**

AS TO LOAD OF TRAINS IN DRY WEATHER.

Down.—The Maximum load for each Engine will be 10 Loaded Waggons, or a gross load of 120 tons, and proportionally less in wet or slippery weather.

The Breaks of every Waggon, and of the Vans, must be carefully examined by the Guard, and those of the Waggons pinned down before starting. The Trains must stop at Llanfoist to take off the Breaks.

Any Waggon with an imperfect Break must be left for repair, and the Guards are to report the number of the Waggons so left to the Station Master at Abergavenny, who will see to their being repaired.

A page from the MTA working timetable for 1867. Caution on the descent was required and the old junction at Abergavenny was called West Midland Junction.

PRO RAIL 946/3

A view looking south from the sidings behind the station at Abergavenny Junction. Part of the large carriage shed features on the right of the picture, while in the distance a GWR train pounds up the main line; July 1953.

John Beardsmore

Many preserved railways would welcome such a carriage shed as this, which the LNWR built at Abergavenny Junction in the early 1920s; 1953. *John Beardsmore*

A further example arose in 1870 in connection with some locomotives and rolling stock borrowed from the Rhymney as security for a loan. Moon was concerned to make sure that these were still of sufficient value as a security; subsequently he received reassurance that far from decreasing in value, their worth was actually enhanced.

In the same year 1867 it was decided to order 20 special 0-6-0 tank engines to be ready for the opening to Rhymney Bridge. In 1879 doubling was completed on the line through the Clydach gorge when the two new tunnels were bored at Clydach and Gelli-felen on the side nearest the mountain, i.e. the upward, down side. The relationship with Crawshay Bailey remained sensitive; he was, after all, a powerful figure with plenty of influence. When in February 1869 it was reported to the Shrewsbury committee that some trains were stopping near Bailey's house in Llanfoist for him to get up or down, it was 'resolved that it be continued on sufferance'.

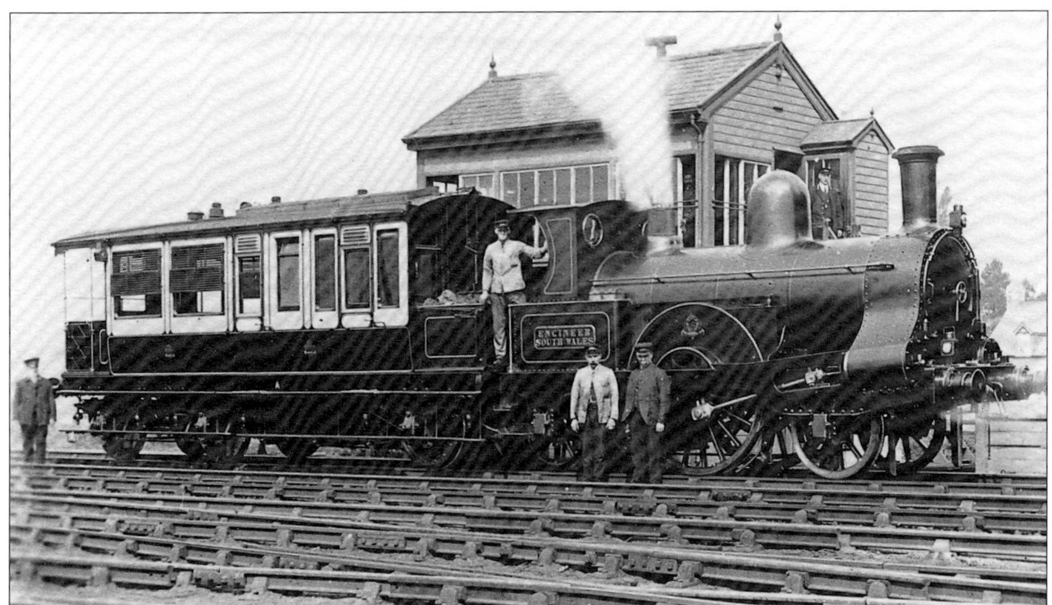

LNWR South Wales inspection train; no date. *Nigel Lewis Coll.*

THREE WAYS TO NEWPORT

In December 1864 the MTA had drawn the attention of the LNWR to a project to build a railway from Brynmawr to Blaenavon at the head of the eastern valley. This was to be the first of three additional routes to Newport over and above the direct NAH and MRCC route through Pontypool.

The first project, the Brynmawr, Blaenavon & Pontypool Railway, failed on Standing Orders in the House of Commons in 1865; this was a line from Brynmawr down the eastern valley to a junction with the Taff Vale Extension of the former NAH, one mile west of Pontypool Road Station. It wound its way down the west side of the Llwyd valley, virtually parallel to the line of the MRCC. It had an eastward branch from near the highest point at Waunavon towards the limeworks above the south side of the Clydach gorge. Its successor the following year was the Brynmawr & Blaenavon Railway; both the Blaenavon ironworks and the MRCC were invited to participate. Indeed, the MRCC paid half the cost of John Gardner's survey, but when it was authorised in 1866 it was immediately leased to the LNWR. It was to be a rather shorter line terminating just south of Blaenavon and with a branch back to the MRCC in the valley; it was also to have a line towards the edge of the Clydach gorge. These branches were never built. One of the directors was John Jayne of the MTA. In 1872 an extension was made to Abersychan & Talywain, and in 1877 a route to Newport over the MRCC was completed.

The LNWR station at Blaenavon in deep snow in the early 1920s, looking towards Brynmawr.
J.M. Dunn/W. Rear Coll.

Spring sunshine at Blaenavon, looking down the valley; early 1920s.
J.M. Dunn/LNWR Soc.

The LNWR station at Blaenavon looking towards Brynmawr; 14 July 1958. *H.C. Casserley*

From Blaenavon Station the scene up-valley was of intense industrial activity; early 1920s. *J.M. Dunn/LNWR Soc.*

By 19 April 1957, the scene had changed: the iron-works had gone, an enormous spoil tip had appeared, and the Western Region had taken over. Locomotive No. 5231. *C.H.A. Townley, courtesy J.A. Peden*

Summer at Abersychan and Talywain, looking up-valley towards Blaenavon; 14 July 1958.
H.C. Casserley

Winter at Abersychan and Talywain, looking north; 31 December 1969.
J.A. Sommerfield, courtesy J.A. Peden

The ironworks at Blaenavon already had the benefit of connection with Newport by means of a branch of the MRCC, but the attraction offered by the LNW was a shorter route over the MTA to the north of England. The line was vested in the LNWR in 1869. It was a remarkable railway, heading off eastward from Brynmawr and then south-east across the moor, climbing to a height of 1,400 ft in its 5 mile route to Blaenavon, 1:40 up and down. Waunavon near the summit was the only intermediate station, of which the house survives. It stands in a lonely setting surrounded by open moorland, with wonderful mountain views. On 27 July 1869 Gardner forecast completion by the beginning of October; it opened on 1 February 1870.

The second advance towards Newport was down the Sirhowy valley. We had left the Sirhowy Railway protesting that it did indeed intend to forge the link to the MTA at Nantybwch. This had been authorised by Parliament in the 1860 Act by which the Sirhowy Tramroad was authorised to become a railway; the work was eventually carried out in 1863/64. A slightly different route from the original was chosen, crossing a main road just north of Sirhowy Station by a bridge rather than a level crossing, and this was retrospectively approved by Parliament in the 1865 Sirhowy Railway Act.

Much of the early history of the railways in the Sirhowy valley lies beyond the scope of this book, but the affairs of the Sirhowy Railway cast interesting light on the minor railways of the time and provide a slightly different example of how the LNW managed its takeovers.

The enduring character of the location of Waunavon Station, 1,400 ft high on the Blaenavon Branch, is revealed in the following series of photographs and contrasts with the transitory nature of the railway paraphernalia; early 1920s.
J. M. Dunn/W. Rear Coll.

By 13 July 1958 Waunavon was used for waggon storage.
H.C. Casserley

Waunavon after the removal of the track; no date.
National Monuments Record of Wales

Waunavon in the spring of 1997.
DD

An unidentified 0-8-4T stands outside Blaenavon shed in the early 1920s. *J.M. Dunn/W. Rear Coll.*

The Sirhowy Tramroad was authorised by Parliament in 1802 from an end-on junction at a place known as Nine Mile Point, with a tramroad from Newport owned by the Monmouthshire Canal Co. It was financed by the lessees of the Tredegar ironworks and was opened as a horse-drawn tramroad of 4 ft. 2 ins gauge in about 1804. It was a historic line, being one of the first in Britain to convey fare-paying passengers, and Samuel Homfray, one of the directors, was also a director of Tredegar Iron Works. His son, also called Samuel Homfray, was a steam engine enthusiast, who was responsible for introducing the first steam locomotive on the line in 1829. Indeed, he had been present with his father at Penydarren when Trevithick had demonstrated his historic steam engine in 1804. Son-in-law of Sir Charles Morgan, whose house near Newport gave its name to the town of Tredegar, Samuel junior lived at Bedwellty House, which still stands near the centre of what is now Tredegar, and

Tredegar High Street; late 1940s. *Old Bakehouse Publications*

Bedwellty House, home of the Homfray family, in the middle of Tredegar. *Old Bakehouse Publications*

Coal tank No. 58915 at Tredegar on the 10.31 a.m. train to Nantybwch on a damp 13 September 1951. *H.C. Casserley*

became the first chairman when the company was re-incorporated as a Railway in 1860. He and his brother, the Rev. Watkin Homfray, resigned when they sold their shares in 1861, and from that time Rowland Fothergill, son of one of the other founders, took over the chairmanship. He died in office and was succeeded by Major Browne in 1871. S.H. Yockney was appointed engineer and general manager in 1860 at a salary of £500 a year, plus a house, coals and a horse. He remained until his summary dismissal in February 1868. Henry Davis was the secretary until 1867.

The 1860 Act authorised a route which followed the old tramroad for most of the way, diverging slightly to avoid running down the middle of the main street in both Blackwood and Argoed. It also covered an extension from Sirhowy up to a westward junction with the MTA at Nantybwch. At the point where the line crossed the TVE at Pontllanfraith, soon to become Tredegar Junction, it was originally intended to make the crossing just east of the Bryn tunnel; this would have been west of the pub which gave its name to the later Bird-in-Hand Junction. The bridge was eventually built to the east of the pub and was to be the subject of arbitration between the GWR and the Sirhowy Railway due to its faulty construction. The authorised work on building the railway was carried out by a firm called Griffiths & Thomas; serious disagreement with them led to another arbitration case which lasted for most of 1865 and 1866.

Sirhowy Station, looking down-valley towards Tredegar; date unknown. *National Monuments Records for Wales*

Pontllanfraith in 1939, looking towards Tredegar. *LGRP 19379/NRM*

Pontllanfraith Station, formerly Tredegar Junction, with the 7.52 p.m. Tredegar to Newport train leaving the platform; 10 July 1958. *H.C. Casserley*

Photographs of trains on both lines at Pontllanfraith are rare. During the last days of the Sirhowy branch, when the line had been singled and most of the signals removed, a short mixed freight approaches the bridge over the Vale of Neath line, on which can be seen part of a train; 27 July 1963.
Alan Jarvis

The work on the line was almost completed by August 1863 and it was therefore planned to open for passenger traffic at the end of October, provided the Monmouthshire were ready at Nine Mile Point. In September this was postponed and on 3 December it was decided to give notice to the Board of Trade of the intention to open on 1 January 1864. At the same time a meeting was held with the MRCC to discuss traffic arrangements and to request a proposal from the MRCC. They were warned that as the Sirhowy directors were 'in treaty for the sale of their property' it might not be possible to make any general arrangements. The identity of the potential purchaser referred to is not certain. Both the GW and LNW were locally believed to be interested. Their failure to complete and the Sirhowy's subsequent independence for ten years is hard to understand at this distance in time. Perhaps the adverse inspection report from Captain Rich deterred at least the GW, who were implicated. Perhaps frustration over Nantybwch discouraged the LNW. They may have set a priority on getting to Cardiff with the Rhymney and in 1864 those negotiations were at a critical stage.

Nine Mile Point, facing south, in 1939.
LGRP 11531/NRM

On 24 December 1863 the MRCC wrote proposing a morning train from Tredegar to Newport, which waited in Newport for a quarter or half hour before returning, and the same in the afternoon. Dock Street, the MRCC terminus for the Western Valleys trains was to be used. This was little more than a wooden shed with a single platform. The Sirhowy were to provide the carriages and locomotives, staff, tickets and luggage labels; the MRCC would provide porters and booking clerks at Risca and Newport. Their charges would be:

> 2d per mile..........................1st class
> 1½d per mile........................2nd class
> 1d per mile..........................3rd class
> . . . and a scale of charges for parcels.

In March the MRCC made a fresh proposal:

> normal rate for parcel traffic as if in MRCC trains
> running rights for MRCC goods trains to Tredegar Jc.

The key objective of the MRCC was to gain mineral rights to Tredegar Junction as the price of access for the Sirhowy to Newport; this was agreed in July 1864 and was later to become of great importance to the GWR.

Then a bombshell struck. The 10 March inspection report by Captain Rich of the Board of Trade was unfavourable and he suggested withdrawing the notice of the intention to start a passenger service until the line was ready for a new inspection. The main problem was the supporting columns of the GW bridge at Tredegar Junction, though there were many other faults. The report casts fascinating light on the state of the railway and is reproduced below:

> The new line is 13 m. 31 ch. long and is single throughout with sidings. Land has been purchased for a double line and the works have been constructed accordingly. The guage [*sic*] is 4ft 8½ in, the rail used is flat bottomed. It is laid in 20 ft lengths and weighs 72 lbs per lineal yard. The joints are fished, the rail is keyed in chairs weighing 25 lbs each with compressed elm keys. The chairs are bolted to sleepers laid transversely about 3 feet apart, those next the rail joints being only 2 feet apart. The line is well ballasted with cinders and broken stone and the permanent way generally is in good order though some of the rails are considerably worn and many of the fish joints loose. It is an old mineral line which it is now proposed to convert into a passenger line. The coal and goods sidings are very numerous and require in all cases to be protected with distant signals. A box will be wanted at each siding for the man in charge of the points and signals. In some cases repeating signals will also be necessary when the auxiliary signal cannot be seen for at least 700 yards on that side from which the sidings are approached on falling gradients. Nine Mile Point, Tredegar Junction, Blackwood and Tredegar are the only passenger stations on the line.
>
> At Nine Mile Point there is no station and no approach to a station. A platform has been erected for the purpose of landing the passengers from the Sirhowy carriages and enabling them to re-enter the Monmouthshire carriages at the same platform. The Sirhowy Railway expect to work in connection with the Monmouthshire Railway Company but desire at the same time to provide for independent working. They have not yet made any arrangements with the Monmouthshire Railway Company and it will be necessary that there should be a passenger platform at each side of the Sirhowy Railway which is doubled at Nine Mile Station and further that there should be up and down lines at each of the two platforms so that the passengers may change carriages and that the risk of a collision shall be avoided by the trains of each company coming up at different sides of the up and down platforms
>
> No turntable has yet been erected at the terminal station of the Sirhowy Railway. A raised signal box from which the signal and point lever can be worked in connection with each other should be erected at this junction and the north distant signal requires moving so as to be seen by the signalman.The double line which now becomes single and again becomes double before reaching the weighbridge should be carried out continuously as a double line to a point north of the weighbridge and the weighbridge points will require the further protection of a distant signal and a repeating signal if the latter cannot be seen at 700 yards distance. The whole of the Sirhowy Railway is on a steep ascending gradient.
>
> Tredegar Junction Station is intended to be a passing station for trains. Platforms are necessary at each side of the line and the loop should be extended for about 60 to 80 yards beyond the station.

The Sirhowy Railway has two junctions for mineral traffic with the West Midland Railway near this station. The loop or second line of rails should be extended outside both junctions and the signalman at the south junction should have a raised box from which he can work his signal and point lever in connection with each other. The south distant signal of the south junction requires moving to a place where it can be distinctly seen from the signal box. The north auxiliary signal for Tredegar Junction Station requires a repeating signal. Upper Argoed mineral siding if worked as a passing place for trains as now proposed will require to have the line doubled for some distance and one of the two north auxiliary signals may be abolished. The watering place for engines requires a south distant signal and Blackwood Station which is on an incline of 1:150 should have a blind siding taken out of the second or western line of rails to catch run-away carriages.

Blackwood Station in LNWR days, looking up-valley.
Old Bakehouse Publications

Blackwood Station, looking north, shortly after closure to passengers.
J. Peden Coll.

Station staff at Blackwood; no date.
Old Bakehouse Publications

> The gates of the authorised public level crossing at Tredegar Junction require lamps and the stations want clocks. There is an unauthorised public level crossing at 13 miles – 18 chains. It is outside the limits of the present inspection and will be abolished immediately by a diversion of the road through an adjacent underbridge. There are 6 over bridges, one of stone and the rest of timber.
>
> 14 underbridges are constructed of stone. Three have wooden beams stiffened with iron rails and the 10th consists of wrought iron girders 110 feet long supported in the centre with circular cast iron columns. The whole of these works appear substantially constructed and of sufficient strength except the last underbridge which is constructed for two lines of rails and carries the Sirhowy Railway over the West Midland (now the Great Western Railway) at Tredegar Junction. I have no drawings of the columns but they appear too light and are fixed in an unsteady manner. The main girders and cross beams of the bridge are only half the strength they should be.
>
> I have received no undertaking as to the proposed mode of working. I beg to submit that the Sirhowy Railway cannot by reason of the incompleteness of the works be opened for passenger traffic without danger to the public using the same.

On 28 February 1865 Yockney was again asked to give 10 days notice of opening to the Board of Trade, but this was hopelessly premature as on 29 March it was reported that the bridge at Tredegar Junction would not be ready until 8 April. The line eventually opened for passengers on 19 June 1865. The Board of Trade required third-class carriages to be fitted with two lamps. Hitherto they had been unlit. Stations at Argoed and Nine Mile Point were authorised in August at a maximum cost of £50 each. By the Sirhowy Railway Act of 1865 mentioned earlier, minor deviations from the original on the line up to Nantybwch were authorised and the direction of the junction was changed from west to east, much to the disgust of the B & M who still hoped to reach it from Dowlais. The railway was authorised to make arrangements with the GW and LNW and the authorisation of three through trains a day from Tredegar to Newport obviated the need to change trains on to the MRCC at Nine Mile Point.

The railway then pursued a relatively uneventful existence until 1875. In 1866, with GWR backing, the Sirhowy deposited plans and introduced a bill for a railway from Nine Mile Point to the GW's south Wales main line west of Newport with another branch across the north of Newport to the prospective Pontypool, Caerleon & Newport (PCN) line. This was subsequently

Tredegar Station in 1939. *LGRP 11529/NRM*

Curiosity 22 years old

SIRHOWY RAILWAY SERVICE TIME TABLE, from FEBRUARY 1st, 1866, until further Notice.

DOWN TRAINS.

WEEK DAYS.

Distance	Stations and Sidings	1 arr.	1 dep.	2 arr.	2 dep.	3 Pick Up arr.	3 Pick Up dep.	4 Colliers and E. Trucks arr.	4 Colliers and E. Trucks dep.	5 Passenger arr.	5 Passenger dep.	6 arr.	6 dep.	7 arr.	7 dep.	8 arr.	8 dep.
		a.m.	a.m.	a.m.	a.m.	a.m.	a.m.	a.m.	a.m.	a.m.	a.m.	a.m.	a.m.	a.m.	a.m.	a.m.	a.m.
	Sirhowy	...	...	...	...	...	...	...	...	.	7 50	...	8 15	...	...	...	...
1	Tredegar	...	4 15	...	4 20	...	5 30	...	6 30	8 0	8 2	8 20	9 0	...	9 10	...	11 4
1¼	Ty Trist (Lower)	...	...	4 23	4 28	...	...	...	...	...	...	...	...	...	...	...	...
2¼	Bedwellty (Lower)	...	...	4 35	4 40	...	...	6 38	...	...	8 6	...	...	9 20	...	...	...
4	Pontygwaith	...	...	...	...	...	5 50	...	...	...	...	...	...	...	...	...	...
4¼	Hollybush	...	...	...	...	...	5 55	...	...	...	...	...	...	...	...	...	...
4½	Ancient Druid*	...	...	...	...	...	6 2	...	...	...	...	...	...	...	...	...	...
6½	Argoed	...	...	...	...	...	6 16	...	...	...	8 20	...	...	...	...	...	...
7¼	Upper Argoed	...	...	...	...	...	...	...	...	...	...	...	...	...	...	...	...
7½	Lower Argoed	...	...	...	...	...	...	...	...	...	...	...	...	...	...	...	...
8	Upper Rock Colliery	...	...	...	...	...	6 18	...	...	...	...	...	...	...	...	...	...
8¼	Cwm Gelly	...	...	...	...	...	6 24	...	...	...	...	...	...	...	...	...	...
8½	Blackwood	...	5 0	...	5 23	6 32	6 55	...	...	...	8 29	9 40	9 45	...	...	...	11 42
10	Bryn Siding	...	...	...	...	...	7 5	...	...	...	...	...	...	...	...	...	...
10	Tredegar Junction Station	...	5 7	...	5 30	...	7 7	...	...	...	8 36	...	9 51	...	...	...	11 50
10¼	Junction with G.W.R., Upper	...	...	...	...	...	...	...	...	...	...	...	...	...	...	...	...
10½	" " Lower	...	...	...	...	7 9	7 21	...	...	...	...	...	10 0	...	...	...	...
	Ynysddu	...	...	...	...	...	...	...	...	...	...	...	...	...	...	...	...
12½	Duffryn Chemical Works	...	...	...	...	...	7 39	...	...	...	...	...	...	...	...	...	...
14½	Nine Mile Point (S.R.)	...	5 27	5 50	...	7 55	...	...	...	...	8 50	10 15	...	...	...	12 20	...
	Mon. Railway Company's Goods and Mineral Trains Nine-Mile-Point	...	6 0	...	6 20	..	8 30	...	...	...	...	...	11 5	...	...	...	12 10
	Risca	...	...	...	...	...	...	...	...	...	9 0	...	...	...	...	...	...
	Newport	...	...	...	...	...	...	...	...	9 25	...	...	...	...	...	...	...

Distance	Stations and Sidings	9 Passenger arr.	9 Passenger dep.	10 arr.	10 dep.	11 arr.	11 dep.	12 arr.	12 dep.	13 Passenger arr.	13 Passenger dep.	14 arr.	14 dep.	15 arr.	15 dep.	16 Colliers and Minerals arr.	16 Colliers and Minerals dep.	17 Passenger arr.	17 Passenger dep.
		p.m.	p.m.	p.m.	p.m.	p.m.	p.m.	p.m.	p.m.	p.m.	p.m.	p.m.	p.m.	p.m.	p.m.	p.m.	p.m.	p.m.	p.m.
	Sirhowy	...	12 28	...	...	...	...	...	...	...	4 46	...	2 44	...	...	...	...	...	8 18
1	Tredegar	12 31	12 34	...	1 0	...	1 10	...	2 32	4 50	4 52	2 50	4 57	...	5 12	...	6 16	8 [illegible]	...
1¼	Ty Trist (Lower)	...	...	...	...	...	...	2 35	2 44	...	...	...	...	...	...	...	...	...	...
2¼	Bedwellty (Lower)	...	12 38	1 13	1 18	1 20	...	...	...	...	4 56	...	...	...	...	6 21	...	...	...
4	Pontygwaith	...	...	...	...	...	...	...	...	...	...	...	...	...	...	...	...	...	...
4¼	Hollybush	...	...	...	...	...	...	...	...	...	...	...	...	...	...	...	...	...	...
4½	Ancient Druid*	...	...	...	...	...	...	...	...	...	...	...	...	...	...	...	...	...	...
6½	Argoed	...	12 52	...	...	...	...	...	...	...	5 10	...	...	...	...	...	...	...	...
7¼	Upper Argoed	...	...	...	...	...	...	...	...	...	...	...	...	...	...	...	...	...	...
7½	Lower Argoed	...	...	...	...	...	...	...	...	...	...	...	...	...	...	...	...	...	...
8	Upper Rock Colliery	...	...	...	...	...	...	...	...	...	...	...	...	...	...	...	...	...	...
8¼	Cwm Gelly	...	...	...	...	...	...	...	...	...	...	...	...	...	...	...	...	...	...
8½	Blackwood	...	12 58	1 45	1 50	...	...	3 14	3 32	...	5 19	...	5 27	...	5 42	...	...	...	...
10	Bryn Siding	...	...	...	...	...	...	...	...	...	...	...	...	...	...	...	...	...	...
10	Tredegar Junction Station	1 3	1 10	...	1 58	...	...	.	3 37	...	5 26	...	5 35	...	5 50	...	...	...	...
10¼	Junction with G.W.R., Upper	...	...	...	...	...	...	3 39	3 45	...	.	...	...	...	...	...	...	...	...
10½	" " Lower	...	...	...	2 8	...	...	...	...	...	...	...	...	...	5 55	...	...	...	...
	Ynysddu	...	...	...	...	...	...	...	...	...	...	...	...	...	...	...	...	...	...
12½	Duffryn Chemical Works	...	...	...	...	...	...	...	...	...	...	...	...	...	...	...	...	...	...
14½	Nine Mile Point (S.R.)	...	1 25	2 28	...	...	...	4 12	...	...	5 40	6 5	...	6 20	...	...	...	...	...
	Mon. Railway Company's Goods and Mineral Trains Nine-Mile-Point	...	...	..	3 50	...	...	...	4 15	...	...	...	...	...	...	...	...	...	...
	Risca	...	1 32	...	...	...	...	...	...	...	5 50	...	...	...	...	...	...	...	...
	Newport	1 52	...	...	...	...	...	...	...	6 15	...	...	...	...	...	...	...	...	...

SUNDAYS.

Distance	Stations and Sidings	1 Passenger arr.	1 Passenger dep.	2 Passenger arr.	2 Passenger dep.	3 Passenger arr.	3 Passenger dep.
		a.m.	a.m.	p.m.	p.m.	p.m.	p.m.
	Sirhowy	...	7 50	...	4 5	...	7 27
1	Tredegar	7 53	8 2	4 8	4 10	7 30	...
1¼	Ty Trist (Lower)	...	...	...	...	...	...
2¼	Bedwellty (Lower)	...	8 10	...	4 14	...	...
4	Pontygwaith	...	..	...	...	...	...
4¼	Hollybush	...	..	...	...	...	...
4½	Ancient Druid*	...	...	...	...	...	...
6½	Argoed	...	8 16	...	4 26	...	...
7¼	Upper Argoed	...	...	...	...	...	...
7½	Lower Argoed	...	...	...	...	...	...
8	Upper Rock Colliery	...	.	...	...	...	...
8¼	Cwm Gelly	...	...	...	...	...	...
8½	Blackwood	...	8 25	...	4 [illegible]	...	...
10	Bryn Siding	...	...	...	...	...	...
10	Tredegar Junction Station	8 30	8 30	...	4 41	...	...
10¼	Junction with G.W.R., Upper	...	...	...	...	...	...
10½	" " Lower	...	...	...	...	...	...
	Ynysddu	...	...	...	...	...	...
12½	Duffryn Chemical Works	...	...	...	...	...	...
14½	Nine Mile Point (S.R.)	...	8 48	...	4 55	...	...
	Mon. Railway Company's Goods and Mineral Trains Nine-Mile-Point	...	...	...	...	...	...
	Risca	...	8 56	...	5 5	...	...
	Newport	9 20	...	5 30	...	...	...

Those of the Sirhowy Trains proceeding to Newport stop at Bassaleg for the examination of Tickets.
Nos. 14 and 15 Down Trains will run, if required, but in no case without a due observance of the regulations having reference to Special Trains. See Book of Rules and Regulations.
Nos. 8, 10, 12, 14 and 15 will call at Ty Trist or Bedwellty, if required. No. 8 Down must not start before arrival of No. 7 Up.
Previous to despatching Nos. 4, 7, 11, and 16, for Bedwellty, a man with Signals must be sent 800 yards in advance to protect them.
No. 16 Down must not be despatched until after the arrival of No. 13 Up.
On Wednesdays and Saturdays, all Up and all Down Passenger Trains will stop at Ynysddu and Pontymoile Farm Crossing, for the purpose of taking up and setting down Passengers.

CROSSING ARRANGEMENTS.

No. 3 Down to cross Nos. 1 and 2 Up
No. 6 Down to cross No. 5 Up
No. 10 Down to cross No. 9 Up
No. 12 Down to cross Nos. 11 and 12 Up
} At Blackwood.

UP TRAINS.

WEEK DAYS.

Distance	Stations and Sidings	1 arr.	1 dep.	2 arr.	2 dep.	3 Colliers and E. Trucks arr.	3 Colliers and E. Trucks dep.	4 Passenger arr.	4 Passenger dep.	5 Pick Up arr.	5 Pick Up dep.	6 arr.	6 dep.	7 Passenger arr.	7 Passenger dep.	8 arr.	8 dep.
		a.m.	a.m.	a.m.	a.m.	a.m.	a.m.	a.m.	a.m.	a.m.	a.m.	a.m.	a.m.	a.m.	a.m.	a.m.	a.m.
	Newport	...	...	...	...	...	...	...	...	...	...	...	...	...	9 40	...	...
	Risca	...	...	...	...	...	...	...	...	...	...	...	...	...	10 5	...	...
	Mon. Railway Company's Goods and Mineral Trains Nine-Mile-Point	5 50	...	...	...	...	...	...	...	7 0	..	...	...	...	...	10 55	...
	Nine-Mile-Point, S.R.	...	6 0	...	6 20	...	...	...	...	...	8 52	...	...	...	10 15	...	11 0
2	Duffryn Chemical Works	...	...	...	...	...	...	...	...	...	9 2	...	...	...	...	...	...
	Ynysddu	...	...	...	...	...	...	...	...	...	...	...	...	...	...	...	...
4	Junction with G.W.R., Lower	...	...	...	...	...	...	...	...	...	...	...	...	...	...	...	...
4¼	" " Upper	...	...	...	...	...	...	...	...	...	9 30	...	...	...	...	..	11 31
4½	Tredegar Junction Station	...	6 23	...	6 43	...	...	...	...	...	9 34	...	...	10 27	10 34	...	11 32
4¾	Bryn Siding	...	...	...	...	...	...	...	...	...	9 36	...	...	...	...	...	...
5½	Blackwood	...	6 33	...	6 50	...	...	...	...	...	9 44	...	...	...	10 41	11 40	11 44
6	Cwm Gelly	...	...	...	...	...	...	...	...	...	9 46	...	...	...	...	..	...
6¼	Upper Rock Colliery	...	...	...	...	...	...	...	...	...	9 57	...	...	...	...	...	...
7	Lower Argoed	...	...	...	...	...	...	...	...	...	...	...	...	...	...	...	...
7¼	Upper Argoed	...	...	...	...	...	...	...	...	...	...	...	...	...	...	...	...
7½	Argoed	...	...	...	...	...	...	...	...	...	10 2	...	...	...	10 49	...	...
9½	Ancient Druid*	...	...	...	...	...	...	...	...	...	...	...	...	...	...	...	...
10¼	Holly Bush	...	...	...	...	...	...	...	...	..	10 26	...	...	...	...	...	...
10½	Pontygwaith	...	...	...	...	...	...	...	...	...	10 31	...	...	...	...	...	...
12¼	Bedwellty (Upper)	...	...	7 21	7 31	...	6 40	...	...	...	...	...	9 25	...	...	...	...
	Bedwellty (Lower)	...	...	...	...	...	...	...	...	...	...	...	...	...	11 0	...	...
13¼	Ty Trist (Upper)	7 10	7 20	...	...	...	...	...	...	...	...	...	...	...	...	...	12 17
13½	Tredegar	7 23	...	7 40	8 4	6 48	...	...	7 50	10 52	...	9 35	...	11 4	11 6	12 20	...
14½	Sirhowy	...	...	8 9	...	...	...	7 53	...	...	...	...	...	11 9	...	...	...

Distance	Stations and Sidings	9 arr.	9 dep.	10 arr.	10 dep.	11 Passenger arr.	11 Passenger dep.	12 arr.	12 dep.	13 arr.	13 dep.	14 Minerals arr.	14 Minerals dep.	15 arr.	15 dep.	16 arr.	16 dep.	17 Passenger arr.	17 Passenger dep.
		p.m.	p.m.	p.m.	p.m.	p.m.	p.m.	p.m.	p.m.	p.m.	p.m.	p.m.	p.m.	p.m.	p.m.	p.m.	p.m.	p.m.	p.m.
	Newport	...	...	...	...	...	2 20	...	...	...	...	...	...	...	...	...	...	..	6 50
	Risca	...	.	...	...	...	2 40	...	...	...	...	...	...	...	...	...	...	...	7 10
	Mon. Railway Company's Goods and Mineral Trains Nine-Mile-Point	12 0	...	...	...	...	...	...	...	3 35	...	...	...	3 55	...	...	...	...	...
	Nine-Mile-Point, S.R.	...	1 26	...	...	...	2 55	...	3 0	...	4 40	...	..	...	6 20	...	6 35	...	7 20
2	Duffryn Chemical Works	...	...	...	...	...	...	...	...	...	...	...	...	...	...	...	...	...	...
	Ynysddu	...	...	...	...	...	...	...	..	...	...	...	...	...	...	...	...	...	...
4	Junction with G.W.R., Lower	...	...	...	...	...	...	...	...	...	...	...	...	...	...	...	...	...	...
4¼	" " Upper	...	...	...	...	...	...	...	3 20	...	5 0	...	...	...	...	...	...	...	...
4½	Tredegar Junction Station	...	1 34	...	...	...	3 10	...	3 22	...	5 6	...	...	..	6 44	...	6 59	..	7 35
4¾	Bryn Siding	...	...	...	...	...	...	...	...	...	...	...	...	...	...	...	...	...	...
5½	Blackwood	...	1 49	...	...	...	3 18	...	3 30	5 15	5 43	...	...	...	7 0	...	7 15		7 42
6	Cwm Gelly	...	...	...	...	...	...	...	...	...	...	...	...	...	...	...	...	...	...
6¼	Upper Rock Colliery	...	...	...	...	...	...	...	...	...	...	...	...	...	...	...	...	...	...
7	Lower Argoed	...	...	...	...	...	...	...	...	...	...	...	...	...	...	...	...	...	...
7¼	Upper Argoed	...	...	...	...	...	...	...	...	..	...	...	...	...	...	...	...	...	...
7½	Argoed	.	...	...	...	...	3 26	...	...	...	...	...	...	...	...	...	...	...	7 51
9½	Ancient Druid*	...	...	...	...	...	...	...	...	...	...	...	...	...	...	...	...	...	...
10¼	Holly Bush	...	...	...	...	...	...	...	...	...	...	...	...	...	...	...	...	...	...
10½	Pontygwaith	...	...	...	...	...	...	...	...	...	6 10	...	...	...	...	...	...	...	...
12¼	Bedwellty (Upper)	...	2 16	...	1 25	...	...	...	...	...	...	...	6 25	...	...	...	...	...	...
	Bedwellty (Lower)	...	...	...	...	...	3 38	...	...	...	...	...	...	...	...	...	...	...	8 [illegible]
13¼	Ty Trist (Upper)	...	2 21	...	...	...	...	...	...	...	...	...	...	...	...	...	...	...	...
13½	Tredegar	2 30	2 35	1 35	...	3 42	3 44	4 10	...	6 15	...	6 30	...	7 40	...	7 50	...	8 [illegible]	8 10
14½	Sirhowy	2 40	...	...	...	3 47	...	...	...	...	...	...	...	...	...	...	...	8 1[illegible]	...

SUNDAYS.

Distance	Stations and Sidings	1 Passenger arr.	1 Passenger dep.	2 Passenger arr.	2 Passenger dep.	3 Passenger arr.	3 Passenger dep.
		a.m.	a.m.	a.m.	a.m.	p.m.	p.m.
	Newport	...	...	...	10 0		6 0
	Risca	...	...	...	10 25		6 20
	Mon. Railway Company's Goods and Mineral Trains Nine-Mile-Point	...	...				
	Nine-Mile-Point, S.R.				10 [illegible]		[illegible]
2	Duffryn Chemical Works		...				
	Ynysddu						
4	Junction with G.W.R., Lower						
4¼	" " Upper						
4½	Tredegar Junction Station		..	10 52	10 5[illegible]		6 4[illegible]
4¾	Bryn Siding		...				
5½	Blackwood	...	...		11 [illegible]		6 52
6	Cwm Gelly						
6¼	Upper Rock Colliery						
7	Lower Argoed						
7¼	Upper Argoed						
7½	Argoed				11 14		7 1
9½	Ancient Druid*						
10¼	Holly Bush						
10½	Pontygwaith						
12¼	Bedwellty (Upper)						
	Bedwellty (Lower)				11 26		7 14
13¼	Ty Trist (Upper)						
13½	Tredegar	...	7 50	11 30	11 32	7 1[illegible]	7 2[illegible]
14½	Sirhowy	7 53	...	11 35	...	7 2[illegible]	...

CROSSING ARRANGEMENTS.

No. 8 Up to cross No. 8 Down
No. 13 Up to cross Nos. 13, 14, & 15 Down
} At Blackwood.

* Mineral and Goods Trains to stop at Ancient Druid for water.

Nos. 15 and 16 will run, if required, but in no case without a due observance of the regulations having reference to Special Trains.—See Book of Regulations.
Nos. 12 and 13 to call at "Junction with the G.W.R.," if required.
Nos. 15 and 16 to call at Bedwellty or Ty Trist, if required.
On Wednesdays and Saturdays, all Up and all Down Passenger Trains will stop at Ynysddu and Pontymoile Farm Crossing, for the purpose of taking up and setting down Passengers.
No. 13 Up will call daily at Bedwellty for Colliers.
No. 5 Up Train must not start from Nine Mile Point before the arrival of No. 15 Down.

This working timetable from the first year of operations as a railway was sent by the station master at Tredegar to his Head Office in Abergavenny in 1888. No doubt he came across it when clearing out the drawers of his desk, as the handwritten comment suggests, and felt that its survival for 22 years had given it curiosity value.

PRO RAIL 981/436

Tredegar Station, looking north, in 1939. *LGRP 11530/NRM*

withdrawn. In 1868 the junction at Nantybwch was at last completed and on 27 February Yockney was suddenly told not to act in any way for the company in the future; there is no evidence in the papers as to the cause, though the case went to arbitration. The new general manager, R. Bond, started at a salary of £300 a year which he negotiated up to £500 by January 1874. The LNW clearly found the service between Nantybwch and Tredegar unsatisfactory as, already in June 1868, Findlay was recommending that the LNW take over the train operation.

In April 1872 the GWR requested that the line from Tredegar Junction to Nine Mile Point be doubled. They were now moving 400,000 tons of coal a year from Aberdare down the route from Tredegar Junction, made possible by the narrowing of the broad gauge through Newport on the old south Wales main line. This was agreed in August. At the same time a carriage was bought from the LNW for £40. In March 1874 the Sirhowy were still pushing their independence and arguing that they should now only pay one third of the operating costs at Nantybwch on the basis that the Rhymney made a third partner; the LNW of course argued that they and the Rhymney were one. Relations with the LNW do not appear to have been particularly good, and in January 1875 the Sirhowy was stoutly asking the LNW to subvent the losses on the passenger operation over the extension to Nantybwch.

But events were beginning to move to a crescendo of negotiating activity which was to lead to the abrupt ending of that sturdy independence. In November 1873 the MRCC approached the Sirhowy with an offer to buy the shares for £295,000 or £12,000 a year for the ordinary and preference shareholders. The Sirhowy directors were not opposed to the idea provided parliamentary approval could be obtained, though Major Brown, the Sirhowy chairman appears to have had a preference for a lease. Throughout 1874 negotiations continued between the MRCC and the Sirhowy, with the Tredegar Iron Co. also in the picture. It seems that the GW were also involved and the LNW must have got wind of this because, on 5 March 1875, Moon wrote to Gooch asking as to the truth of reports that the GW were negotiating purchase of the line. The GW did not reply. On 3 March Gooch had been authorised by the GWR board to negotiate with the Sirhowy following a satisfactory inspection of the line. Perhaps it was because the GW had indeed made a draft agreement with the Sirhowy, on the strength of which they promoted in 1875 a

LNWR train at Hollybush, heading up-valley.
Lens of Sutton

BR auto train at Hollybush. The view up-valley is little changed.
J. Peden Collection

re-run of the 1866 Sirhowy Extension Bill, that the MRCC felt threatened. In separate negotiations the MRCC had been discussing with the Midland joint purchase of the B & M (see Chapter 6). When the Midland backed off, the MRCC turned instead to the GWR. On 16 June the GWR board approved a proposal to the MRCC to make an approach jointly to the Sirhowy. At about the same time, the LNW lept into action and did a secret deal with the Sirhowy effective from 1 July but formalised on 21 August. The Sirhowy debenture holders received LNW debentures, and the ordinary and preference shareholders received 10% and 5% LNW stock respectively. The whole was subsequently authorised by the LNWR (Sirhowy Railway Vesting) Act 1876. The GWR had to be content with a lease of the MRCC. The Midland was left without a partner and henceforth had to concentrate on Swansea (see Chapter 6). Once again the LNW had snatched a prize from the GWR's grasp.

On 1 July the LNW effectively took over the Sirhowy. Unlike the cautious and diplomatic approach adopted with the MTA, the initiative was swiftly seized, key personnel were changed, and matters requiring attention were speedily identified and action pressed. Major Browne resigned the chairmanship and was replaced by Benjamin Whitworth; J. Bishop, a LNW man, replaced Bond as general manager, and S. Reay, the LNW secretary, became company secretary. Henceforth board meetings were held at Euston. On 21 August Moon himself became a director.

On 27 July the LNW carried out a major inspection; Findlay, Reay, Bishop, Webb, Roberts and Bradford made a detailed tour. The highlights of their observations were: that although the GWR had diverted its Aberdare coal traffic, facilities should nevertheless be kept in place in case the business returned; much fencing was incomplete (this stemmed from the early days of the railway when a conscious decision had been taken to use hedges where possible); a post was required in the ground to mark the boundary at Nine Mile Point; deeds of conveyance held in an iron box three feet long were to be sent to London; improvements in the service for goods customers between Aber-gavenny and Tredegar were required; and the LNWR would provide guarantees for the company's agents as was its usual practice. These points were all taken up at the board meeting on 14 October. Preparation of the accounts presented a problem and half yearly meetings had to be postponed from 14 October to 18 November, 2 December, 15 February, 21 February and eventually 26 February before the accounts were ready to be presented. On the 26 May 1876 the company was vested in the LNW.

The final development of the LNWR's approaches to Newport was to complete the MRCC line up the Ebbw Fach valley by closing the gap between Nantyglo and Brynmawr. This link was not made until 1905 in spite of earlier requests from the people of Brynmawr; indeed, in 1874 a deputation to the MRCC sought such a line, and it is perhaps interesting to understand why it took so long. It was not that there was a gap in the rail network between Nantyglo and Brynmawr because a line owned by the Nantyglo & Blaina Iron Co. had been converted from tramway status by the Baileys and in 1881 leased to the LNWR. This purely freight line was of great importance as it was the means by which the LNW and later the LMS gained access to the Rose Heyworth Colliery. However, it was only developed as a freight line and joined the MTA east of Brynmawr station and would have been expensive to adapt for passenger use. Accordingly, when the Brynmawr & Western Valleys Railway was promoted in 1899, the GW and LNW jointly agreed under pressure to take it over and to use it primarily as a passenger carrying line. It ran parallel to the freight line for just over a mile.

CHUMS WITH THE RHYMNEY

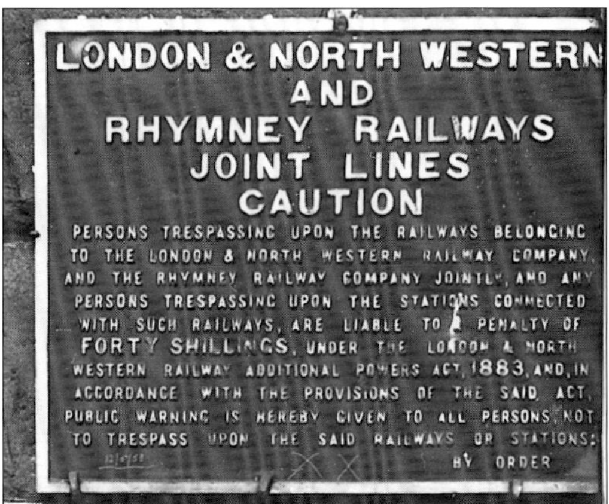

A joint notice-board at Rhymney Station; August 1955.

Ian L. Wright

We now need to turn back to 1861 in order to follow events west of Nantybwch where we have already been aware of moves by other companies to fill the gap between there and Dowlais. The position was made complex by the rivalry between the Rhymney and the Brecon & Merthyr for access to the Rhymney valley and for control of the extremely shakey so-called 'Old Rumney' railway. These differences eventually played into the hands of the LNWR. The first challenge to the LNW was when the B & M, by its Extensions Act of 1861, obtained authority to build a line from near Dowlais to Nantybwch, amended slightly in its Act of 1862 and again in 1863 and 1864. This followed closely the original concept of the MTA (see Chapter 4).

However, since 1860 the LNWR and the Rhymney had been developing a relationship. In October that year the LNW loaned the Rhymney £30,000 and as security hired some rolling stock. In May 1861 the Rhymney were leasing locomotives from the LNW. In that year John Boyle, who had been chairman of the Rhymney since its inception, resigned from the board of the B & M, as a head-on conflict with the Rhymney was being pursued by the B & M in the Bargoed Rhymney valley. In October that year he had a meeting with Moon and the LNW secretary, Stewart. When Boyle reported this meeting to his board, he was urged to assure the LNW of their 'readiness to cooperate with them in arrangements for developing the traffic of the district'. In June 1862, when the Bill for the LNW to lease the MTA was in Parliament, Boyle told his board that they should now start working on their own Bill for the next session to build a line from Rhymney Bridge to join the MTA at Nantybwch.

Rhymney Railway 0-6-2T No. 82 at Rhymney Bridge; 25 July 1922.
GBJ Coll.

On 13 August 1863 John Boyle had another meeting with Richard Moon. This time Cawkwell and Blenkinsop, the lawyer, were present and the meeting continued with them the following day. This must have been the seminal meeting at which joint ownership of the line from Nantybwch to Rhymney, LNW access to Cardiff and reciprocal running powers were discussed, for afterwards the Rhymney board asked Boyle to write to Moon to seek an assurance that the LNW would treat the Rhymney Railway's projected direct line as their 'principal or main route' to Cardiff, in return for which the Rhymney would agree to extend running powers to the LNW over the rest of their line. In September Boyle was asked to get the LNW to agree to calculate rates over their system, where theirs were not the shortest route, by dividing LNW mileage by that of the shortest route; this applied particularly to the link between Worcester and Hereford which was not available to the LNWR. When Boyle met Moon again he was told somewhat patronisingly, 'It would be of very little use to

Rhymney Station, looking up-valley; 6 November 1971.
J.A. Sommerfield, courtesy J.A. Peden

Rhymney Station in its setting, looking south in BR days; 1981.
GBJ

Rhymney Station, looking south; 6 November 1971.
J.A. Sommerfield, courtesy J.A. Peden

the RR to insist upon the point.' The LNW might after all have wished to do the same in reverse. On 20 October Moon reported to the Shrewsbury & South Wales Committee, of which he was the chairman, that he had had a meeting with Boyle at which they had agreed that the Rhymney would deposit a Bill for the line from Rhymney Bridge to Nantybwch, over which the LNW was to have running powers, and had agreed to endeavour to make an agreement with the B & M to avoid duplication.

In 1864 the two important RR Bills were passed enabling them to go ahead with the Cardiff direct line and the northern extension from Rhymney. The Rhymney Railway (Northern Lines) Act authorised the construction of a line northward from Rhymney to join the previously authorised line of the B & M

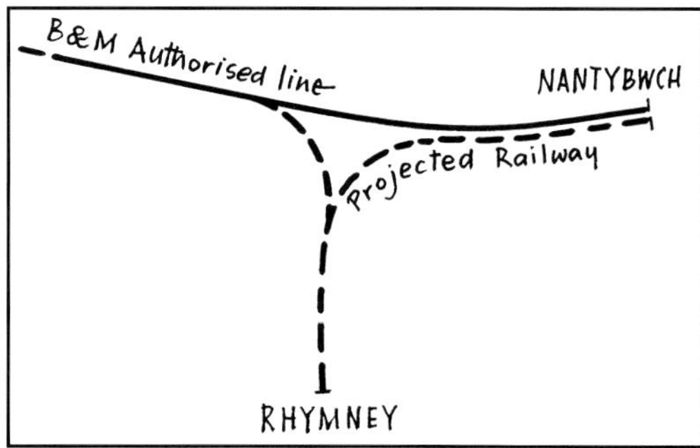

Rhymney Railway (Northern Lines) Act, 1864.

from Dowlais at Rhymney Bridge with lines facing both east and west. A further line from Rhymney Bridge was to extend eastward to join the MTA end-on at Nantybwch. In the same year, as is revealed in more detail in Chapter 4, an agreement was made with the B & M, who now gave up their plans to extend from Dowlais to Rhymney Bridge and beyond. With the LNW, the agreement was made to share the line from Nantybwch to Rhymney and to allow running powers to the LNWR all the way to Cardiff, and to the Rhymney over the MTA. In January 1865, as an interim measure, the LNW, being able now to declare in all honesty to the GWR that it would not pursue its own line from Nantybwch to Merthyr, was able to extract a discount off the GWR rates from Merthyr on the grounds of the distance being greater along the TVE.

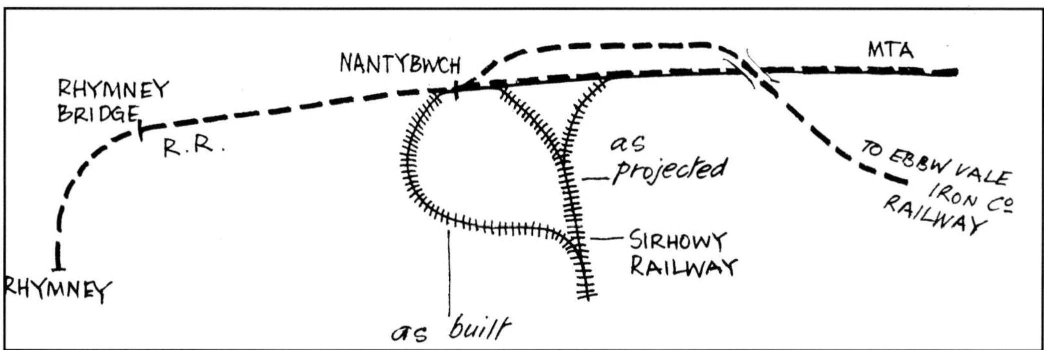

Rhymney Railway (New Lines) Bill, 1866.

In 1866 the Rhymney was ready with the next phase: the line from Rhymney to Rhymney Bridge was now complete and further plans were deposited for the line from Rhymney Bridge to a point just west of Nantybwch; a new oddity was a line east from there parallel to the MTA but to the north of it, which was then to cross it and descend the Ebbw valley; in addition, a spur line was projected from the Sirhowy Railway westward to enable a direct link between the top of the Sirhowy valley and Cardiff. This last proposal generated serious debate in the committee proceedings, with the business men of the Tredegar area interested in improved connections with Cardiff and the landowner down the valley anxious to maintain the income from trains going down loaded to Newport.

The resulting Rhymney Railway (New Lines) Act of 1866 repeated the planned link between Rhymney Bridge and a point a little west of Nantybwch but excluded all the rest. The spur from the Sirhowy towards Rhymney was never built though the issue was by no means dead. The additional line to the Ebbw valley was not needed, and final agreement to exchange running powers between the LNW and the Rhymney was made while the Bill was in committee. The agreement as to joint ownership between Nantybwch and Rhymney was confirmed in the 1867 LNWR (New Lines) Act.

Completion of this piece of the chain took longer than expected to the evident irritation of the LNW; already in 1866 Boyle had had to write to Moon from his holiday at Pontresina in Switzerland apologising for having given an over-optimistic impression of progress and pleading that ground problems with the Rhymney Iron Co. were 'giving trouble and vexation'. It sounds as though there had not been total unanimity within the Rhymney, as he went on, 'You know how personally anxious I have always been about this line. Now I am happy to say all my people are desirous to have it made.' When Moon and his entourage made their grand tour of south Wales in 1867 and saw the railway system of Cardiff, they met Lundie, general manager of the Rhymney, and reported, 'The arrangements with the Rhymney Co. are satisfactory and as far as practicable they exchange all their traffic with the LNWR.'

It was not until 18 December 1867 that Lundie was ready with plans of the Nantybwch to Rhymney Bridge section. The cost was now estimated at £50,000, up from the original

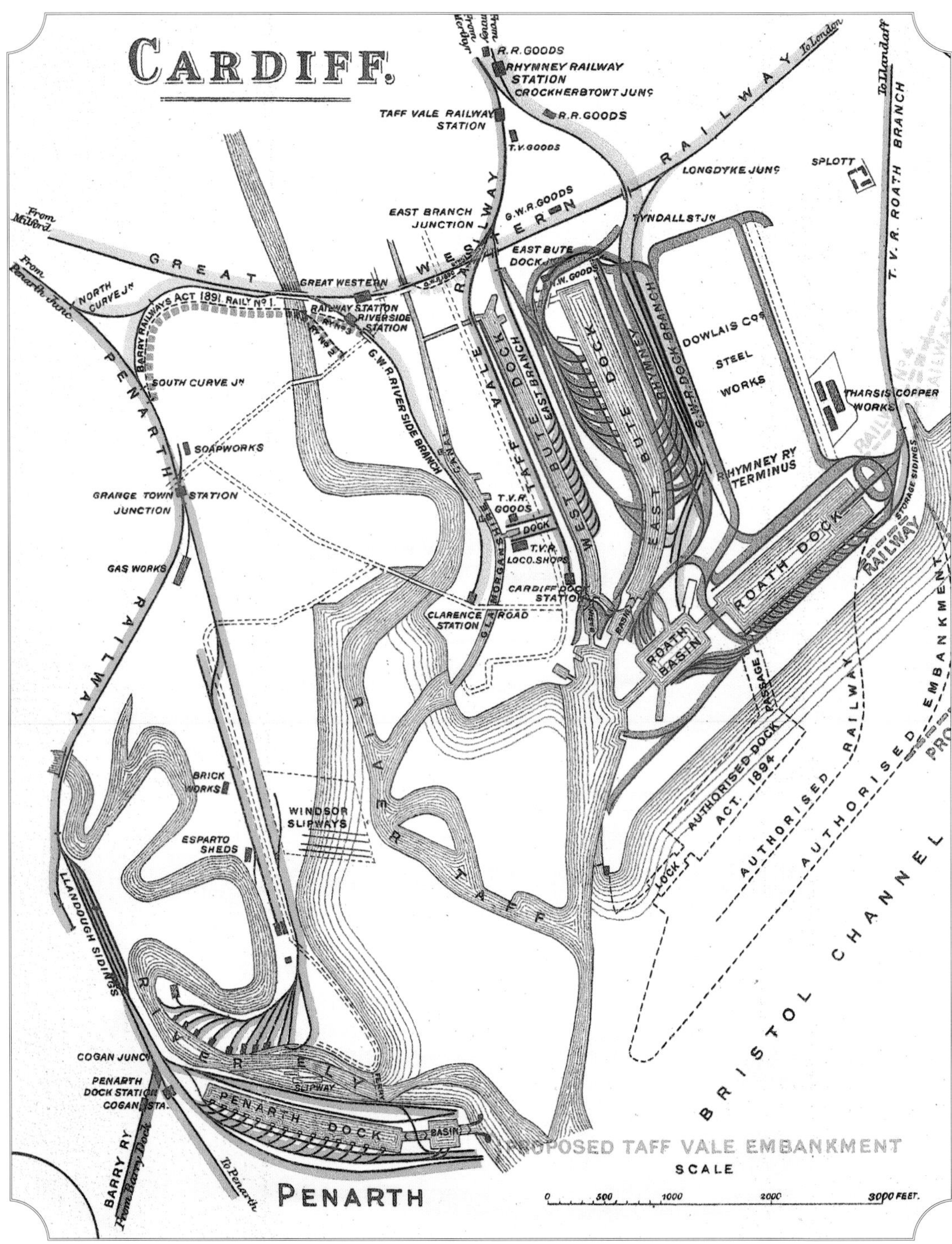

The LNWR at the heart of Cardiff from a plan accompanying an 1895 Rhymney Railway Bill.

PRO RAIL 1057/1656

The former LNWR goods warehouse at Tyndall Street, Cardiff, now the Cardiff Bay Hotel; spring 1997.

DD

Gardner forecast of £30,000. As soon as this connection was made in 1871, the LNWR began operations through to Cardiff, and as early as 13 March 1872, was receiving complaints that inadequate warehousing there was causing delays to customers. Findlay suggested the company should have its own warehouse near the Bute Docks instead of using the Rhymney Station, and in due course in 1875 the LNW built its own goods station at Tyndall Street. This and the half mile of connecting track was authorised by the LNWR (Joint & Various Powers) Act of 1877 which approved the lease of the site from the Rhymney.

The opening of the joint line was clearly regarded as a matter of importance for at the official opening on 5 September, not only was Richard Moon present, but the Lord Mayors of London and Cardiff also judged that the event justified their attendance. The Rhymney held most board meetings at this time in London, so it was not a stranger in the City and this, as well as commercial logic, may have contributed to the building of the close relationship with the LNWR. Still to be completed was the original concept of the MTA for a line into the heart of Merthyr and Dowlais. The complexity of this process calls for a separate chapter.

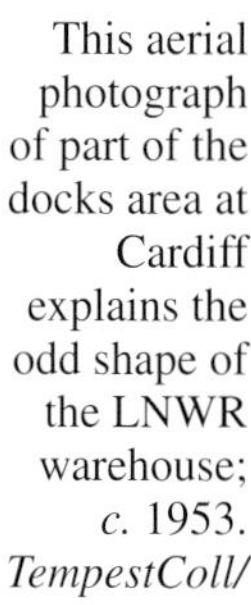

This aerial photograph of part of the docks area at Cardiff explains the odd shape of the LNWR warehouse; *c.* 1953. *TempestColl/ WIMM*

The former RR shed at Cardiff Docks still bore evidence of the LNW connection in August 1924 in the form of coal tank No. 3739. The other locomotive was RR No. 65, at that time GW No. 1324.
Tudor Watkins Coll.

C A R D I F F.

The L.& N.W. secured running powers over Rhymney Company by Agreement June 4th, 1864.

Working expenses at 20% allowed.

Under Agreement November 12th, 1875, the L.& N.W. may convey by their own engines to and from Cardiff all through Goods and Mineral traffic for points east of Brynmawr. In practice the L.& N.W. work over the Rhymney Line with traffic for places on M.T.& A. West of Brynmawr.

L.& N.W. receive usual terminals and 45 chains mileage at Cardiff, plus 20% on 24 miles for working expenses over the Rhymney Line.

L.& N.W. to maintain, use and work a junction with the Rhymney Company's Bute Dock, Low Level Line, together with all signals, etc. Pointsmen and signalmen to be appointed by Rhymney Company and L.& N.W. to pay Rhymney Company the wages paid.

L.& N.W. to pay Rhymney Company £50 per annum as rent for land for junction, signals, shunts, etc.,

Agreement for 99 years as from September 29th, 1875.

Passenger train traffic is dealt with at Cardiff G.W. and exchanged at Hereford.

An internal document for briefing LNWR management on the arrangements at Cardiff; 1912.
PRO RAIL 1007/130

However, before we move on to Merthyr, it is worth pausing to consider the different fates of the Sirhowy and the Rhymney: the one glad to sell out, the other stoutly independent until the grouping by Parliament. The Sirhowy shareholders had been looking for a way out for some ten years; their original objective of gradually improving communication from the ironworks and collieries to the markets had been achieved and there was no further value to be added out of forming part of a national trunk route. Indeed, much of the coal from the Sirhowy valley moved northward to England, so the Sirhowy was dependent on other railways. The Rhymney was much more independent, was financially very robust and had close links with the Bute family. There was little value to be added by uniting with an English company; better to benefit from an alliance. The arrangement between the Rhymney and the LNWR suited both and had clearly worked so well that, when the 1923 grouping was being discussed, there was a strong body of opinion in favour of the Rhymney becoming part of the LMS, in order both to reflect this relationship and to maintain competition. The GWR successfully argued against it.

Chapter 4

THE MERTHYR TANGLE

The growth of Merthyr, 800 ft up in the mountains, to become by the middle of the nineteenth century the largest town in Wales was a phenomenon brought about by the presence in those mountains of the three precious ingredients of iron manufacture: iron ore, limestone and coal. With a population of 70,000 people to be fed, housed and clothed, as well as the need to move minerals and mineral products, it was hardly surprising that there was a crying need for transport, and something better than the appalling mountain roads.

Merthyr lies in a bowl, open on the south side where the Taff runs out and down a long valley to Cardiff; to the north are two steep, narrow and picturesque valleys where the two Taff rivers run down from the Brecon Beacons. Just below the confluence of these rivers, the town grew up around two ironworks, the Penydarren and the Plymouth. On the northern side of the bowl was Cyfarthfa ironworks and at some 1,200 ft up on the eastern rim stood Dowlais with the world famous Guest-owned Dowlais ironworks, founded in 1759 and named after the stream which powered the first bellows; by 1845 it was the largest ironworks in the world.

This pulsating, heaving, smokey, dirty place attracted railway promotion early in the nineteenth century, for as business expanded, the canals and tramroads proved inadequate and too expensive. The ironmasters saw the opportunity railways provided for improved transport and it was they who produced the early stimulus. The Taff Vale was the first to be created, in 1841, running from a station near the Plymouth works down the Taff to the docks at Cardiff. Second on the scene in 1851 was the steeply inclined Dowlais Railway, branching from the Taff Vale up the eastern side of the bowl for nearly two miles to the Dowlais ironworks. Third came the broad gauge Vale of Neath entering the bowl in

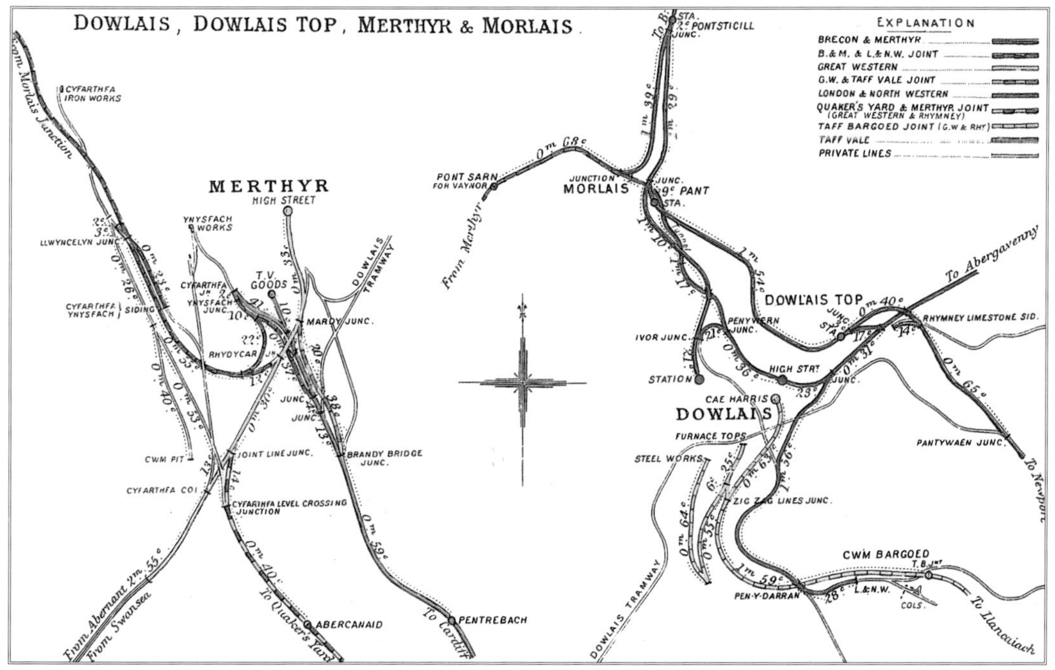

The final shape of the tangle at Dowlais and Merthyr; 1913.

Railway Clearing House

1853 through a tunnel on the western flank, crossing the TVR and turning northward to a new station, High Street, in the centre of the town. In 1857 the Merthyr Junction Railway had been floated as a line down the east side of the Taff from Penydarren to Quakers Yard; it was designed by Liddell, engineer to the NAH, but made no progress. In the following year a further link was forged when the TVR was reached four miles down the Taff valley at Quakers Yard, by the Taff Vale Extension (TVE) of the NAH.

From now on there was complex manoeuvring between other companies anxious to share in the potential profits, and in spite of the unpropitious lie of the land, further assaults on Merthyr were made from the north, east and south. The principal assailants were the B & M from the north and the LNW from the east. Later, in 1876, the GW and Rhymney, in an unlikely alliance, arrived at Dowlais up the Bargoed Taff valley and then, in 1886, drove a line up the west side of the Taff from Quakers Yard.

'Cornwall' at Merthyr at the turn of the century. On gradients such as those found on the MTA, this locomotive, with its 8' 6" driving wheels, would have been best restricted to hauling the inspector's saloon. *Ken Davies Coll.*

In 1859, the original deposited plans of the MTA envisaged a frontal assault on Merthyr with a line sweeping down the side of the mountain across the Dowlais Iron Co.'s inclined railway and arriving in High Street Station from the east, down a gradient of 1:39 for more than five miles. This bold concept was included in another Bill in 1865 which was withdrawn. The LNW were clearly concerned at the potential cost as Findlay was asked by Moon to speak to Joshua Williams about the possibility of the Vale of Neath contributing. Eight years later the LNW adopted a rather more cautious and circuitous approach, though hardly less costly.

In 1871 we left the LNW celebrating with the Rhymney the opening of their joint line to Rhymney Bridge. This now became the new bridgehead for the assault on Dowlais, which had been under consideration for the last ten years. The initial prize was the opportunity to bring in iron-ore from Northamptonshire and to take out iron products, especially rails, from the Dowlais ironworks, but the ultimate goal was Merthyr. Across the LNW's path, the ambitious but impoverished B & M was coming down from the north, aiming to gain access to Newport down the Rhymney valley, but also apparently seeking to control the movement eastward from Dowlais by building and thus controlling a link to the MTA at Nantybwch.

In order better to understand the LNW's slow progress in the area west of Nantybwch, it will be instructive to look more closely at the B & M which generated an immense amount of legal and parliamentary work in the course of its pursuit of a route from Brecon through Dowlais to the Bristol Channel. Its initial Act of 1859 had granted authority for a railway from

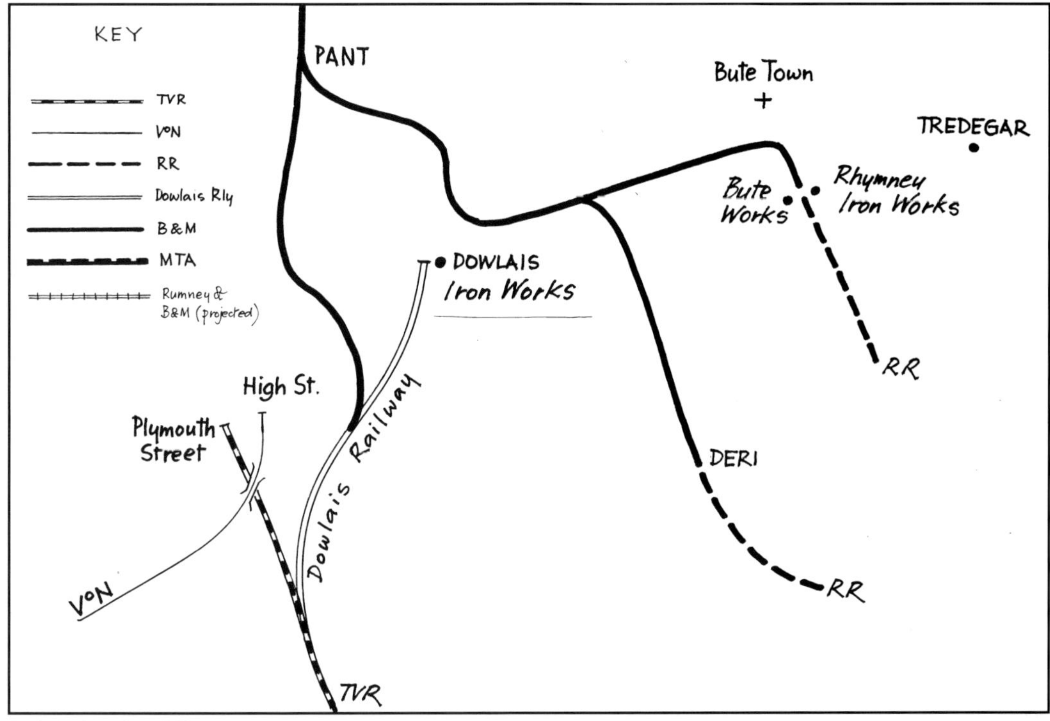

B & M Jc Rly 1859.

Brecon to a junction with the Dowlais Railway. As noted earlier, this industrial line ran from a point near the Dowlais works down the steep side of the mountain to a junction with the Taff Vale in the heart of Merthyr. Just north of Dowlais a branch of the B & M was to head south-east to join the Rhymney Railway head-on in the Bargoed Rhymney valley, and a further branch was to run eastward into the next valley, the Rhymney valley, to another end-on junction with the Rhymney. There then followed a succession of negotiations and Bills aimed at gaining access to Newport, but also intended to block the path of the LNWR. In the end all parties obtained some satisfaction but it was a slow and expensive process.

The first step was the B & M (Extensions) Act of 1860. This may be ignored here as it was only

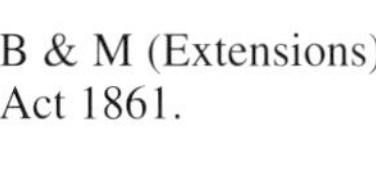
B & M (Extensions) Act 1861.

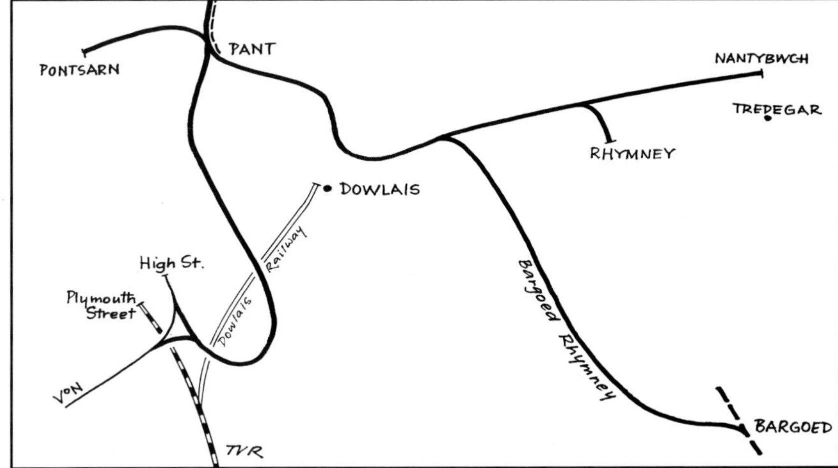

concerned with some deviations near Brecon. The first round of serious negotiations about the Merthyr area led to the B & M (Extensions) Act of 1861. This was an ambitious elaboration of the 1859 Act; it introduced the start of a westerly branch around the north of Merthyr and altered the link with the Dowlais Railway. In its place the Act introduced a bold sweep across the mountainside, cutting across the Dowlais Railway, and then making a sharp curve leading to a steep drop all the way down the side of the mountain to a junction just south of Merthyr. The fact that this route bore a marked resemblance to John Gardner's original concept, expressed in the 1859 MTA Act and repeated in the LNWR Bill of 1865, can be explained by the fact that in about 1860 Gardner and Conybeare, the B & M engineer, were working together. The projected B & M line into the Bargoed Rhymney valley was now to run all the way down this valley to the point where it joins the Rhymney river, and, most alarming of all for the MTA, was a new line from the head of the Rhymney valley eastward towards Nantybwch.

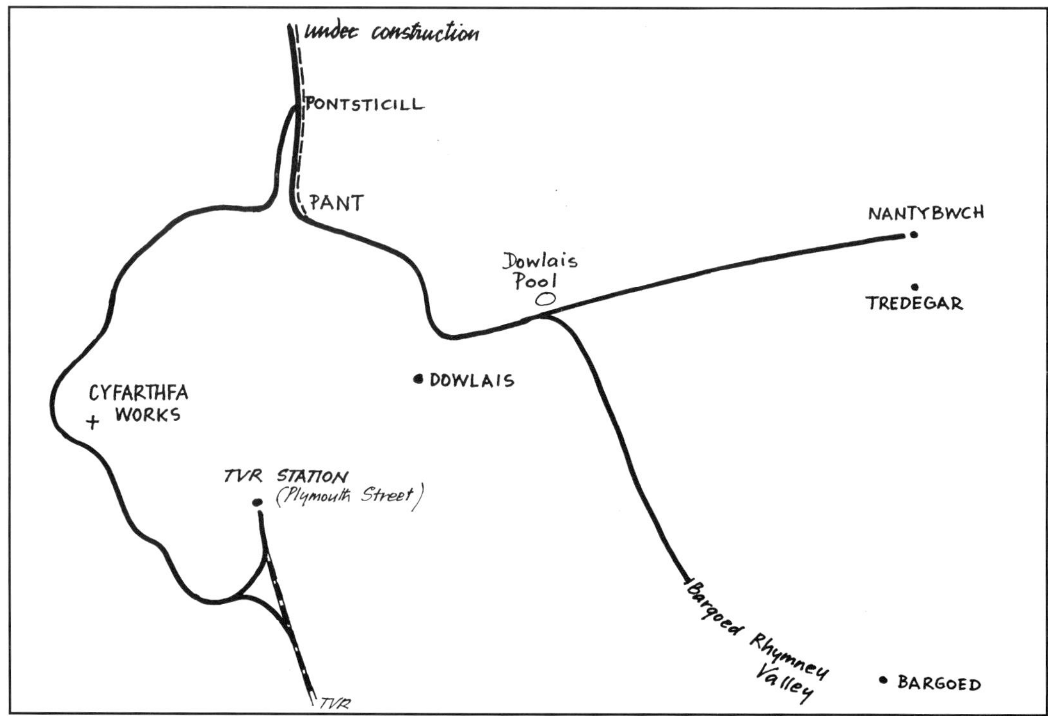

B & MR 1862.

The B & M Act of 1862 repeated the eastward move with some deviations, dropped altogether the link with the Dowlais Railway of 1859 and the steep drop down to Merthyr of 1861, and substituted an extension of its 1861 idea of a line across the north of Merthyr and round the Cyfarthfa Works; it then described a semi-circle and ended up facing north in a two-way junction with the Taff Vale. As a result the TVR was now to be approached from the west instead of the east. The B & M Act of 1863 added to this last design an additional link to the Vale of Neath. This was to be the means by which both the B & M and the LNW ultimately reached Merthyr. The Rumney and B & M Act, also of 1863, introduced a line southward from the Nantybwch extension to join end-on the 'Old Rumney' Railway which ran down the east side of the Rhymney valley. By acquiring this company the B & M reached Newport, though the link to it was eventually made lower down the valley at a junction with the line running down the Bargoed Rhymney valley.

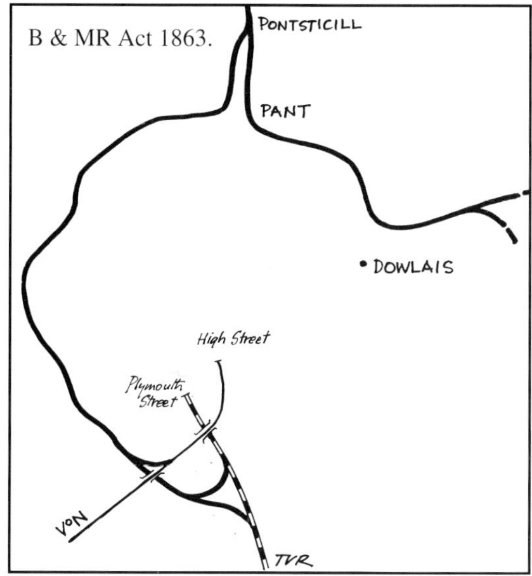

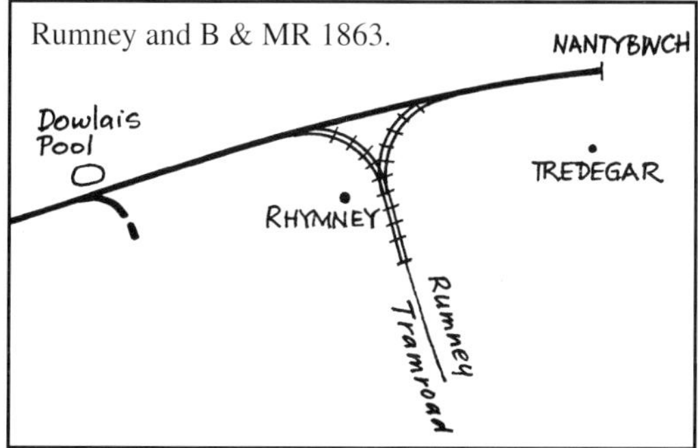

In 1864 three Bills were presented which were distilled into the B & M (No. 1) Act and the B & M (New Lines) Act. The first made some minor deviations in the area east of Dowlais, one of them rejoicing in the name of the Dowlais Road-side Pond Deviation. The New Lines Act again redrew the line between

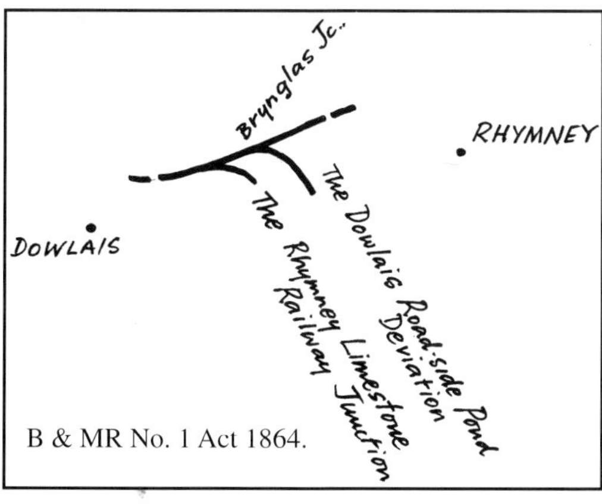

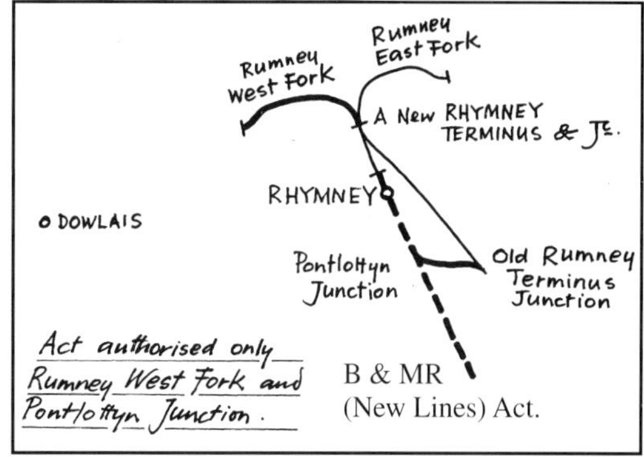

the Rhymney valley and Dowlais and altered the point of contact with the 'Old Rumney'. It was significant because it marked the end of the struggle, for it coincided with the Rhymney's Northern Lines Bill and contained a schedule repeating the agreement now reached between the B & M and the Rhymney as a result of negotiations between them.

In 1865, the last of the series, the B & M (Various Powers) Act was passed. This

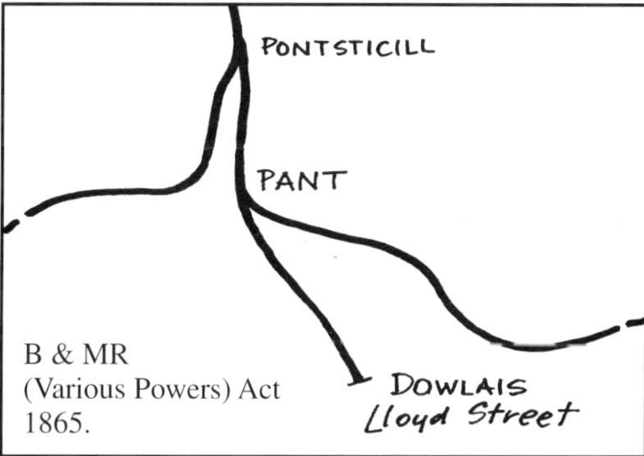

permitted a branch from the north straight into the heart of Dowlais, near the Ivor Works, to a passenger station at Lloyd Street. This and the passage in 1867 of the LNWR (New Lines) Act effectively cleared the way for the LNWR. By this last Act authority was obtained to build a line westward from Rhymney Bridge to join the B & M line to Dowlais Lloyd Street at Ivor Junction and to acquire running powers over the final one mile of the new B & M line. Although only three miles long, it took the LNW until 1 January 1873 to complete it, necessitating an appeal to Parliament for an extension of time; this was granted by the LNWR (Additional Powers) Act of 1870.

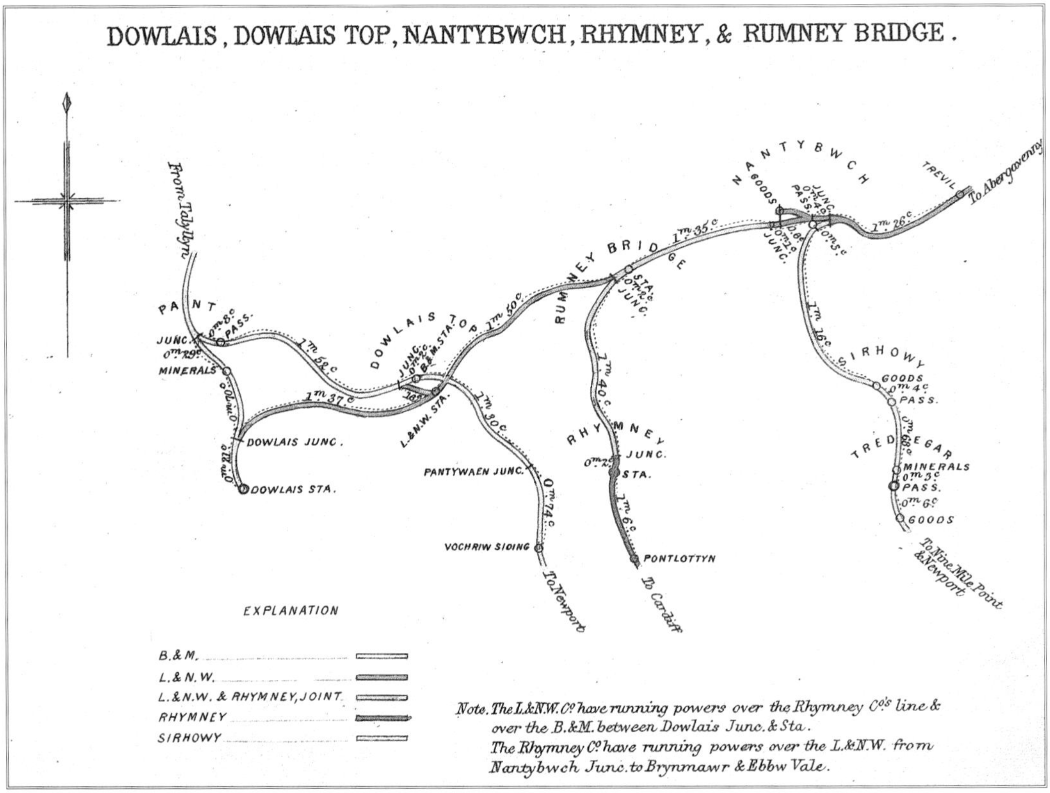
DOWLAIS, DOWLAIS TOP, NANTYBWCH, RHYMNEY, & RUMNEY BRIDGE.
From Talyllyn
PANT
JUNC.
MINERALS
PASS.
DOWLAIS JUNC.
DOWLAIS STA.
DOWLAIS TOP
L.&N.W. STA.
PANTYWAEN JUNC.
VOCHRIW SIDING
To Newport
RUMNEY BRIDGE
RHYMNEY
JUNC.
STA.
PONTLOTTYN
To Cardiff
NANTYBWCH
GOODS
TREVIL
To Abergavenny
SIRHOWY
GOODS
PASS.
TREDEGAR
MINERALS
PASS.
GOODS
To Nine Mile Point & Newport
EXPLANATION
B.& M.
L.& N.W.
L.&N.W. & RHYMNEY, JOINT
RHYMNEY
SIRHOWY
Note. The L.&N.W. Co. have running powers over the Rhymney Co's line & over the B.&M. between Dowlais Junc. & Sta.
The Rhymney Co. have running powers over the L.&N.W. from Nantybwch Junc. to Brynmawr & Ebbw Vale.

The Railway Clearing House plan of Dowlais in 1870, before the LNWR had made its final thrust to Merthyr through the Morlais tunnel.

PRO RAIL 1082/8

That was not, however, the end of the story, for although the B & M had by 1868 obtained most of its objectives, it was in sufficient financial difficulty for some cooperation with the LNW to be desirable. However, it had not survived as an independent entity by pursuing a policy of accommodation, cooperation and compromise with anyone. In June of that year it was agreed that the LNWR would build a connection to the B & M at Dowlais Top; initially this was thought to be within the limits of the deviation lines on either side of the line on the parliamentary plans, but subsequently an Act was sought, presumably on legal advice, that a branch was a branch even if within the lines of deviation. It was agreed between the two companies that all those works on the line involving both parties were to be shared or

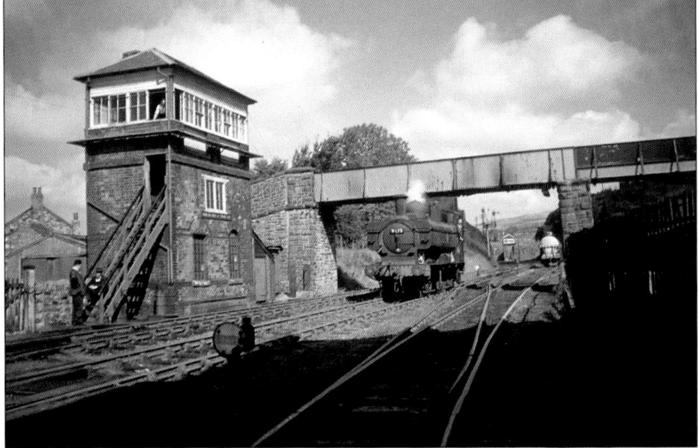

The B & M line from Ivor Junction to Dowlais Central (formerly Lloyd Street) over which the LNWR gained access to Dowlais. Ivor Junction signal box is visible in the distance beneath the bridge. 9625 is shunting ammonia tanks; 1950s. *Alan Jarvis*

allocated equitably. This was the intention, but nothing concerning the B & M was straightforward and negotiation of the terms with the LNW for making the junctions and the granting of running powers over the single mile of B & M line into Lloyd Street Station and to the Ivor Works took from 1872 to 1875; it then had to be referred to an arbitrator and was not finally settled until 1877.

Ivor Junction signal box with the B & M line to Pant to the left of it; early 1920s.
E.T. Miller/Brian J. Miller (Both photographs)

This closer view of Ivor Junction signal box shows the LNWR curving away to the right towards Penywern Junction and Dowlais High Street. The ruins to the right of the box are the remains of the LNWR engine shed which supplied locomotives for the shuttle between Dowlais Top and Lloyd Street between 1873 and 1885.

The confident LNW had not, however, allowed this minor dispute to delay making the next step into Merthyr. D.S.M. Barrie has an amusing word picture of the LNW poised dissatisfied on the hilltop at Dowlais gazing down 'into the lucrative industrial reek in the Merthyr bowl'. It was to pay dearly for the privilege of joining this particular club. With the passing of its 1863 Bill, the B & M had been getting on with building its line round the north and west of Merthyr. This involved two viaducts, at Pontsarn and Cefn Coed, over the two Taff rivers, and was completed in 1868. Its construction was a slow process, partly because of the need to construct the viaducts, the second of which, the Cefn Coed, coincided with the bankruptcy of the builder, Thomas Savin, in 1866, and partly because the B & M were caught in a vicious circle over access to the Vale of Neath station at Merthyr. The Taff Vale had extracted as their price of acquiescence in this part of the enabling Act that the B & M were also to link with their line; this the B & M were hard pressed to afford at £4,500, and it was only when they were able to acquire some ready laid track from the Baileys that they were able to get into Merthyr.

On 23 April 1873 Gardner submitted to the LNW's Shrewsbury Committee plans for a line from the Dowlais Extension to join the B & M

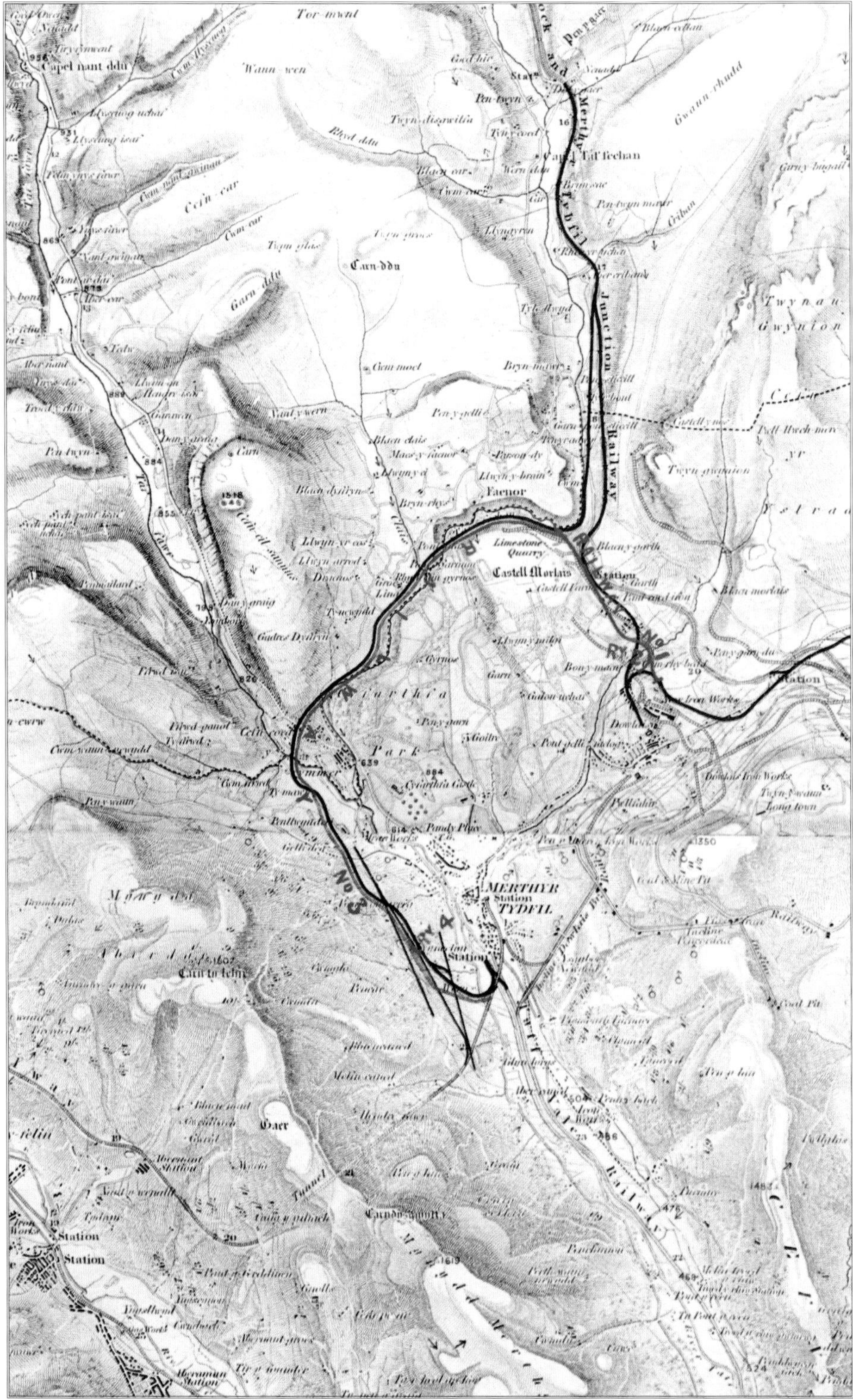

Final assault on Merthyr. The LNW eventually forced the hand of the B & M with this forthright approach in 1873.
Glamorgan Record Office

north of Cyfarthfa. Later that year the LNW submitted a Bill for an independent and separate line from Dowlais, shadowing the B & M and curving round the north side of the Merthyr bowl, and descending virtually parallel to the new B & M line. The Bill has the flavour of brazen swashbuckling confidence with a dash of sheer cheek. The B & M's financial position placed it in no position to withstand such a powerfully played hand and, while the Bill was in committee, an agreement was made. The LNW would build a link from Penywern Junction in Dowlais to the B & M at Morlais by digging the 1,040 yd Morlais tunnel beneath the B & M; this was to be double track and finely engineered on a continuous slope of 1:60 and was completed by over 500 men working around the clock for two years. The second part of the agreement was that the LNW would become joint owners of the B & M line from Morlais Junction into Merthyr by paying the B & M half the cost of their line for the nearly five miles down to Rhydycar Junction and the Vale of Neath. This included the Pontsarn and Cefn Coed viaducts. The Act was ambiguous as to whether the quoted cost of £25,000 was the total cost per mile or the LNW's half share per mile, though the latter seems more likely. In evidence in Parliament in 1867 it was stated that the five mile line had cost the B & M £90,000 in the twelve months up to March 1867, that is after the bankruptcy of Savin. With the Cefn Coed viaduct costing £25,000 and the Pontsarn probably not much less, it seems likely that the line cost in total some £250,000, which represents about £50,000 a mile. The LNW's access to Merthyr therefore cost them £125,000, plus the cost of the line from Penywern Junction to the Morlais tunnel, plus the cost of the tunnel itself, which was hardly likely to have been less than £50,000. This solution was authorised by the LNWR (Wales) Act of 1874 and the agreement became a schedule of the LNWR (New Lines & Additional Powers) Act of 1875. LNWR trains started using Merthyr Station on 9 June 1879.

The construction of the Cefn Coed viaduct almost certainly contributed to the bankruptcy of Thomas Savin, the principal contractor, in 1866.
National Tramway Museum

Pontsarn viaduct with the mountain which the railway had to scale to reach Dowlais; *c.* 1900.
GBJ Coll.

Merthyr Station in August 1951 with a Stanier Class 3 2-6-2T No. 40145 at the head of a train for Abergavenny.

R.W.A. Jones

An Abergavenny train at Merthyr headed by 41203 and consisting of two ex-L & Y carriages; 13 September 1951.

H.C. Casserley

The LNWR achievement can be reviewed by tracing an imaginary train journey. In 1920 Merthyr Station was still a busy place, shared by five railway companies responsible for some fifty train departures every working day. A typical train for the journey to Abergavenny would consist of five wooden four-wheeled carriages, in LNWR purple-lake and white. Our train stood at the furthest left platform, number five. At its head a small tank engine hissed quietly, issuing steam from several joints; it was one of the many 'coal tanks' which had been the main LNW motive power in this part of south Wales since they took over from the 0-6-0 'special tanks', in 1890. On the other side of the platform a smart black engine brought in a red and white Taff Vale train from Cardiff. At the narrow platform beyond, which had been put in when the broad gauge track was removed in 1872, a Great Western auto train for the Vale of Neath line to Hirwaun was waiting, and beyond that at Platform One stood a Brecon & Merthyr saddle tank at the head of an assorted collection of brown carriages, waiting to set off over the Brecon Beacons for Brecon.

It was a grey day in Merthyr, with a blanket of misty rain combining with the smoke pouring from the chimneys on the rows of terraced houses, and from the great works. Merthyr Station still had its Brunel overall roof and was gloomy inside, even when the sun penetrated the cloud cover, but our carriage was outside in the open and it was possible to look up and make out through the haze the line of mountains between Merthyr and Aberdare, through which the Vale of Neath line had tunnelled in 1853. To the east, the blackened mountainside leading up to Dowlais, 400 ft above, was harshly scored by tram tracks and distorted with pits and slag heaps. Somehow our train was going to get up there to take us to Abergavenny.

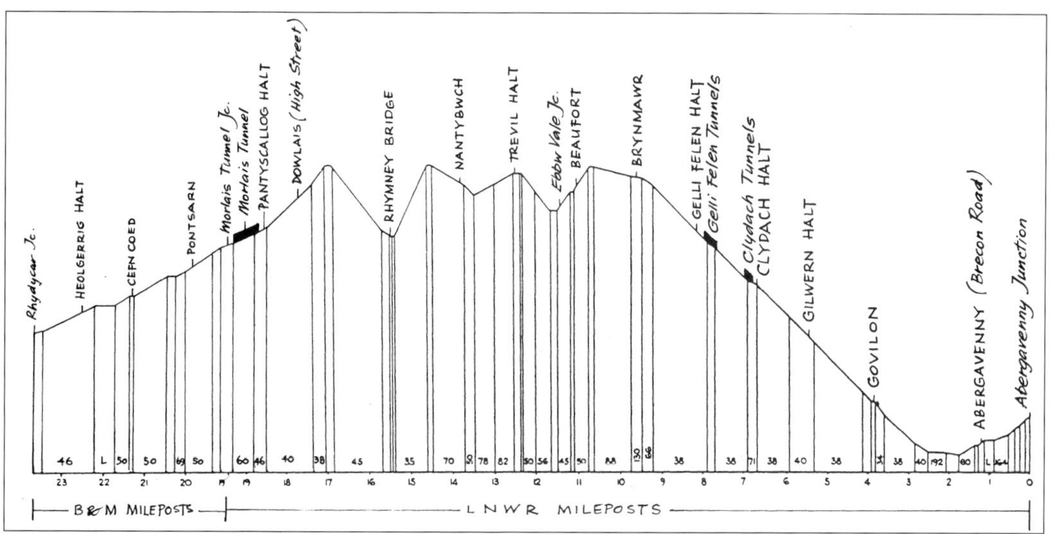

The gradient profile of the MTA illustrates not only the up and down route across the Heads of the Valleys but also the long drop from Brynmawr to Abergavenny and the relative height of Merthyr.

GBJ Coll.

We slowly edged out of the station, past sidings with carriages and waggons from many different owners. Over to the left lay the famous Penydarren ironworks. At Maerdy Junction the Taff Vale double track bore away to the left down the valley, while we headed right across the river and began to describe a huge semi-circle, in the opposite direction from that in which we had started. Now on single track, to our right and slightly below us we could just see the station we had left; we had crossed the Glamorganshire Canal, then an oasis of calm surrounded by industry, and for a mile headed upward at 1:38 for the Cefn Coed viaduct, built for the B & M with 15 arches on a graceful curve 725 ft long and 122 ft above the Taff Fawr. The fine view from the top over the Merthyr bowl can still be enjoyed as the viaduct is a preserved monument. At its northern end the train entered Cefn Coed Station, a solid stone building which had served as the B & M's station for Merthyr while the viaduct was under construction, and then while access to Merthyr over the Vale of Neath was negotiated.

The train headed by 41203 approaches Cefn Coed Station on its way to Abergavenny; 13 September 1951.

H.C. Casserley

Cefn Coed Station looking down towards the viaduct; 13 September 1951.
H.C. Casserley

Cefn Coed Station, looking up the gradient towards Pontsarn, the Morlais tunnel, Dowlais, Brynmawr and Abergavenny; no date.
NMRW

Auto train to Abergavenny approaching Cefn Coed Station; late 1950s.
R.W.A. Jones

Pontsarn Station, looking up the line. Part of the parapet of the viaduct may be glimpsed through the arch in the road bridge. The large crowd of Sunday School children demonstrates how the railway was used to convey people relatively short distances for a day out; *c.* 1910.

Lens of Sutton

This postcard view of the Pontsarn viaduct from the far side gives some clue as to the appeal of this area as an escape from Merthyr; *c.* 1900.

GBJ Coll.

The line then climbed for just over a mile at 1:50 through the outskirts of Merthyr to Pontsarn Station, set on the wooded side of the hill at the edge of the steep ravine carved by the Taff Fechan and crossed by the Pontsarn viaduct. The station had an ephemeral appearance, being built of wood, reflecting something of the role it originally played as a holiday place to which one escaped from the town. Both viaducts were laid for double track but remained single throughout. As the train crossed the Pontsarn viaduct, the mountain to the right rose steep and forbidding, an imposing and formidable massif, which the railway edged around for half a mile before plunging into it, in the Morlais tunnel. Just before the tunnel entrance the B & M main line bore away to the left for Brecon and the LNW line became double track. The tunnel was 1,040 yds long at a gradient upward of 1:60, so we became acutely aware of the pungent smoke from the Rose Heyworth Colliery steam coal being burned by our labouring locomotive. We burrowed beneath the B & M's Pant Station. This was the junction where the branch to Lloyd Street left the B & M main line from Brecon to Newport. On emerging in a deep cutting we opened the window and looked back at the finely finished tunnel entrance, in dark brick, built to last a thousand years—and still standing, idle and damp in 1998.

The southern portal of the Morlais tunnel, seen from a Brecon train; *c.* 1920.
E. T. Miller/WIMM

The northern portal of Morlais tunnel after closure; January 1983.
GBJ

The stone which surmounted the northern portal; January 1983.
GBJ

Further along this cutting the B & M Lloyd Street branch crossed our path by an overbridge alongside a road bridge. As we emerged from the cutting we passed Pantyscallog Halt. This wooden platform stood in open pasture with a row of Edwardian villas in the distance. Then we were in another cutting, this time only some 30 foot deep and, as the line bore left towards the east, we were joined on our right at Penywern Junction by the short spur coming in from Lloyd Street.

The B & M branch from Pant to Dowlais crossed the LNWR twice while it was in the Morlais tunnel and again after it had emerged. This view of the LNW's Pantyscallog Halt is from the B & M overbridge, looking towards Dowlais; *c.* 1930. *NMRW*

Pantyscallog Halt from a road bridge and looking in the opposite direction towards the B & M bridge, beyond which is the Morlais tunnel; *c.* 1930. *NMRW*

We were still climbing, now at 1:40, and in half a mile drew into Dowlais High Street Station, a typical minor LNW station constructed of wood, but with an unusually fine view. This had been opened in 1885 to avoid the need for the LNW to provide a shuttle service into Lloyd Street from Dowlais Top Station which, as a result, was closed. The cloud lifted and we were able to see for miles across what was once rolling moorland but which for 200 years had been ravaged by man in his search for iron and coal. The view to the south-west over-looked the roof-tops of Dowlais, the massive ironworks and the misty, smokey hollow where Merthyr lay; south, beyond the Rhymney Railway's nearby Cae Harris Station, the

Dowlais High Street Station opened in 1885, looking towards Merthyr; 1920s. *E.T. Miller/Brian J. Miller*

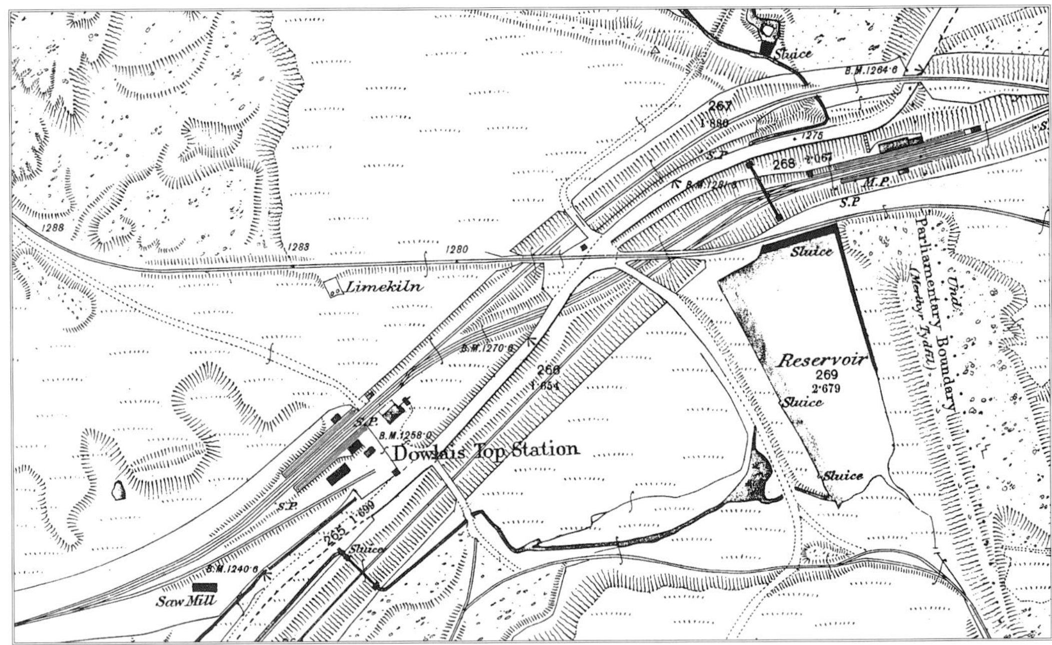

In 1876 there were two stations at Dowlais Top; the B & M station, of which the station master's house survives in 1998, is at the lower part of the map; the LNWR station is top right. At that date the LNWR was single track but a double track link line between the two companies was already in place, as were the complex road bridges and drainage duct.

O.S. Crown Copyright

This photograph taken at Dowlais Top, looking east, reveals something of the complexity of the layout between the LNWR and the B & M. In the centre is the LNWR line and the former LNWR Dowlais Top Station, closed in 1885. The B & M line to Newport crossed the LNWR on the bridge in the distance. The overbridge in the foreground is an enclosed culvert. The lines leading to the left, at the bottom of the picture, are the link line which joined the B & M just east of its own Dowlais Top Station; 1920s.

E.T. Miller/Brian J. Miller

A later view of the LNWR station at Dowlais Top and its setting, looking in the same direction but from a slightly different viewpoint; no date.

NMRW

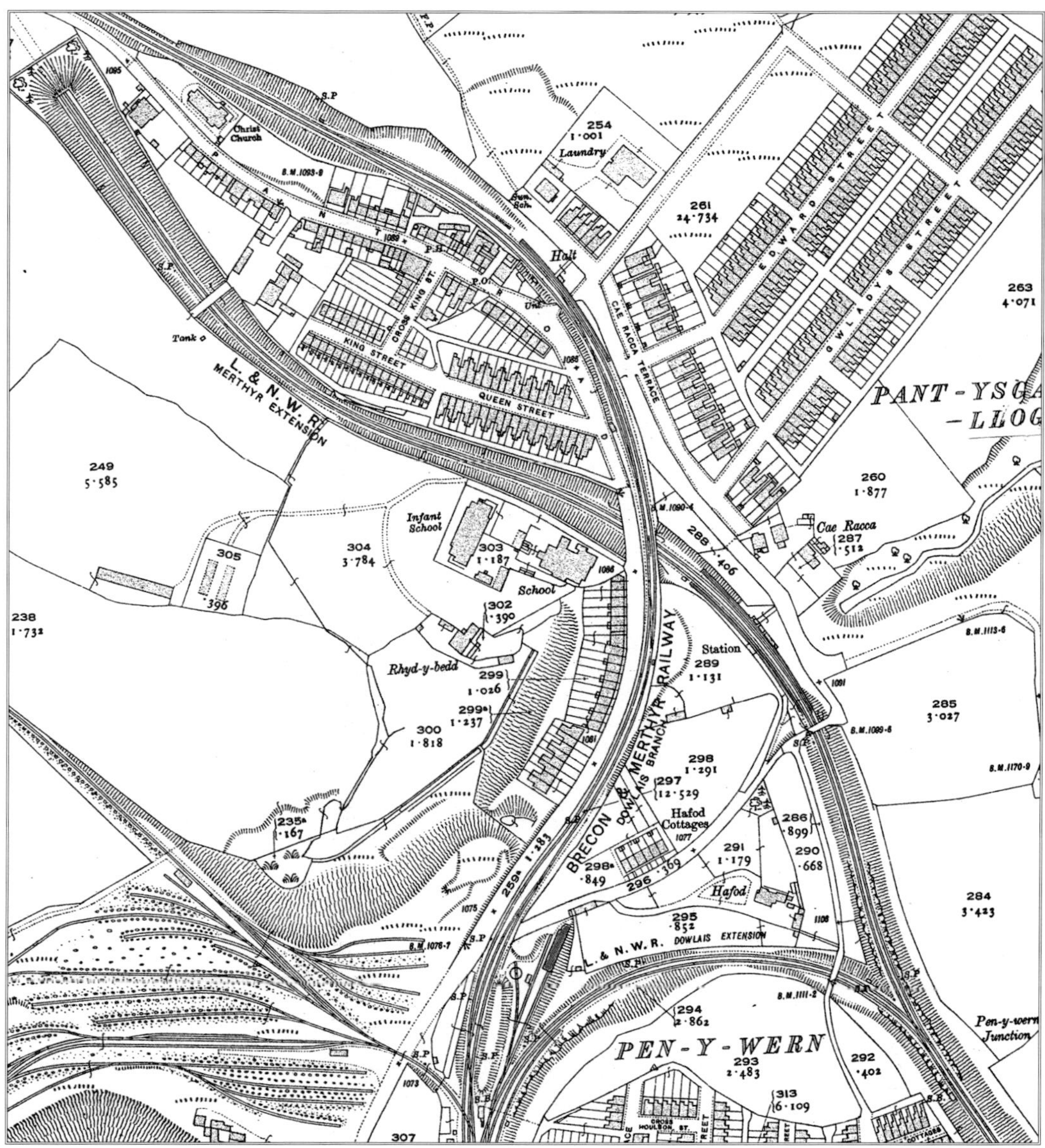

Pantyscallog in 1920 showing the network of LNW and B & M lines and the two Pantyscallog halts.
O.S. Crown Copyright

hillside was scored and misshapen with remnants of tips and opencast mining. To the north lay rolling mountainside, heavily contorted by old workings, whilst ahead to the east—where we were going—the open mountainside rose gradually towards the closed Dowlais Top Station. Not to be confused with the B & M station of the same name, the LNW station was a mile from High Street, at the summit of this part of the line. Although it had only been in use for 12 years from 1873, the brick building still stood, just beyond the link line from the B & M. After Dowlais Top, the B & M's Brecon to Newport line crossed our path on its way to the Bargoed Rhymney valley. Just east of High Street, the LNWR had put in a mineral line from Cwm Bargoed mine in 1881, but this was closed by 1920.

This view from the signal box at the former Dowlais Top Station looks in the opposite direction from the previous two photographs, towards Merthyr, beneath the enclosed culvert and the two road bridges. The path of the link line to the B & M led away to the right of the picture; 1 April 1922.
J.M. Dunn/W. Rear Collection

Another view of the site of the LNWR's Dowlais Top Station from the B & M overbridge to the east, looking towards Merthyr; 18 May 1959.
Alan Jarvis

Having twisted and burrowed around and beneath the B & M for some 5 miles, the locomotive then had a respite as the line descended for a mile and a half at 1:45 to Rhymney Bridge. This was the point at which the Rhymney joint line arrived on the right from the valley below. From here to Nantybwch we were on the joint line opened in 1871 and, as D.S.M. Barrie has pointed out, each company placed its own mile posts, measuring from opposite directions; the LNW from Abergavenny, the Rhymney from Cardiff. The

Rhymney Bridge Station, looking towards the east; January 1951.
LGRP

Rhymney Bridge Station, looking east; 13 September 1951.
H.C. Casserley

station at Rhymney Bridge Junction was a single-storey brick building, resembling a peasant's dwelling from the bleak wastes of northern China, but a covered bridge provided some protection against the weather.

The next two miles to Nantybwch lay across open mountain-top, with a climb for the first mile at 1:35 to the summit at 1,135 ft. Nantybwch had a similar layout to that at Rhymney Bridge, with the Sirhowy valley line coming in from the right, but the station buildings here were only wooden and the bridge uncovered. For a time it was the operational centre for the line and there were extensive sidings on the north side. If we were lucky we might have seen one of the LNW-designed 0-8-4 tank engines, introduced to the line in 1923, working a train up from the Sirhowy valley collieries. When first introduced some of these impressive machines were resplendent in Midland red paint. From Nantybwch the line continued its descent for half a mile to cross the Sirhowy, at this point merely a stream, by the Blaen-y-cwm viaduct. This was to remain standing as a monument. The line then climbed for about a mile at some 1:80 to Trevil Halt

An atmospheric portrait of coal tank No. 7752, recently arrived at Nantybwch with the 9.05 a.m. from Newport; 10 May 1951.
Ian L. Wright

No. 58915 at Nantybwch; 1951.
H.C. Casserley

A LNWR train on the Beaufort viaduct.
Old Bakehouse Publications

where a siding connected with the Ebbw Vale ironworks, and the old tramway entered on the right. Then down again to the junction for the Ebbw Vale branch, another single track line like the other branches, entering from the south, and joining in the direction of Abergavenny. From here to Brynmawr there were extensive earthworks as the landscape became more turbulent. First was the Beaufort viaduct across the Ebbw, and then Beaufort Station, a solid stone building with elaborate awning on the down side and a standard wooden shelter on the up side. Then the line entered the Beaufort cutting and a short tunnel, before descending at 1:88 for a mile and a half to Brynmawr.

Beaufort Station, looking east; no date.
Old Bakehouse Publications

Beaufort Station, looking west; no date.
Lens of Sutton

Here lay a railway complex. Before reaching the station, we crossed the LNW line which linked the Western valley lines at Nantyglo directly to the MTA. Then the joint Brynmawr & Western Valleys line entered on the right and terminated at a wooden bay platform. This had been built-on as an extension to the down platform. At the far end was another bay platform, this one being for the Blaenavon branch, now operated by the GWR all the way down to Newport. The station buildings had something of a wild-west air, being single storey and built of wooden planking, the whole pitched quite high and on the outskirts of the town. In spite of being the highest town in Wales, Brynmawr had an intense passenger train service with, for many years, nearly 100 arrivals and departures a day.

H.C. Casserley's Hillman helps to emphasise the elevated position of Brynmawr Station; 13 July 1958.
H.C. Casserley

An early view of the Merthyr platform at Brynmawr; c. 1910.
Old Bakehouse Publications

Coal tank No. 7720 and LNWR carriage stand at the Merthyr platform at Brynmawr; 7 July 1938. *H.C. Casserley*

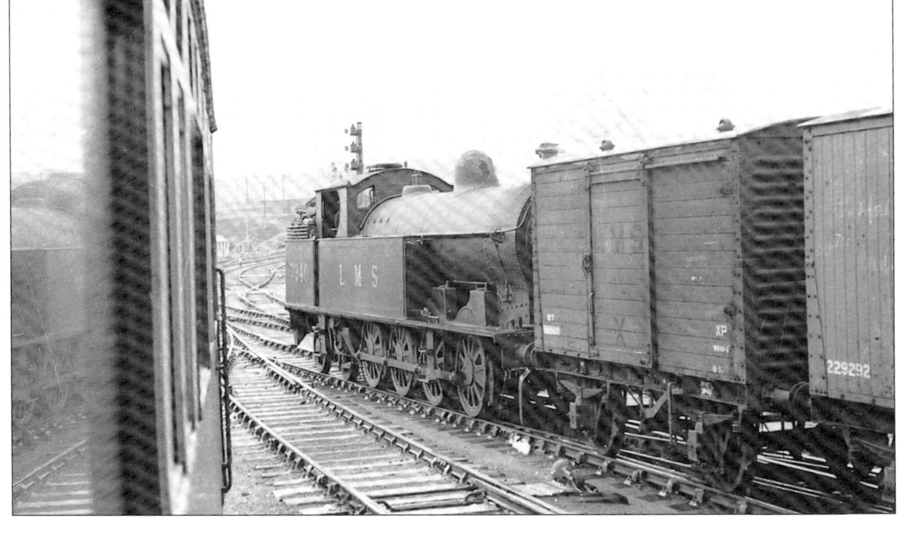

Seen from an Abergavenny train, 0-8-4T 7940 shunts at Brynmawr; 7 July 1938. *H.C. Casserley*

As we continued our journey eastward, our line to Abergavenny bore left under a road bridge and headed downhill, while the line to Blaenavon headed straight towards the rising ground. The next four and a half miles down to Gilwern were surely among the most spectacular in the country. As we felt our way cautiously down the south side of the Clydach gorge, perched on a ledge high above the ravine, steep limestone cliffs and crags rose threateningly above us; to our left the rocky mountainside, scored with the lines of early industrial tramways, rose from the floor of the ravine. After a mile and a half we entered the original Gelli-felen tunnel, emerging after 386 yds, beneath a high escarpment. Then, as we bore right round the breast of the hill, there, dramatically displayed below us on our left, lay the Vale of Usk, and rising above it, like a crinolined lady, the Sugar Loaf mountain. Just beyond Llanelly level crossing, we crossed over the track-bed of a former tramway leading from the Llanelly stone quarry on our right, a vast amphitheatre carved into the mountainside. When the railway was doubled, the up (downward) line had to be carried on a short girder bridge at this point. We continued downhill, heading straight for the steep shoulder

At Gelli-felen, a passenger's view of the Clydach gorge from a Merthyr-bound train; 13 September 1951.
H.C. Casserley

A view looking across the Clydach gorge from the north side, which demonstrates the gradient of the MTA near Gelli-felen as it cuts across the cliff-like face of the mountain; *c.* 1930.
Old Bakehouse Publications

A similar view but from the south side of the Clydach gorge.
Old Bakehouse Publications

of mountain in front of us, over a short viaduct spanning a steep wooded dingle, and then entered the first of the twin Clydach tunnels, 302 yds long. Clydach Station, a charmingly romantic stone cottage, was just beyond the eastern end of the tunnels, on the downward side, and just before the elegantly curved Clydach viaduct. This crossed another steep sided dingle; on the right were extensive stone quarrying activities with rows of limekilns built into the side of the hill. Then came the Cuckoo's Nest Siding which had so interested Richard Moon; still on a down gradient of 1:38 we descended to Gilwern Station, on the side of the

Gilwern Station, looking down the line; 8 September 1957. *GBJ Coll.*

Govilon Station with a Merthyr-bound train at the platform; no date. *Lens of Sutton*

The MTA bridge over the Usk at Abergavenny, looking towards the Brecon Road engine sheds, whose saw-toothed roof is just visible; no date.

Nigel Lewis Coll.

hill, a mile above the village which was situated on the banks of the Brecon & Abergavenny Canal lower down the slopes of the valley. The gradient remained at 1:38 for a further three miles through Govilon, now amid gentler farming country and woodland, before easing for the crossing of the Usk, on the bridge built by the MTA to replace the old tramway bridge. A short climb brought us past extensive locomotive sheds, over two road bridges in quick succession, and into Abergavenny Brecon Road Station, located at a considerable height above its surroundings. The line skirted the north-western side of the town as it climbed almost continuously to Abergavenny Junction and terminated at an island platform on the GWR main line from Newport to Hereford. Here, shortly before the grouping, the LNW built large carriage sheds.

This was the remarkable railway which Crawshay Bailey envisaged and which took 20 years to build. In Chapter 7 we look at the traffic it generated.

Stanier Class 5 4-6-0 No. 5378 makes for Abergavenny Junction as it passes the Brecon Road engine sheds, with a train from the Merthyr direction; *c.* 1939.

Oscar Elsdon/Nigel Lewis Coll.

A friend who commuted every day for most of his life from Gilwern to Merthyr was probably typical of the majority who travelled on the line and frequently complained about it, finding the journey slow, with too many stops, and bitterly cold in winter. He hardly knew what he missed as he dozed or read his paper. But for those passengers who took an interest, it provided a memorable experience.

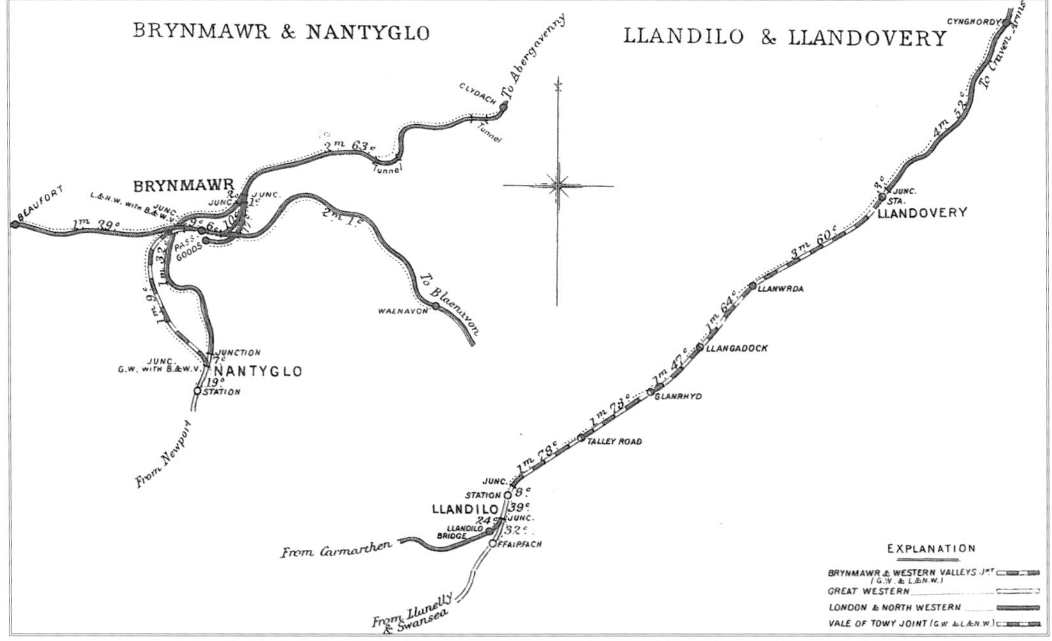

Two contrasting LNWR operations: the busy hub at Brynmawr and the pastoral joint line in the Tywi valley; 1913.

Railway Clearing House

Chapter 5

THE HARD WAY TO SWANSEA

Chapter 2 revealed how the LNWR had been frustrated by Parliament's rejection of the Swansea Junction Extension Bill and how this had contributed to the loss of enthusiasm for the NAH as a vehicle for expansion. But Swansea remained an important objective. It was a major centre of industry and a fast growing port, and as noted earlier the Shrewsbury & Crewe line was promoted in 1853 with a view to speeding traffic between Swansea in particular and the north of England; its completion in 1858 refocussed attention at Euston on alternative means of reaching Swansea. Shrewsbury held the key, but before tracing the birth of the Central Wales Line, it will be logical to leap to the early developments at the western end.

The exterior of Swansea Victoria; 2 April 1964.
T.B. Owen

Interior of Swansea Victoria with BR Standard Class 5 No. 73095; 25 April 1963.
Alan Jarvis

Llanelly can lay claim to some of the oldest railways in the country. As long ago as 1799 a tramroad had been built from a dock in Llanelly to an ironworks, just over a mile away. In 1802 it was extended by an Act of Parliament authorising the Carmarthenshire Railway or Tramroad Company. In 1828 the Llanelly Railway & Dock Company was authorised. In 1835 this company obtained approval to build a railway up the Loughor valley and over to Llandilo in the Tywi valley. The first six miles were opened to Pontardulais in 1839. The little

Pontardulais Station, looking south, with, on the left, the line to Swansea and, on the right, the original 1839 line from Llanelly; date uncertain.
Mowat Collection, courtesy N.T. Wassell

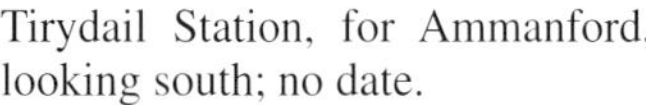

Tirydail Station, for Ammanford, looking south; no date.
NMRW

company was extremely profitable yielding in 1839 a dividend of 12%. This was mainly due to the rich anthracite seams along its route and the ability to charge a high rate of 1½d per mile. Progress in extending the line was accordingly rapid though it stopped some six miles short of Llandilo; in 1842 a branch up the Amman valley from Pantyffynnon reached Brynamman. This was only for mineral traffic and so no passenger station was built at this time, but it laid the ground for the odd railway arrangement which developed at this small town in the hills (see Chapter 6).

The first permanent station at Llandilo, with early signalling arrangements on the left of the picture; *c.* 1880.
John Thomas Collection/National Library of Wales

When the station at Llandilo was extended, the height of the platform was raised and the signal box was moved. The date is uncertain but shunting horses had left their mark in the foreground and the plus-fours on the platform suggest *c.* 1920.

GW/WIMM

Then the management appear to have run out of breath. In 1846 the first four steam engines were in such bad condition that the railway had to revert to the use of horses. In 1853 a combined horse-drawn bus and train service was inaugurated between Swansea and Llandilo which lasted for two years. In the same year a branch was laid into the main station at Llanelly on the broad gauge South Wales Railway. Eventually, after very slow progress, the railway reached Llandilo in 1857, 22 years after the enabling Act. It is possible that the mainly rural activity in the area did not offer the inducements or rewards of the locations already reached, but the protracted arrival was cause for a major celebration. John Biddulph, chairman of the Llanelly, was hailed at the *déjeuner* held in Llandilo Town Hall as the hero of the day and in his speech referred to the impact the railway was likely to make on Llandilo; he foresaw excursionists visiting the area and filling the houses and hotels, merchants would come seeking health and fresh air, and the prices of commodities would be reduced. Our friend J. Palmer Budd was also present and rose to make some pious remarks about the contribution railways made to 'extending liberty of thought and intellect'. He even linked this thought with his own involvement with the Welsh Midland, whose failure he blamed on 'the war of the guages [*sic*]' (see Chapter 1). The news reporter of *The Çambrian* looked forward to Llandilo eventually being connected with ports in the north of England. This was an allusion to the forthcoming opening of the line onward to Llandovery, for in 1854 there had been an important development. In that year the Vale of Towy Railway was incorporated to build a 12 mile line from Llandilo to Llandovery. After failing two inspections it was opened in 1858 and leased to the Llanelly for ten years. This gave the Llanelly Railway a continuous line from Llanelly to Llandovery. By 1858 there were 40 collieries, 30 tin-plate works, and many brickworks and limeworks, all served by the Llanelly Railway.

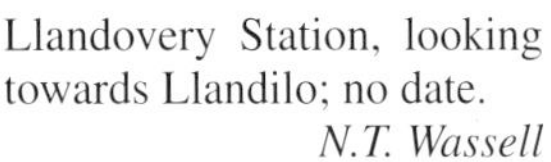

Llandovery Station, looking towards Llandilo; no date.
N.T. Wassell

An idle moment at Llandovery.
D. Harries Collection/National Library of Wales

John Biddulph who was the chairman of the Llanelly Railway & Dock Company was a Swansea banker, and this was probably just as well, since, for the next ten years, finance was to become something of a nightmare for the company. On 31 January 1860, Henry Robertson attended a board meeting held, as was frequently the case, at the London Coffee House on Ludgate Hill. He was the engineer-in-chief of the Knighton and Central Wales (CWR) Railways; the former was under construction and the latter was the subject of a Parliamentary Bill that year. He expressed interest in the idea of uniting the Llanelly and the CWR. (At the same board meeting an interesting little side-light on Victorian business practices occurred when the board agreed to pay an entrepreneur called George Webb £50 if, within three months, he could get the French government to abolish the import duty on anthracite for agricultural purposes.)

Robertson attended again on 24 July 1860; the Llanelly board decided that through traffic arrangements with the CWR would be of interest but any talk of amalgamation would have to await the completion of the CWR; meanwhile 'unity of action' with the CWR was desirable especially with regard to approaches to Parliament, for example in connection with possible extensions to Carmarthen from Llandilo and to Swansea from Pontardulais.

Then a new party came into the picture. Richard Kyrke Penson, who was an architect and director of the Kington & Eardisley and who appears in Chapter 6 as an antagonist to W.L. Banks, came to a Llanelly board meeting at 9, Villiers Street on 9 October. He brought with him Thomas Savin and his partner Johns.

Savin was a draper turned Welsh railway promoter who had the charisma to give confidence where others quailed. They proposed that the Llanelly promote a Swansea branch from Pontardulais, a Carmarthen branch from Llandilo, and another from Llandovery to Brecon, the whole to be financed by the partners, who would take a lease of the whole of the Llanelly for ten years at a fixed rate of 2½% for the first five years and 4% for the following five, to be followed by full amalgamation. At the time the Llanelly was only earning 1%. Provided they could be satisfied as to the security of the partners, the directors of the Llanelly were in favour of the scheme.

Relaying the level crossing at Pontardulais; September 1960. *Huw Daniel*

The next day Robertson and the CWR party were at Villiers Street. They offered joint promotion of the Carmarthen and Swansea lines and running powers from Craven Arms on the S & H. The Llanelly turned this down. In the light of subsequent events, this was a bad decision as it led the Llanelly into a position where the two dubious new undertakings threatened the integrity of its core activity. Belief in independence and the ability to build successful railways with promoters like Savin was strong and at that time the LNWR was seen more as a threat than a saviour. With the confidence of a promoter rather than the prudence of a banker, the Llanelly chose the more risky course, and accordingly, the Penson party were called in and told that the Llanelly would hold an Extraordinary General Meeting on their proposal on 31 October; Savin and Johns both attended the meeting which agreed the proposition. A Bill was to be prepared to seek powers to build the three lines and to prepare the lease. Conybeare was recruited as Savin's engineer.

Then, almost immediately, things began to go wrong. First, on 28 November, Johns withdrew altogether; then on 29 January 1861, Savin withdrew the Brecon to Llandovery line, for a year he said, allegedly due to the state of the money market. On 5 June, he withdrew from the lease. The Llanelly decided nevertheless that they would continue on their own. Savin still appeared able and willing to provide finance. Accordingly, on 10 June they replaced him as engineer with Conybeare of the B & M.

Then over the next four years the Llanelly besieged Parliament with a succession of Bills as opinion waivered and the management was led from one idea to another. Biddulph seems to have presided with good nature but a signal lack of decisive leadership. The project was hardly complex. The Carmarthen line was a straightforward 14 miles down the broad valley of the Tywi; the Swansea line a mere 12 miles across the neck of the Gower peninsula and along the coast of Swansea Bay. But the Llanelly ran into one problem after another.

Swansea Bay Station, looking west; 10 September 1951. *H.C. Casserley*

Swansea Bay Station, facing Swansea; 10 September 1951. *H.C. Casserley*

The first Bill in 1861 covered the two lines from Llandilo to Carmarthen and from Pontardulais to Swansea, the latter including a branch to Penclawdd. In addition, the line from Llandovery to Brecon was reinstated. Trouble arose with the Oystermouth Railway at the point where the line was to run along the coast; the mortgagee of the Oystermouth, George Byng Morris, was of a litigious nature and was reputed locally to be idle and to prefer the good life of Cheltenham. He petitioned against the Bill. First, he feared for the safety of the passengers in the horse-drawn carriages if one of the horses were to take fright at the noise and sight of a steam engine on the neighbouring track; he accordingly sought to have screens

Sand on the line near Swansea Bay Station, looking towards Swansea.
L.C. Turner, courtesy N.T. Wassell

The removal of sand between Victoria and Swansea Bay stations. While aiding adhesion, the fine sand presented a permanent problem to the moving parts of locomotives; 29 March 1953.
GW/WIMM

erected. Secondly, as a resident accustomed to being able to walk from his house across the road along which the Oystermouth Railway ran and to go bathing in Swansea Bay, he wanted a gate in the railway fence. This was offered by the Llanelly who wrote to him suggesting what was described as a 'V gate'. Somewhat obtusely, he chose to interpret this as an offer for five gates and attempted to make an issue of the fact.

The Carmarthen branch had a delicate problem with the Bishop of St David's across whose front lawn the railway was planned to go, spoiling the view from the drawing-room of Abergwili Palace. A clause had to be inserted in the 1861 Act forbidding any construction of this part of the line before the end of August 1862 without the Bishop's permission, and putting a stop to any use of this route thereafter, whether or not they obtained consent for a deviation

The main entrance to the palace of the Bishop of St David's at Abergwili, now Carmarthen Museum; 1996.

DD

behind the palace in 1862. This was in fact obtained in a new Act in 1862 which added a high level extension to the newly projected Swansea & Neath in Swansea, a branch to the south side of the new South Dock, a link with the South Wales at Gower Road, and finally a branch leading to a terminus in the centre of Carmarthen which, if constructed, would have provided the town with its third station.

The third Act in 1863 improved the approach into Swansea, and reverted to the original approach to Carmarthen over the broad gauge Carmarthen and Cardigan by the laying of a

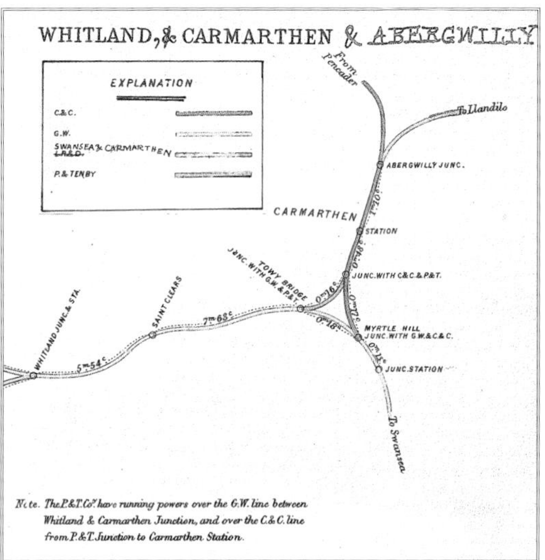

Railway Clearing House plan of the railways at Carmarthen in 1870.

PRO RAIL 1082/85

third rail. The 1863 Act also increased the authorised capital by £114,000 for the Swansea line and £8,000 for the Carmarthen, the latter being to pay for the cost of avoiding a bog which lay in the path of the diversion round Abergwili Palace.

The 1861 Act contained important provisions with regard to the capital structure of the company which, as things turned out, were later to provide the means for the LNW to gain control. Up until this Act the share capital consisted of £364,000. This was increased by £270,000, £155,000 being in respect of the Swansea line and the Penclawdd branch, and £115,000 for the Carmarthen branch. Section

42 of the Act said, 'with respect to the company's three separate undertakings, the total capital of the company is by this Act divided into and shall consist of the following three separate capitals.' According to section 66, 'shareholders of Swansea line capital and Carmarthen line capital may appoint one of themselves to be a director of the company.' Such directors were not to vote concerning undertakings of which they were not shareholders. Section 69 required separate accounts to be kept and section 70 made amalgamation automatic in the event of the main undertaking and either of the other two achieving dividends of 5% for three consecutive years. At that point all shareholders would have equal rights. This desirable state of affairs was never achieved.

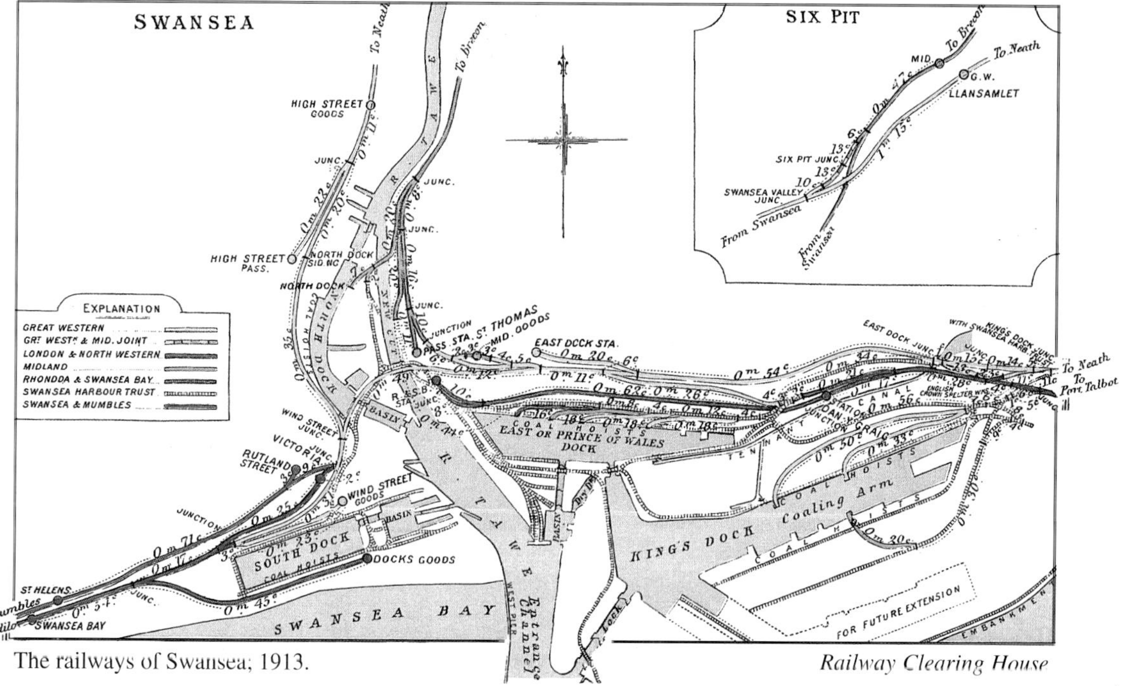

The railways of Swansea, 1913. *Railway Clearing House*

By 27 November 1861, after the first Act had been passed, the Llanelly must already have been concerned about the financing of the 'new lines'. In October, they invited the South Wales to participate, to no apparent avail, and accordingly they were amenable when the Central Wales Extension Railway (CWE) invited them to meet to discuss arrangements

An unidentified coal tank heads for Swansea through the sand dunes; date uncertain.
H.T. Hobbs, courtesy R.C. Riley

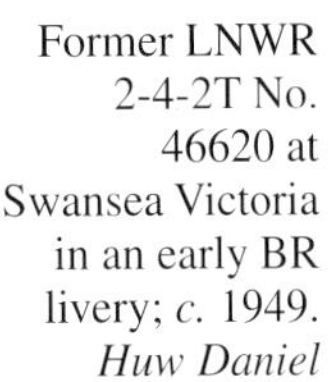

Former LNWR 2-4-2T No. 46620 at Swansea Victoria in an early BR livery; *c.* 1949. *Huw Daniel*

for 'the new lines'. The CWE had in 1860 obtained approval to link Llandrindod and Llandovery and appear to have refrained from pursuing their own plans for an extension from Pontardulais to Swansea. This meeting led to a decision by the Llanelly on 12 December to write to the LNWR, inviting them to subscribe to the 'new lines', with one stipulation: that they give no favours to any line competing with the Llanelly. To assist in the process of warming the Llanelly to the idea of association with the LNWR-backed group, a copy of the CWE agreement with the LNWR was lent to them. This was followed on 7 January 1862 by a copy of the agreement between the LNW, S & H, Knighton and CWR. Following a meeting at Euston, the Llanelly agreed to the terms including the offer of a rebate from the LNWR. The Llanelly then sought confirmation of the LNW's agreement.

In October 1862 discussion of amalgamations reached a crescendo. An agreement was to be drafted covering the Llanelly, the Vale of Towy, the 'new lines', the Knighton, the CWR, the CWE, the Mid-Wales and a projected new railway from Craven Arms to Birmingham. Overend was pressing to take over the construction of the CWE. Robertson favoured an amalgamation of the Llanelly, CWE and Mid-Wales by putting their combined capital in what he called a 'hotchpot', and then taking a lease of the Knighton and the CWR. This was debated by the Llanelly and the board was divided on whether or not to support it. Biddulph was in favour though failed to exercise his casting vote, yet again displaying a lack of resolve and leadership. The matter rested pending a response from the LNWR on the rebate, but this never came. The LNWR was playing a waiting game. To add to the general confusion, in 1863, a stream of new railway projects burst upon the market. The following Bills the Llanelly board noted as requiring their attention:

Llandilo & Teifi Valley
Carmarthenshire
S. Wales, Tenby & Milford Haven
Whitland, Tenby & Milford Haven
Pembroke & Tenby
Carmarthen & Cardigan
Swansea Vale & N & B Jc.
Swansea & Oystermouth
Llanelly Harbour
Swansea Harbour

They also had notice of a line from Llandilo to Lampeter to be called the Swansea & Aberystwyth, and in 1863 the Swansea Vale (SV) was also building its branch to Brynamman, confronting the Llanelly head-on.

Meanwhile the financing and construction of the 'new lines' were causing problems. Savin had originally required that the financing of the 'new lines' be quite separate from what came to be called the 'original undertaking' of the Llanelly but was now getting cold feet about the viability of the 'new lines' as a stand-alone project. Penson told the Llanelly in August 1862 that he thought Savin would be glad of an excuse to break off the negotiations; matters came to a crunch over the insistence by Savin that if he built the line for shares, he should work the combined Llanelly Railway for 45% of gross receipts. At that point the Llanelly decided to make an alternative agreement with another bidder for the business, Watson & Overend. Now it was they who were to finance and build the two 'new lines'.

The new contractors appear to have been somewhat casual in their management of finance; not only did they pay for the third rail to Carmarthen and some additional station investment out of their own funds, but they also built the earthworks for a link line to the South Wales, now GW, at Gower Road which were never used. With the waivering which characterised the whole project, these were authorised by Parliament in the 1862 Act but discontinued in 1863 and revived in 1864. In the latter Act the capital of the Swansea line was increased by a further £18,000 of shares to pay for this link line. By agreement with the contractor, the allowance for vehicles was raised from £30,000 to £60,000.

Just north of Gowerton South Station, the Penclawdd branch bore away to the left. No. 8708 was working a train from Pontarddulais to Swansea on 19 May 1959. *T.B. Owen*

During 1863 and 1864 work proceeded on the 'new lines', but the board continued to dither. In April 1864 consideration was given to economies of construction on the Swansea line. Some £20,000 could be saved if the number of coal hoists was reduced to two, if the line were singled from Gower Road to Swansea, and if provision were not made for mixed gauge track. In August 1864 the board inspected the work. At Pontardulais they were concerned that the station facilities should be the cheapest possible, but at the same time they were concerned that a road should be made on the outside of the Swansea line for access.

In 1865 further capital was authorised (Llanelly Capital Act) with £120,000 of shares to cover the cost of doubling from Gower Road to Swansea and additional coal hoists at the South Dock, though these items were not progressed. In that year too the contractors promoted yet another Bill in the name of the company to construct a railway to Mumbles from the point where the Swansea line met the shore in Swansea Bay, at a place called

Killay Station lay in thick woodland where the Swansea line crossed the neck of the Gower peninsula. This view is towards Swansea; 1965.
Mowat Collection, courtesy N. T. Wassell

North of Killay, Dunvant Station was in the vicinity of coal mining. Again looking towards Swansea; 1961.
Alan Jarvis

Blackpill. This was thought to be tactically advisable in view of Dickson's efforts on behalf of the N & B to extend from Neath to the Oystermouth Railway. Parliament required the Llanelly to build a pier at Mumbles as a condition of consent. This was not proceeded with, but the Mumbles Extension and Pier were formed into a fourth separate undertaking of the Llanelly; some might feel that three were already proving too many. The abandonment of this project on which no work was done was finally authorised by the Central Wales & Carmarthen Junction Act of 1873.

As to rolling stock, in May 1864 Overend proposed the following for the 'new lines':

2 1st cl. carriages	at £350 each
2 2nd cl. carriages	at £275 each
3 compo. 1st/2nd	at £365 each
4 compo. 2nd/3rd	at £275 each
20 3rd cl. (5 compartments)	at £250 each
3 pass. brake-vans	at £230 each
4 goods brake-vans	at £180 each
15 timber trucks	at £70 each
20 covered goods	at £90 each
150 open goods	at £67 each
200 coal waggons.	at £70 each
5 goods engines	at £2380 each
2 pass. engines	at £1870 each
	£52,395

Mumbles Road Station with 'Jubilee' Class No. 45689; undated. *Huw Daniel*

A Swansea-bound train at Mumbles Road Station headed by Class 5 No. 44835; 25 July 1957. *Huw Daniel*

Jinty No. 47479 on push-pull duty near Swansea Bay Station; May 1959. *Alan Jarvis*

Two more passenger engines were also to be considered, bringing the total value to the £60,000 budgeted. In August Overend produced a drawing showing how communication could be provided between the passengers and the guard. But they were short of funds and only

LNWR 'Whitworth' Class No. 739 'Sutherland' near the original station at Carmarthen; *c.* 1897. *Terry James Collection*

managed to buy one locomotive and 80 waggons. For the opening of the Carmarthen line in November 1864, instead of new vehicles, rolling stock was taken from the Mid-Wales, which the contractor alleged was his in spite of the fact that the vehicles bore the plate of the Mid-Wales; in 1866, when the Mid-Wales insisted they be returned, they were purchased by the Llanelly for £6,650, £4,000 of which had to be borrowed at 11%. They consisted of the following :

1 1st cl. carriage
1 2nd cl. carriage
10 3rd cl. carriages
12 goods vans
50 open trucks
1 pass. brake-van

The Carmarthen line was opened for goods traffic in November 1864, but early in 1865 the financial indicators were not good. By 10 June 1865 shares to the value of £607,900 had been handed over to the contractors on the strength of engineer's certificates, but the last of these were in advance of actual outgoings as the contractors were having cash flow problems. Furthermore, during 1865 the Llanelly board had been asking their contractors for the documents covering the conveyances of land alleged to have been purchased, as these had not yet been produced. On 25 August, nearly a year before the great crash of the banking firm, Overend Gurney, the Llanelly board met unusually at Swansea. The contractor had failed to meet £10,000 of acceptances due to the Llanelly on advances made. Biddulph reported a meeting he had attended at the Great Western Hotel in London at which Watson had told him that his company was short of £315,000 owed to the London Financial Association. Although the Carmarthen line was open, the Swansea line was far from complete, with £60,000 worth of works exclusive of vehicles still required. There was then feverish activity to hold the position together.

The north end of Pontardulais Station with an unusual engine change; 19 November 1960. *Huw Daniel*

The main building at Gowerton South was on the Swansea platform. *N.T. Wassell*

In the open country around Gowerton, a freight train near Grovesend hauled by pannier tank No. 4676; 13 August 1965. *T.B. Owen*

In September the contractor proposed that the company give him acceptances of the 'new lines' for the total sum of £315,000 and £30,000 of Lloyds Bonds (high interest unsecured promises named after a barrister, one John Lloyd, not the bank) to pay for the land outstanding. The board agreed to the latter on the understanding that the proceeds should be paid to their bankers, and the chairman would monitor the payments to landowners. It was later discovered when no payments were made, that the contractor disposed of the bonds and used the proceeds for his own needs. He obtained possession of the land by offering acceptances of three, six and nine months, but before the first of these bills became due, the contractor became insolvent and entered into an arrangement with creditors; under a Deed of Inspection the appointed inspector was a Mr Dunn, manager of the London Financial Association.

In spite of interruptions in the work during 1865, the company began operating mineral trains on the Swansea line in January 1866, and when the bills were dishonoured it was the company who had to pay to regain possession of the land, including that at Swansea Station. To make matters worse, the traffic on the Swansea line did not live up to expectations. Coal movements were barely 20,000 tons in the first year against the 300,000 originally expected. Furthermore, a fixed rental had to be paid to the Duke of Beaufort for sidings in Swansea, and gradients of 1:70 against the load made operating expensive.

On 1 February 1867 the board woke up to the importance of Swansea and asked for a map of the town to be available at the company's office at 34 Great George St, Westminster. For the Llanelly board were under pressure to progress their Swansea Station as work had stopped in September 1865. It was decided that the 'original undertaking' would advance £40,000, and a further £13,000 would be raised by the Lloyds Bond holders and the preference shareholders of the Swansea line. This was authorised by an Act of July 1866. It took over a year to execute and it was not until September 1867 that work was resumed to complete the station and the line. Due to the panic of 1866 many of the loans were at high rates of interest and short term; for example, some were at 11% and others were at 8% with 1% commission. Furthermore, the traffic being generated on the Carmarthen line was very small and insufficient to cover the interest due. When the Llanelly's support was exhausted, interest on the debentures could no longer be paid and the London Financial appointed a receiver, a Mr Koch. Swansea Station was eventually completed in December 1867 after a considerable effort by the contractors.

In January 1866 an attempt was made to find a way for Swansea to have the benefit of a single passenger station. The Vale of Neath (now part of the GWR) had opened their temporary station at Wind Street, the GWR were at High Street, while the Swansea Vale had their primitive arrangements at St. Thomas on the east side of the Tawe; the Llanelly were planning Victoria near the site of Wind Street and were willing to subscribe £150 towards the cost of a Bill for a Swansea General Station provided the GWR also subscribed. The plan envisaged a station at both high and low level on the site of the Llanelly and Vale of Neath stations with a large hotel and station building on the city side of the tracks; possibly the prospective cost was the ultimate deterrent, as the bridge and permanent way infrastructure alone were estimated to cost £20,000, but, for whatever reason, the Bill was withdrawn. As a result of this failure by the railway companies to concentrate on one location, Swansea was to enjoy the benefit at one time of six separate passenger terminal stations (High St, St Thomas, East Dock replacing Wind Street, Rutland Rd, Victoria and Riverside). In 1946, shortly before nationalisation, the LMS and GWR discussed concentrating their activities on High Street Station but nothing was done and St Thomas closed completely in 1950, leaving Victoria to struggle on until 1964.

Just to add to John Biddulph's problems there was a suit in Chancery brought by the Oystermouth Railway for alleged trespass by the Llanelly's contractor. Vice Chancellor Stuart decided against the company but his decision

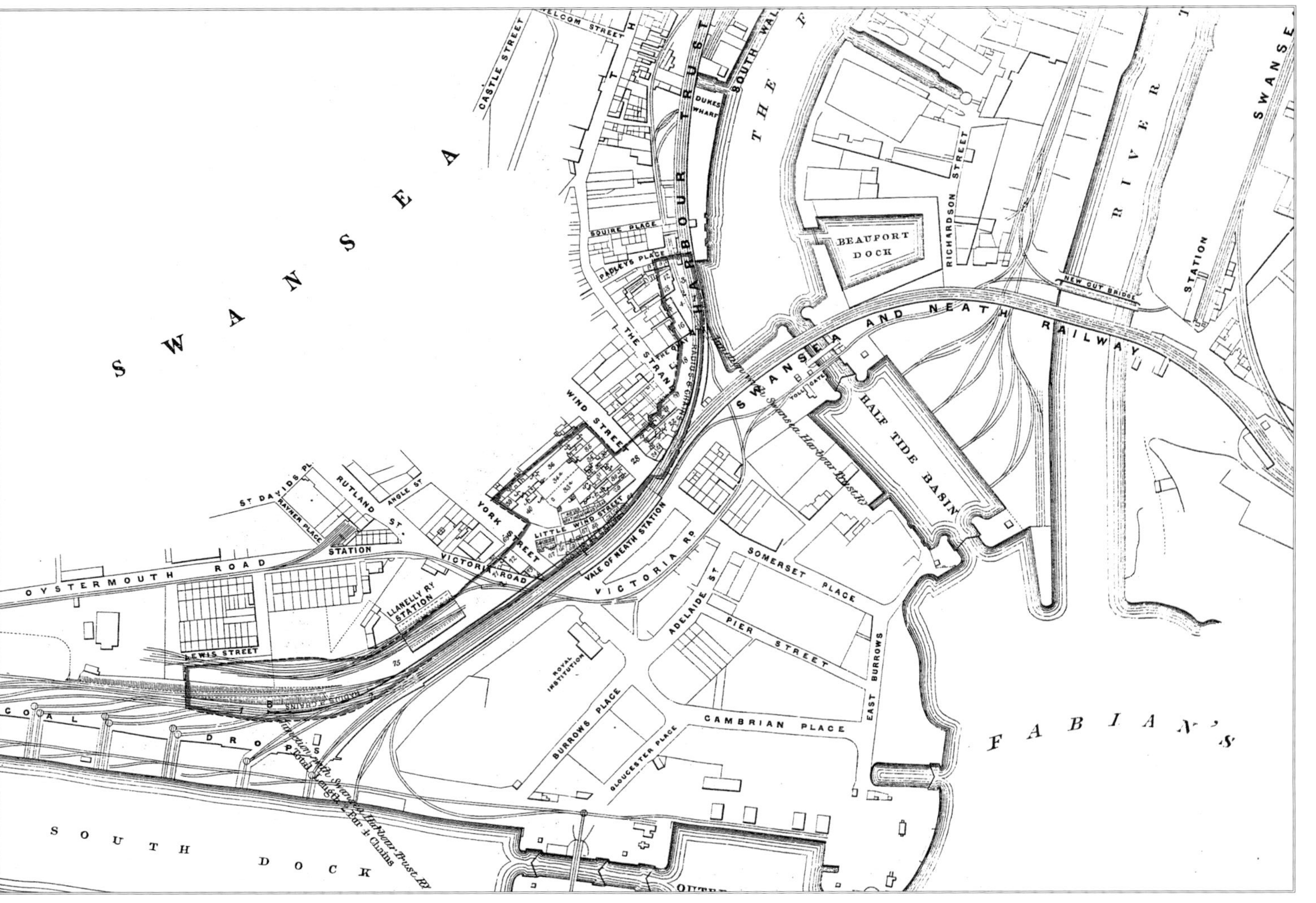

Plan of Swansea prepared for the abortive Bill promoting the General Station in 1866. The restricted location of the Wind Street Station platform is clearly shown and removes the uncertainty of whether this was an island platform or not.

House of Lords Library

Interior of Swansea Victoria; date uncertain.

NMRW

The LNWR bridge over the Mumbles Road; early 1920s.

Librarian, Swansea City and County

was later reversed on appeal. The Llanelly needed to use some of its alignment in order to make its chosen approach to Swansea along the coast. George Byng Morris also went out of his way to pick a quarrel over the dimensions of a bridge over the Oystermouth. There was a genuine difficulty in fitting the railway between the sea wall and the road alongside the Oystermouth and there was a need for sensible co-operation to resolve it. Morris did nothing to facilitate the process. His litigious nature brought him at various times into dispute with the Swansea Harbour Trustees, the Duke of Beaufort, the local Board of Health and Swansea Corporation, as well as the Llanelly.

However, salvation was at hand. The July 1867 grand tour of south Wales by the LNWR management was well timed; Richard Moon, George Findlay and their immediate assistants on the Shrewsbury and South Wales Committee visited the Llanelly Railway after the Swansea Vale. They met John Biddulph and made a tour of the line as far as Brynamman and Carmarthen. They saw what was described as a vast mineral district with coal pits, limekilns, lead works, tin-plate and copper. They foresaw great potential for the Central Wales Line and interestingly mentioned for the first time the potential on it for the tourist trade. An evening meeting was held with Biddulph, Henry Robertson and Sir Richard Green-Price. He was M.P. for Radnor and had been influential in promoting the Knighton and Central Wales. He was an enthusiast for railway speculation and held several directorships, among them the Central Wales and the S & H. His son Dansey inherited his taste and between them they heavily mortgaged the family estate of some 9,000 acres, being in particular somewhat over-enthusiastic about the commercial merits of the Golden Valley Railway.

Coal tank No. 27625 at Swansea Victoria with a local train for Pontardulais; 20 April 1949. *Huw Daniel*

Fowler 2-6-4T No. 2387 arriving at Swansea Victoria; undated. *Huw Daniel*

The carriage shed and approaches to Swansea Victoria with Webb 0-8-0 No. 9376; 20 April 1949.

Huw Daniel

Coal tank No. 7741 at Swansea; 27 August 1948. *H.C. Casserley*

At this critical meeting, the LNW were offered running powers over the Llanelly which Moon agreed to consider. There was also a question of a possible loan to the financially troubled Llanelly. In the light of the subsequent legal dispute about these running powers which in the end went as far as the House of Lords, it is noteworthy that, according to the LNW record, the approach was initiated by the Llanelly and not the LNW.

The following day the LNWR party travelled to Shrewsbury, by that time being able to use the railway from Llanwrtyd. When they stopped briefly at Builth Road, Moon said the cost of the

Builth Road Station with a Swansea train headed by No. 73091; 9 August 1961.
T.B. Owen

Builth Road Station with a Shrewsbury train headed by Class 5 No. 44835, about to cross over the Mid-Wales line; 20 April 1960.
T.B. Owen

0-8-0 No. 49117 approaches Builth Road with a Swansea to Craven Arms freight train; 16 April 1955.
Ian L. Wright

platforms at £2,500 should be passed to the Mid-Wales plus 5% for interest, presumably on the argument that it was they rather than the LNW who would benefit most from the interchange. On the same line of thought, Moon considered the receipts at Builth Road should be retained by the LNW and not shared with the other party. Moon, Green-Price and Robertson discussed the relationship of the LNW with the CWR and CWE. In 1868 G.P. Neele of the LNW followed up this tour by making an inspection of the 72 miles of Llanelly line. He was not impressed as there had been a tendency to exhaust the capacity of the plant with insufficient attention to maintenance let alone any enhancement. No doubt the root of the problem lay in the need to syphon funds into the Swansea project.

As early as 1864 the Llanelly had been holding discussions with the Vale of Towy about their lease, due to expire at the end of March 1868. The Towy directors were out to get what

LLANELLY & VALE OF TOWY RAILWAYS.

LLANELLY, LLANDILO, LLANDOVERY & CWMAMMAN

On and after MAY 1st., 1858.

UP-TRAINS.

STARTING FROM	1, 2, & 3 Class.	1, 2, & 3 Class.	1, 2, & 3 Class.	FARES. 1st Class. s.	d.	2nd Class. s.	d.	3rd Class. s.	d.
Llanelly	9.10	12.10	5.0						
Dock ...	9.14	12.14	5.4	0	3	0	2	0	1
Bynea	9.22	12.22	5.12	0	9	0	6	0	[illegible]
†Llangennech ...	9.28	12.28	5.18	1	0	0	8	0	5
Pontardulais ...	9.35	12.35	5.25	1	6	1	2	0	8
*Garnant *departure*	9.20		5.10						
Cross-Inn „ ...	9.45		5.35						
Cross-Inn *arrival*	10.0		5.50	2	6	1	10	1	2
*Garnant „ ...	10.25		6.15	3	3	2	3	1	6
Llandebie	10.0	12.55	5.50	3	3	2	3	1	3
†Derwydd Road ...	10.5	1.0	5.55	3	6	2	7	1	5
Fairfach	10.15	1.10	6.5	4	0	3	0	1	7
Llandilo ...	10.20	1.15	6.10	4	0	3	0	1	8
†Glanrhyd	10.30	1.25	6.20	4	9	3	7	2	0
Llangadock ...	10.35	1.30	6·25	5	2	3	9	2	2
Lampeter Road ...	10.40	1.35	6.30	5	6	4	1	2	4
Llandovery ...	10·50	1.45	6·40	6	3	4	8	2	8

DOWN-TRAINS.

STARTING FROM	1, 2, & 3 Class.	1, 2, & 3 Class.	1, 2, & 3 Class.	FARES. 1st. Class. s.	d.	2nd. Class. s.	d.	3rd. Class. s.	d.
Llandovery ...	9·0	12.45	6.40						
Lampeter Road ...	9·10	12.55	6.50	0	9	0	7	0	4
Langadock ...	9·15	1.0	6.55	1	2	0	11	0	6
†Glanrhyd	9.20	1.5	7.0	1	6	1	2	0	8
Llandilo	9.30	1.15	7.10	2	3	1	9	1	0
Fairfach	9.35	1.20	7.15	2	6	1	11	1	1
†Derwydd Road ...	9.45	1.30	7.25	2	10	2	3	1	3
Llandebie	9.50	1.35	7.30	3	0	2	6	1	5
*Garnant *departure*	9.20		7.0						
Cross-Inn ...	9.45		7.25						
Cross-Inn *arrival.*	10.0		7.40	4	3	3	3	1	8
*Garnant... ...	10.25		8.5	4	9	3	8	2	1
Pontardulais ...	10.15	1.55	7.55	4	9	3	6	2	0
†Llangennech ...	10.22	2.2	8.2	5	3	4	0	2	3
Bynea	10.28	2.8	8.8	5	6	4	2	2	4
Dock	10.36	2.16	8.16	6	0	4	6	2	7
Llanelly... ..	10.40	2.20	8.20	6	3	4	8	2	8

* *Garnant Passengers will be set down or taken up at Gellyceidrim or Cross Keys, if required.*

Cross Inn Passengers by Middle-day Trains will in like manner be set down or taken up at Pantyffynon.

†The Trains will stop at Llangennech, Derwydd Road, and Glanrhyd by signal only; Passengers wishing to alight must give notice to the Guard at the next Station of their intention.

A Coach from Brecon to Llandovery daily, arriving at 12.0 and returning at 12.30.

REGULATIONS.

Dogs will be charged Sixpence each.

Children under three years, no Charge; above three years and under twelve, at Half-price.

Tickets issued at intermediate Stations are so issued conditionally upon the chance of there being room in the Carriages, on the arrival of the Train, and if there be no room, the money will be returned for any Ticket produced at the Booking Office, immediately after the departure of the Train for which it had been purchased. Tickets must be shown to the Company's Servants, or delivered up to them the Trains shall start or arrive at the time specified in the Bills; nor will they be accountable for any loss, inconvenience, or injury which may arise from delay or detention.

Luggage—First Class Passengers are allowed 100lbs. of Luggage; and Second and Third, 60lbs. of Luggage, Free of Charge, not being merchandize or other articles carried for hire or profit: all excess will be charged for. Passengers are requested to place on each article, their Name and Address; and Notice is Hereby Given that the Company will not be responsible for the care of the same unless booked and paid for accordingly.

Opening timetable of the Vale of Towy Railway, 1858. *PRO RAIL 981/231*

they could by playing off the potential bidders for their rather unprofitable railway. On 25 August 1864 they offered to lease their company to the Llanelly at £7,500 per mile, cash. On 5 September the Llanelly countered with a price for the 11 miles of £70,000, £18,000 in debentures, £52,000 in shares. Not surprisingly this was rejected. On 24 November the offer was increased by £5,000 in cash. There was no more cash available to offer so on 25 January 1865 agreement was reached to extend the lease from 1 October 1866 at 4¼%. No sooner had this been done than a counter-offer was made by Green-Price on behalf of the CWR which caused the shareholders of the Vale of Towy to reject the Llanelly offer. The latter were understandably irritated by the CWR action and refused to respond to a peacemaking approach from the CWE made in March. It seems at first sight odd that in view of earlier discussions and the strategic interest of the LNW, this was allowed to happen, but it was presumably a way of weakening the Llanelly's position and forcing a joint share in the lease. Then on 30 March the Vale of Towy flexed their muscles and rejected a proposed arrangement between their company, the Knighton, CWR and CWE. By June 1866 Biddulph and Robertson, the peacemaker, were again talking about cooperating on a lease of the Vale of Towy which by November had led to heads of agreement being ready. By March 1867 the lease at 5% was agreed, the Llanelly only being concerned that the CWR should make the LNWR fully aware. They need hardly have worried.

In March 1868, with the Llanelly's lease of the Vale of Towy about to expire, Moon took advantage of Biddulph's offer made over dinner the previous July, and gave the seal of approval to the LNW and its allies sharing the new lease with the Llanelly, and accepted the offer of running powers to Swansea, Brynamman, Llanelly and Carmarthen. A promise of a £40,000 loan acted as a sweetener. This offer was accepted and, as a result, once the Central Wales Extension had been completed between Llandrindod and Llandovery, the LNW would be in a position to operate trains through to Swansea. The share in the lease was vested in the LNWR on 1 July 1884, and was in due course inherited by the LMS.

At this point we must return to Shrewsbury and the line from Craven Arms to Llandovery. In 1858, the year the Vale of Towy linked Llandilo to Llandovery, and the direct LNW line from Crewe reached Shrewsbury, the Knighton Railway was authorised to build a line from Craven Arms & Stokesay on the S & H for 12 miles to Knighton. After delays caused by weather and a shortage of labour, the engineer, Henry Robertson completed the line in March 1861 and it was agreed that it would be operated by T. Brassey under a lease. From the outset, close working relations were established with the S & H and the LNW; the latter took a lease and agreed to operate the railway from 1 July 1862, the same date as the start of the joint GW/LNW/West Midland lease of the S & H.

In 1859 a year after the formation of the Knighton, much attention was focussed on

The station at Knighton, looking towards Llandrindod Wells; no date.
N.D. Mundy, courtesy N.T. Wassell

Llanbister Road Station in BR days.
Keith Jones

Llandovery. With the arrival of the Vale of Towy from the south in 1858, there was a general awareness of the importance of reaching Swansea. From the north there were two rival schemes for contact with Llandovery; one the Mid-Wales from Llanidloes, the other, the Central Wales, from Knighton. Parliament preferred the latter but only authorised the Central Wales Railway to build a line for 20 miles from the Knighton as far as Llandrindod. Many of the promoters were the same as those backing the Knighton, and Robertson was again the engineer. In July 1860 a traffic agreement was made between the Knighton, the CWR, the S & H and the LNW which was to cover the gradual opening of the line. Unfortunately, opening of the CWR took longer than expected, due partly to finance but also to the difficulty of the terrain, and in 1862 the LNW had to put up £30,000 to keep work going. This was authorised by the S & H Leasing Act of the same year. On 21 May 1863 the Knighton was merged with the Central Wales, and on 22 June the Central Wales Railway Act approved the working agreements between the LNWR and the two merged companies. However, it was only to be implemented when a third company, the Central Wales Extension, reached Llandovery from Llandrindod.

This company was the result of further negotiation and parliamentary discussion. In 1860 the two rivals for Llandovery had tried again. The Mid-Wales hedged its bets

Shrewsbury train approaching the Sugar Loaf mountain on the Carmarthen/Brecknock border; 25 April 1963.
Alan Jarvis

A north-bound freight train approaches the Sugar Loaf tunnel; 16 May 1964. *Alan Jarvis*

by adding a line to Brecon over the HHB and B & M; this was authorised by Parliament, leaving the Central Wales Extension Railway to build a line over the 26 miles from Llandrindod to Llandovery. Mrs Crawshay Bailey cut the first sod and the whole venture was backed by a similar group to the two other companies, with Robertson once more the engineer. In 1866 the LNWR undertook to manage the operation and maintenance of the line once it was completed and Llandovery was eventually reached in 1868. The last ten miles, involving the tunnel at the Sugar Loaf summit, caused serious delays. On 25 June, with the line complete, the three companies became amalgamated with the LNWR, which, as a result of the agreements with the Llanelly and the Vale of Towy discussed earlier, was finally in a position to operate from Shrewsbury to Swansea.

But the Llanelly was in trouble. Both 'new lines' were in the hands of receivers and the London Financial Association was pressing for amalgamation of the Llanelly and 'new lines' in order to overcome the problems associated with

Close inspection of a Webb 2-4-2T, probably at Llandrindod Wells, early in the twentieth century.
Warwickshire Record Office

determining correct allocations of income and overheads between the component parts of the whole railway. The Llanelly directors were determined to prevent this as they were concerned to continue to isolate the 'original undertaking' and protect what remained of its profit generating ability. The consequence was that in 1871 an Act was passed creating the Swansea & Carmarthen Railway (S & C) as an entirely separate organization to own and operate both 'new lines'.

This child of Parliament had a board consisting of representatives of the various classes of shareholders, under the chairmanship of John Borradale. The London Financial Association was by far the largest shareholder with 12,000 Deferred Shares, 3,700 Preferred Shares and 2,700 Ordinary Shares. Members of the Overend family had some 6,000 shares and R.K. Penson had 300. John Biddulph had probably felt obliged to take 300, and no doubt pressure had been brought to bear on poor old Glascodine, the Llanelly secretary, to take up the 45 that were in his name. The office was at 113 Cannon Street in London.

The first board meeting was held on 23 June 1871, at which Dunn represented the London Financial. Frank Grundy was appointed general manager at £300 a year. This was reduced in 1875 to £150 when the job became part-time, shared with that of managing the Mid-Wales. This first board meeting rejected a proposal from the 'original undertaking' to work the lines; the company's solicitor Samuel Noyes was already in discussion with the LNWR for either the sale of the company or a working agreement. At a meeting with the LNW at Euston on 24 June, Cawkwell and Findlay agreed to work the line for the month of July. By its Act the Swansea & Carmarthen had full running powers over the Llanelly, and full reciprocal booking rights. The situation was complicated further by the Llanelly being bound to grant running powers to the LNW as a result of the agreement of 1867. With a substantial part of their operation now separate and directly under the control of the LNW, this was not an easy relationship to manage. At the June meeting of the S & C board it was agreed that, for July, receipts would be paid to the receiver to pay the staff and those costs other than the LNW's. Bishop and Grundy were to make an inventory and Grundy was to get from Glascodine all the relevant agreements, files, plans and accounting records. Cawkwell was to see the C & C about the use of Carmarthen Station and to discuss with the Llanelly running powers and the joint management of the Vale of Towy. The S & C was to hand over its locomotives and 80 waggons to the LNWR.

In July it became apparent that the books and records were in a poor state and it was decided to put in a complaint in writing, more it seems for the sake of the record than in the expectation that it would have much effect. By 24 October Glascodine had still been unable to produce anything and so it was decided to put the matter in the hands of an arbitrator, as provided under the original agreement. Eventually the arbitrator allocated responsibility for past obligations whereby the burden was placed partly on the Llanelly but mainly on the S & C. The finances were quite clearly in a serious mess for, in June 1872, Glascodine was sued by the receiver for having paid £5,430 S & C profit to the Llanelly instead of to the Court of Chancery.

The LNWR was a large and powerful bed-fellow and the Llanelly board were conscious of the possibility of their most remunerative business being syphoned away. Already in January 1869 they were complaining to the LNW that the passenger mileage allowance was high relative to their receipts on through trains. In April 1870, in desperation at the falling traffic, the management lowered the fares for 1st and 2nd class passengers; on the joint line the LNW insisted that they would maintain their rates and therefore their partner would have to make good the lower proceeds arising from discounted fares. The Llanelly backed down. In the same breath, with the majesterial attention to detail that made the LNW a great railway, Moon turned down an application for a carpet for the cashier's office at Shrewsbury; a piece of matting would suffice.

In August the Llanelly board inspected their lines and were not happy with what they found; at Pontardulais the waiting-room was being

The 12.25 p.m. train to Shrewsbury at Pontardulais, headed by BR Class 4 2-6-4T No. 80099; 6 October 1960.
Huw Daniel

used as a goods shed. This switching of the uses of buildings seems to have been traditional at Pontardulais as, back in 1860, temporary accommodation for the station master had been provided in a stable. At Pantyffynnon there were dangerous steps up to the booking-office and the urinal needed to be moved. At Llandovery the LNW appeared to be using more than their

Pantyffynnon Station, looking south towards Pontardulais. The Brunel-style building is the consequence of the GWR taking over the Llanelly branch in 1873. Over this part of the line, from Pontardulais to Llandilo, the LNWR was dependent on running powers; no date.
N.T. Wassell

Pantyffynnon was the junction for the Llanelly and later GWR branch to Brynamman. A group of railway enthusiasts and Jinty No. 47480 are using the branch platform; no date.
NMRW

share of land for their engine shed. It occurred to the board that it would be useful to find out the profitability of every train and they wondered for the first time how their locomotive costs compared with other railways. Some may feel that a prudent management would have taken these measures sooner and on a routine basis. The contrast in management style is marked.

In October 1870 a typical problem arose over Mr Berry, the station master at Llandovery; a goods train had used a wrong single-line staff from Llanwrtyd to Llandovery and Berry had sent it back to collect the right one. The LNW dismissed the driver, guard and Llanwrtyd station master and proposed the same treatment for Berry. The Llanelly found this hard but felt they had to comply as it was a matter of discipline, but they generously sought to find employment for Berry elsewhere on their own line. Moon himself became involved in a discussion about the 6.30 a.m. early morning train from Swansea which the Llanelly complained was under-utilised; Moon wrote of the need to build up demand gradually, and to maintain times in the timetable so that they became familiar to the public.

Llanwrtyd Wells Station, *c.* 1910.
Courtesy N.T. Wassell

By early 1872, with the 'new lines' now under LNW control, recriminations were coming from both sides. Findlay wrote to complain that the Llanelly were running trains just in front of LNW trains to capture their traffic. He cited five waggons of tin-plate from Llanelly to Liverpool. These were not handed over to the LNW at Pontardulais but taken by the Llanelly to Pantyffynnon (a Llanelly station) and placed on a siding. They were subsequently sent on to Llandovery but missed the connection and arrived 24 hours late at their destination. The same occurred with three waggons of tin-plate for Poplar and a waggon of iron for Dudley. The Llanelly claimed the right to use their trains for any cargo within their own territory. The LNW pressed for the right to run their own trains on the joint Vale of Towy. The Llanelly disputed this and complained that the LNW were putting their own labels on waggons at Pantyffynnon when these were for Llanelly traffic. They also complained that LNW passengers from Swansea to Llandilo were refusing to pay again for that part of the journey over Llanelly lines between Pontardulais and Llandilo. In 1872 delays to traffic were causing the LNW to review their policy of not exercising running powers over the Brynamman branch;

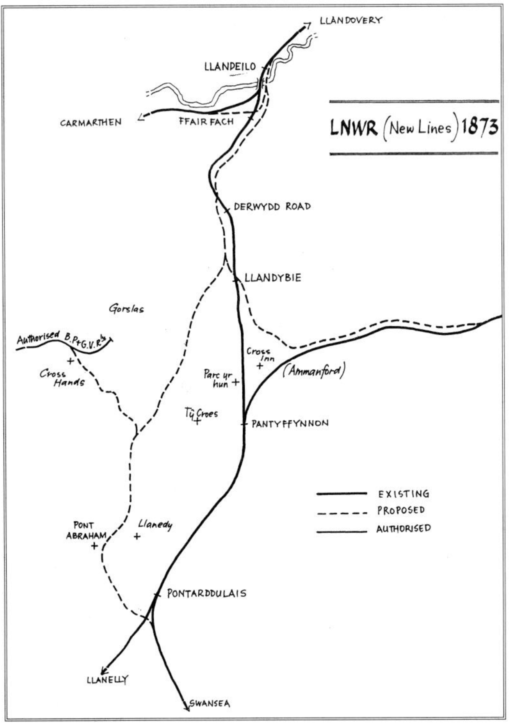

The lines proposed by the LNWR as a means of avoiding use of the Llanelly Railway between Llandilo and Pontardulais. *GBJ*

they even considered extending a line to Ystalyfera, no doubt with J. Palmer Budd's business in mind. In an attempt to step around the problem, the LNW set about planning a separate line from Llandilo to Pontardulais which would by-pass the Llanelly altogether, and submitted a Bill to Parliament.

Circular 5

Llanelly Railway & Dock Company
General Manager's Office
Llanelly June 29th/1872.

Be good enough to note, that upon all traffic from July 1st to 12th inclusive passing from or to or over this Company's Railway between Llandilo and Carmarthen Valley Junction or Stations between Llandilo and Pontardulais inclusive or vice versa this Company will claim their fixed local Tolls in division. After July 12th all [illegible] Through Bookings to from Company's [illegible] line will be discontinued unless [illegible] satisfactory arrangements can be made.
Please note and issue the necessary instructions.

Declaration of War; 1872. *PRO RAIL 377/26*

In desperation, the Llanelly decided in February 1872 to cancel the 1867 running powers agreement and the joint lease and gave notice to the LNW effective from 1 July 1872. The LNW refused to comply and the Llanelly filed a suit in Chancery. The LNW tried to prevent this course. On 28 August Findlay, the diplomat, offered a peacemaking solution; the LNW would lease the whole of the Llanelly undertaking at 5% for the first year, then 6%, or it would work the line for 10 years at 50% of receipts. On 13 August the S & C board added fuel to the fire by agreeing to sell the Swansea line to the LNW for £310,000. On 18 September a large meeting was held at Euston. Moon, Cawkwell, Findlay and Roberts the in-house lawyer were there from the LNW; deputy chairman Kirkwood, Walker and Glascodine represented the Llanelly. Moon was disarmingly courteous. He told the meeting how the LNW

London and North Western Railway.

SWANSEA,
July 6th, 1872.

DEAR SIR,

With reference to a Circular of the 1st July, issued by the Secretary of the Llanelly Railway and Dock Company, withdrawing Through Rates to and from the London and North Western Line and Railways beyond *via* Llandovery, and that Company having made a demand for Local Tolls, and having intimated their intention of Booking the Traffic to and from Llandovery instead of through to destination, which course is in violation of their agreement with this Company, and which must necessarily cause much Public inconvenience and delay.

I am instructed by the General Manager to inform you that the London and North Western Company will undertake that for all Traffic arising at the Llanelly Company's Stations specially consigned by the Public to the London and North Western Company's care, to be conveyed by their Trains, and for all Traffic from the London and North Western System and Stations beyond on other Lines, that the through rates previously existing will be maintained and charged to the public until further notice.

Yours truly,

W. D. PHILLIPPS.

Lofty disdain; 1872. *PRO RAIL 376/26*

was prevented by the 1863 agreement with the GW from leasing the Llanelly; this was because there was a list of Welsh ports to which the LNW was permitted access and un-fortunately Llanelly was not one of them. He therefore suggested withdrawal of the Chancery suit in return for which the LNW would withdraw their planned by-pass. Cawkwell came up with the idea of the LNW working the line north of Pontardulais but this was generally felt to be too complex.

On 30 October the Llanelly board, feeling increasingly desperate, agreed to any solution giving 5% and decided to open discussion with the GW. The LNW started surveying their by-pass. On 11 December the Llanelly board agreed to lease their company to the GW at 5% for four years and 5½% thereafter, the GW to do as they wished with the Chancery suit. This agreement became effective on 1 January 1873. The Llanelly was finally absorbed by the GW in 1899; John Biddulph remained chairman until August 1880, a born survivor; he died a year later. The Lords eventually judged in favour of the LNWR rights and the GWR therefore inherited their running powers to Llanelly and joint ownership of the Vale of Towy.

Thus it was that the LNW's approach to Swansea was first over its own line to Llandovery, then over the joint Vale of Towy to Llandilo, then by running powers over the Llanelly, now GW, to Pontardulais, and finally over its own metals into Swansea. Although the GW inherited the obligation to allow running powers to the LNW, being another national line it was less sensitive to the distinction between local and national traffic and the two companies were able to live together, even agreeing to share traffic from and to points west of Carmarthen. Already by April 1873 the LNW's South Wales committee was noting about the GWR, 'officials appear to have strict injunctions to be very careful to throw no obstacles in the way of LNW traffic'.

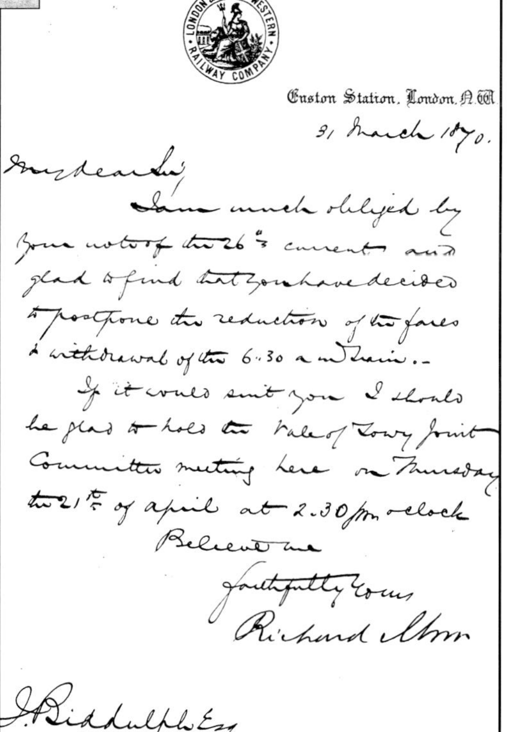

London & North Western Railway Company

Euston Station, London, N.W.
31 March 1870.

My dear Sir,

I am much obliged by your note of the 26th current and glad to find that you have decided to postpone the reduction of the fares & withdrawal of the 6.30 a.m. train.

If it would suit you I should be glad to hold the Vale of Towy Joint Committee meeting here on Thursday the 21st of April at 2.30 p.m. o'clock.

Believe me
Faithfully Yours
Richard Moon

J. Biddulph Esq

The courtesy of the language cloaks the imperial nature of the summons.

PRO RAIL 377/26

The interior of Swansea Paxton Street shed with locomotives Nos 6414, 42305 and 2307; 27 August 1948.
H.C. Casserley

The LNW had played a brilliant game. Swansea had always been the objective. Moon had been convinced since 1852. They then let the players assemble and act. They waited on the side, watchful and alert, ready with finance and working agreements as needed, and working closely with Robertson the go-between. But they did not try to drive events themselves; they waited until the right moment and were then able to move with skill and deliberation. Thus they were active and effective in Parliament when the challenge came; in 1859 the Central Wales Act first created the alliance by permitting the S & H, Knighton, Vale of Towy and Llanelly to make working arrangements. In 1860 the Central Wales Extension Act added the CWR to the club. In 1862 the S & H leasing Act enabled the LNW and the S & H to invest in the Central Wales. In 1863 the Central Wales Extension Act allowed the LNW to work the line. At the other end, they steadily prepared the ground and watched their quarry become weakened, waiting for the right moment to strike, and then, once they were in sight of home, seized every advantage, and mercilessly drove their victim into the ground, and marched into Swansea. The Llanelly directors were at the mercy of the financiers. For a banker, John Biddulph had displayed unusual courage if not foolhardiness in backing the 'new lines' and, in the end, the Llanelly's strategic position was hopeless; dependent on the LNW but squeezed by it and, desperate to protect the 'original undertaking', it was doomed.

Having at last made the connection, the LNW found the station arrangements they took over at Swansea somewhat ramshackle; they accordingly set about replacing the Llanelly's low-cost wooden shed with a rather more permanent structure of iron and glass. This was completed in 1882 and survived until the end, in spite of bomb damage during the Second World War. The line from Pontardulais to Swansea was doubled by 1894. In Swansea, direct contact was made with the high-level GWR lines and the low-level Swansea Harbour Trust system.

However, this was not the end of the story. As a result of the LNW's purchase of the

The Llanelly Railway terminus at Swansea, *c.* 1868. Behind the station buildings may be seen, at a higher level, the short-lived Vale of Neath station at Wind Street.

Librarian, Swansea City and County

Class 5 No. 45190 leaving Swansea Victoria with the 12.25 p.m. train for Shrewsbury. In the background can be seen the high-level line to the East Dock; 20 April 1949.

Huw Daniel

The Penclawdd branch joining the main line at Gowerton South in the direction of Swansea; no date.

J.J. Davies, courtesy N.T. Wassell

Llanmorlais Station with a special train; date unknown.

NMRW

An early photograph of an LNWR train at Penclawdd; *c.* 1870.

Courtesy Stephen Rowson

Penclawdd Station, looking towards Gowerton, during BR days; date uncertain.
J.J. Davies, courtesy N.T. Wassell

Swansea line, together with the Penclawdd branch, which in 1874 was extended to Llanmorlais, the Carmarthen line was left as the S & C's only asset. The sale of the Swansea line was authorised by Parliament effective from 1 July 1873 and the name of the S & C was changed by another Act of the same summer to the grandiose but rather more appropriate Central Wales & Carmarthen Junction Railway (CW & CJ). As owner of nothing but the Carmarthen line, this company was nearly entirely dependent on through traffic and the prime task of its directors was to maintain and, if possible, increase the share value until such time as a suitable sale could be made. In the absence of any new link, the LNW was clearly the most likely bidder, but no doubt the potential traffic for them was not of sufficient importance to warrant more than the working agreement. For the first years the minutes of board meetings consist mainly of minor matters; a farmer's filly killed on the line, a police constable caught riding a horse along the track, a burnt haystack, a theft from the Carmarthen goods station safe due to the key being kept in the office.

A typical locomotive for the Carmarthen branch, ex-LNWR 2-4-2T No. 6619 at Carmarthen in 1939.
LGRP, courtesy N.T. Wassell

2-4-2T No. 6740 at Carmarthen Station; no date.
LNWR Society

Then the excitement began. John Borradale retired as chairman at the end of 1878 and was succeeded by Sir James Kitson, the ironmaster from Leeds, who owned some 1st and 2nd Preference Shares. On 4 November 1879 the LNW requested £233 due to a reduction in the rate for the Burton beer traffic, with effect from January 1873. The board refused to pay.

Market Day at Carmarthen? A rural scene at Dryslwyn Station on the Carmarthen branch; no date.
Courtesy Huw Daniel

Typical country goods yard activity at Llandilo, as a mixed freight moves off in the direction of Llandovery; no date.
Huw Daniel

After much correspondence, on 23 March 1880 the LNW gave notice that they would discontinue working local traffic from 1 April.

It is unclear from the record for how long the impasse continued, though the background appears to be that the LNWR was in dispute with the GWR over rights of transit for goods from the CW & CJ over the joint Vale of Towy. This led to the construction of a new independently-owned station at Llandilo on the Carmarthen line in 1885. This was known as Llandilo Bridge.

CENTRAL WALES

AND

CARMARTHEN JUNCTION

RAILWAY.

THE Central Wales & Carmarthen Junction Railway Company respectfully beg to inform the Public that owing to the refusal of the London & North Western Company to convey traffic between Stations on their Line, the **local Train Service** for Passengers and Goods will unfortunately have to be temporarily **discontinued** on and from 1st April, 1880.

FRANK GRUNDY,
General Manager.

Carmarthen, 30th March, 1880.

C. & D. JONES, PRINTERS, KING-STREET, CARMARTHEN.

David and Goliath at Carmarthen, 1880.
PRO RAIL 1015/2/96

Llandilo Bridge Station on the Carmarthen branch was built by the LNWR as the result of a dispute with the GWR over access to Llandilo from the Carmarthen branch. Looking towards Carmarthen; 6 September 1963.
Andrew Muckley

Kitson resigned after a meeting with the LNW at Euston held on 14 April 1880. He was replaced by Gruning, a 2nd Preference shareholder. The outcome of the meeting is not clear but, from now on, the CW & CJ board spent much more time discussing traffic. In November 1880 they were considering whether to get running powers to Builth Road so that they could link up with the Mid-Wales. They also considered linking up with the N & B and the Pembroke & Tenby with a view to creating a line from Brecon to Pembroke, joined to the Midland's route to Birmingham. They appealed to the Railway Commissioners about the rates on flour between Haverfordwest and Chester and for goods between Hereford and Pembroke. In August 1881, presumably due to a lack of harmony between the two companies, the LNW appointed their own staff at Carmarthen. In November 1882 a CW & CJ Bill was promoted for running powers from Milford to Craven Arms and was approved.

A year later Gruning died and Kitson's son succeeded him. In February 1884 it was decided to support the Usk & Towy Railway Bill by offering running powers over the CW & CJ. This was yet another abortive attempt to make a rail link between Brecon and Llandovery. Kitson queried whether this might prejudice eventual sale of the company to the GW or

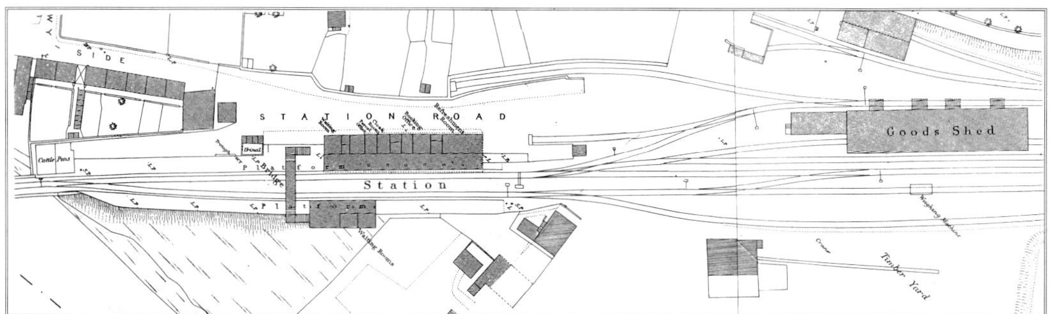

Old Carmarthen Town Station was just to the north of the present station, on the other side of the road bridge. Part of the main station building and the goods shed survive in 1998; *c.* 1885.

O.S. Crown Copyright

LNW since the Midland was involved. Batten, another director, replied that in view of the GW and LNW agreement to divide all traffic west of Carmarthen, it would be vital for a third competitor to have running powers otherwise all traffic would be lost. In the event the Bill was withdrawn.

Then there was an uneasy peace until July 1885, when the board gave notice to the LNW to discontinue the 7.50 a.m. train from Llandilo. The LNW refused. As we saw in an earlier disagreement with the Llanelly about cancelling a train from Swansea, the LNWR was strongly opposed to tinkering with the timetable, believing in the importance of potential passengers becoming familiar with it.

In January 1889 Grundy resigned in order to take up a job as general manager of the Quebec Central. He was succeeded by R. Graham at £150 plus 10% on increases in net profit, but he was dishonest; he fraudulently cheated the GW and LNW, and had to go. His successor John Davies had been station master at Aberdovey and was paid £180 plus commission on net earnings above £2,500 a year.

Then in June 1891 the chairman announced that he had agreed to sell the company to the LNWR for £137,500, the price to be apportioned to the shareholders:

62% to 1st Pref.
31% to 2nd Pref.
15½% to the rest,
the balance less costs to the 1st Pref.

This was unopposed. Indeed, one senses a corporate sigh of relief.

The LNWR took over on 1 July 1891. The authorising Act was dated 21 July. Their motivation for this step is unclear though their lawyers may have been unhappy about their position in the dispute with the GWR due to the independent status of the CW & CJ. The LNWR then, over a period of years, set about upgrading the infrastructure and ran the line as a charmingly peaceful branch. It survived as long as its more august twin, the line to Swansea, but interestingly both 'new lines' have been outlived by the 'original undertaking' from Llanelly to Llandilo.

Carmarthen remained the most distant outpost in south-west Wales, though LNWR through carriages reached Tenby and Pembroke Dock over the Pembroke & Tenby Railway (P & T). In 1895 there was even a possibility of LNWR running powers from Carmarthen over an extended North Pembrokeshire & Fishguard Railway, but this came to nothing as it was dependent on the P & T, which in 1896 became part of the GWR.

Private owner waggon from Penclawdd.

HMRS, courtesy N.T. Wassell

Chapter 6

THE MIDLAND MOPS UP

HEREFORD HEADACHE

Following the failure of a plan to amalgamate with the Great Northern and the Manchester, Sheffield & Lincolnshire, the Midland board under Sir James Ellis, and with James Allport as general manager, had decided in the early 1860s that survival lay in growing their own connections to preserve traditional traffic. This led to a policy of expansion in many directions, such that by 1866 some £5,000,000 was invested in incomplete lines in various parts of the country. With the LNWR making positive progress into south Wales, this was seen as one of the areas where the Midland would need to act to protect its business by the provision of Midland routes to Dowlais, Newport and Swansea. The abortive Welsh Midland project, which had sought to link Worcester to Swansea via Brecon, was still in people's minds. It was not simply a frustrated dream of J. Palmer Budd for in essence it had been revived, though not via Brecon, by the Swansea Junction Extension project (see Chapter 2). In that scheme, J. Palmer Budd had foreseen a branch northward from Colbren to Devynock in the Usk valley, and so to Brecon from the south.

It is now time to return to Hereford where it will be recalled that the sole surviving interest of the LNW/Midland partnership was the Midland running powers over the W & H from Worcester; these had been confirmed by the terms of the amalgamation of the GWR and West Midland in 1863, which had added rights as far as Swansea over the Vale of Neath Railway.

In 1859 the remaining unexploited area around Hereford lay to the west and in that year the Hereford, Hay & Brecon Railway (HHB) was authorised to construct a line from the S & H westward up the Wye valley and then, over the watershed into the Vale of Usk, to a station to be built on the north side of Brecon. The line was to cost £280,000. It was to leave the S & H just north of the NAH link line and a single platform for interchange at the junction was shown on the original plan. Shortly afterwards, in 1860, a Deviation Act shifted the new line slightly southward, this time to join the NAH, south of its junction with the S & H and with a south facing junction, in practice 300 yds north of Barton, though the Act stated that it was to be at Barton Station. This ambiguity was to lead to a complex battle between the companies.

Brecon presented a gap on the railway map of south Wales, but in the next 10 years it was to become host to four railway companies, the Brecon & Merthyr, the Neath & Brecon, the Mid-Wales, and the Midland, and it was to be the focal point of projects to build railway links in five directions. To the east, the Brecknock & Abergavenny Canal was discussing with the NAH conversion of the canal into a railway. To the south was a project to link Brecon to Merthyr and Dowlais. Northward were plans to link up with Llanidloes, projected by the Mid-Wales Railway. Westward there were two

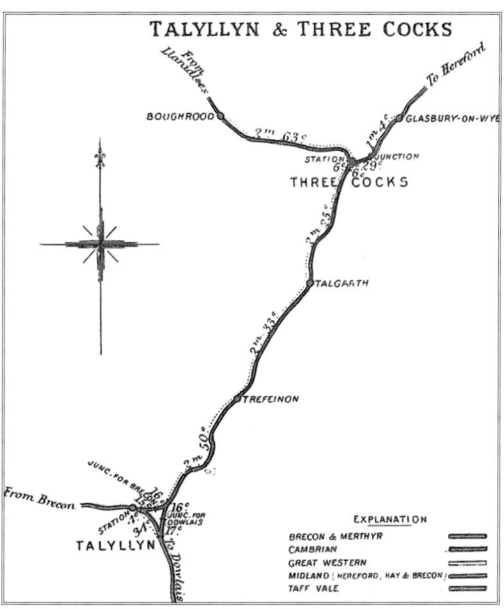

Two strategic junctions, 10 miles apart; 1913
Railway Clearing House

schemes for a line to Llandovery. To the south-west was Swansea with as yet no connection. The Midland sat on the side waiting for an opportunity.

The first meeting of the HHB proprietors was held in February 1860; J.L. Vaughan was chairman and Edward Watkin of the LNW, and later the Great Central, was a member of the board. The projected railway was described as part of the most direct route from London to Milford Haven. This boast rested on an agreement made with the OWW and W & H, that they should work the line, once 20 miles had been completed, at £45 per cent of gross receipts, with 4% payable to the shareholders; at this stage 66% of the capital had been subscribed and the taking up of the balance was urged by the argument that this was 'not a pecuniary speculation but a certain investment'. The relationship with the two constituents of the West Midland does not seem to have survived their merger, as on 24 June 1861, a proposition to allow the working of the HHB by the West Midland was turned down by the shareholders.

One of the peculiarities of the company was that its direction was divided between Hereford/Brecon and London; board meetings were held alternately in each location. From an early stage W.L. Banks, the secretary, emerged as a key player. He became chairman in 1864 in spite of an odd little incident at a board meeting on 5 April of that year, when another member, R.K. Penson, said he could not serve on the same board as Banks; both were asked to leave the room and in their absence Banks was voted to the chair. Penson then remained on the board and managed to overcome his dislike of Banks to the extent of attending meetings throughout the following year. They had possibly crossed swords on the board of the Kington & Eardisley Railway. Penson was an architect, like his father, grandfather and brother. Apart from the minor involvement with the Llanelly noted in Chapter 5, he had an interest in one or two

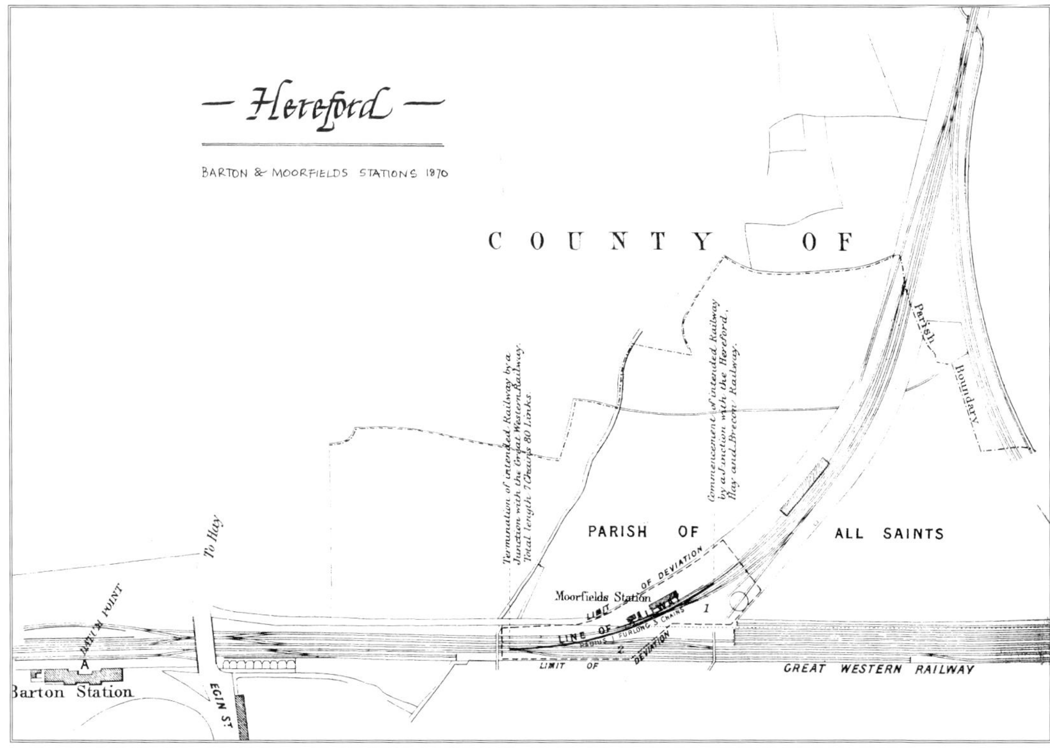

This plan of the 'south fork', which accompanied an aborted Bill in 1870, shows (i) the gap between the HHB junction with the NAH and Barton Station, and (ii) the incomplete 'north fork'.

House of Lords Record Office

William Lawrence Banks, the Brecon solicitor, who played a leading role in creating the Midland's path to Swansea.

By kind permission of the Hergest Trust

minor railways, among them the Bishops Castle. W.L. Banks on the other hand was obsessed with railways and was at one time chairman of three, the HHB, the B & M, and the N & B. Apart from their common focus on Brecon of which Banks was twice mayor, they shared a condition of financial weakness, for Banks' financial judgment was not good. He is reputed to have lost a fortune himself in railway speculation, and, in about 1870, moved with a second wife to north Wales to pursue less risky interests. He is described as an engaging raconteur who in later life had a distinctive appearance with a long white beard, Scotch cap, knickerbockers and stockings. He it was who played a significant part in creating the Midland's path to Swansea.

During 1860 the Hay Tramway was offered for sale. This was an ancient horse-drawn operation linking Brecon with Eardisley. Three railways were interested in taking it over and in the end, after much negotiation, they agreed to split it and give one another running powers. The HHB took the portion from Eardisley to Glasbury, the Mid-Wales from Glasbury to Talyllyn Junction, and the B & M from there into Brecon. Purchase of the HHB part was made by Thomas Savin who was compensated with HHB shares. Glasbury was just east of the point where the line of the Mid-Wales Railway approached the HHB from the north; the junction came to be

Eardisley Station with No. 46518 on a train from Hereford to Brecon; 31 July 1962.

Alan Jarvis

Eardisley Station, looking towards Brecon. This was the junction for the Kington Railway; 23 April 1958.

R.M. Casserley

A romantic scene at Glasbury Station, looking towards Hereford. This was the westward limit of the HHB; 1950. *LGRP 24929/NRM*

Creden Hill with a train for Brecon headed by No. 46505; 14 April 1960. *T.B. Owen*

Moorhampton Station, facing Hereford; 23 April 1958. *H.C. Casserley*

known as Three Cocks after a nearby pub. Part of the deal was that each of the three partners would grant running powers to the others; in this way the HHB was to gain access to Brecon without having to build a line all the way.

The first contract to build the HHB line was let to McCormick who was building the MTA, but he ceased work in June 1861 due to non-payment of his bills and, in August 1861, settled for £10,000 as part of an agreement by which Savin took over the contract. He undertook to build the line from Hereford to Glasbury within 20 months, and onward from there to Brecon. He was to be paid partly in shares, partly in 5% debentures. The line opened for goods as far as Moorhampton on 24 October 1862 and the first passenger train was operated by Savin. It ran from a temporary station at Hereford, called Moorfields, to Eardisley on 30 June 1863; at some stage Savin started using Barton Station for the HHB trains, having completed the south-facing fork just north of Barton, and the first through train to Brecon ran on 19 September 1864. From about 25 April 1865, the Brecon & Merthyr took over operation of the HHB, Banks having become chairman of the B & M. After about a year of using Barton, Moorfields again became the Hereford terminus.

Moorfields goods sidings in 1930, looking towards Brecon. The former MR locomotive depot can be seen in the distance. In later years the lines to the left were occupied by the Bulmer's Railway Centre. *Mowat Collection, courtesy John Miles*

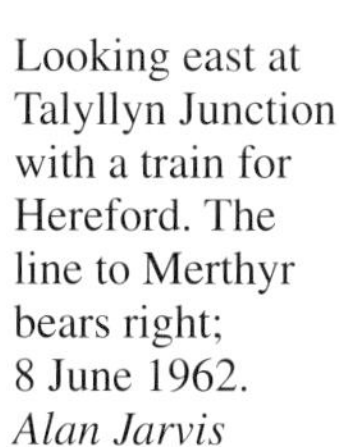

Looking east at Talyllyn Junction with a train for Hereford. The line to Merthyr bears right; 8 June 1962. *Alan Jarvis*

The view towards the east at Talyllyn Junction with the line to Hereford to the left; early 1950s.
Tudor Watkins

Talyllyn Junction with a train for Brecon; 8 June 1962.
Alan Jarvis

Talyllyn Junction with a Brecon train passing behind the former Mid-Wales station, which stood on the line from Moat Lane to Merthyr; 8 June 1962.
Alan Jarvis

The approach to Talyllyn Junction from the east; 8 June 1962.
Alan Jarvis

The close cooperation between the B & M and the HHB became manifest in an agreement to merge which was approved by Parliament in 1865. This happy development then fell foul of the B & M Preference shareholders who successfully brought a writ to prevent the merger. There followed three years of hiatus before the HHB resumed its independent existence; the B & M continued to run the trains but no maintenance was carried out and the accounts became a hopeless tangle; the minute book has two empty pages between a general meeting held on 25 August 1865 and an extraordinary meeting on 10 August 1868. On 1 October 1868, as a temporary measure, the Mid-Wales took over the working of the line for a year.

At this point the LNWR came into the picture; Bolden, the new chairman of the HHB, was also a director of the Cambrian and in that capacity had a close acquaintence with the LNW. When he approached them, he was told that they could not act without the consent of their partner in the S & H. Accordingly, Bolden had a meeting with Grierson of the GW. This appears to have been a most unsatisfactory event. The GW were not prepared to buy the HHB but were willing to work it for a high share of the traffic proceeds, so high that the HHB felt there would be insufficient left for their shareholders. Bolden's view of the meeting was unfavourable and he must have been made to feel distinctly uncomfortable because, when in an effort to demonstrate GW willingness to

Whitney Station, looking towards Hereford, with a fine display of Midland fencing; c. 1910.
Hereford City Library

Repairs in progress to the bridge over the Wye at Whitney; 1887. *R.S. Carpenter, courtesy M. Lloyd*

assist, he was challenged in committee as to how many meetings he had had with the GW. He insisted it was only one, saying, 'I certainly never went to the GW more than once – not several times – I had quite enough of it in that once.' The HHB were looking for what they might reasonably be able to exact as an independent line, yet the viability of the line depended on it being part of a national chain. This led to insoluble confrontation with the GW.

Bolden then approached the Midland and received a letter dated 27 July 1869 proposing a meeting in Derby. On 20 August the Midland board decided to appoint a sub-committee to handle negotiations with the HHB. The matter was clearly considered important as the chairman, deputy chairman, Sir Isaac Morley, Ellis (later chairman) and Heygate were appointed.

A Midland train, bound for Brecon with a through carriage for Swansea, standing at Hay; *c.* 1900. *Courtesy M. Lloyd*

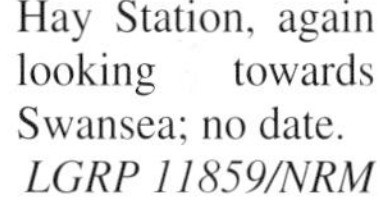

Hay Station, again looking towards Swansea; no date.
LGRP 11859/NRM

A similar view at Hay Station with No. 2287 heading a Brecon train and No. 2275 heading the 4.15 p.m. from Brecon to Hereford; 13 September 1956.
R.M. Casserley, courtesy John Miles

A Brecon train, shortly after leaving Hay, passes a fine display of horse chestnuts; 8 June 1962.
Alan Jarvis

At about this time the Midland had started operating passenger trains into Hereford from Worcester. This was under the terms of the GWR (West Midland) Act of 1863 whereby running powers were granted from Worcester to Swansea; the GW were given five years to double the track in order to be able to accommodate the additional traffic which the Midland were expected to bring. In practice the Midland's passenger traffic was a disappointment and after three years the Midland discontinued their Worcester to Hereford service. On the other hand, goods traffic from Worcester began in November 1868 and was continued. A group of Midland directors travelled over the HHB and clearly saw an opportunity, for on 4 August the Midland board agreed to look for a two-year contract with the HHB. Their only concern about the HHB seems to have been the fear that, if they operated on the line, their carriages would be siezed by the HHB's creditors. Subsequently, Bolden met the Midland chairman at Lancaster and the upshot was that, from 1 October 1869, the Midland took over from the Mid-Wales the working of trains on the line.

The GW were appalled by this development and on 31 August asked for a meeting of the Joint Midland/GW committee to discuss it. The Midland replied, saying they hardly thought a meeting was called for, and assumed that the agreement would not prevent the temporary use of Barton when they started operating on the HHB. This was a serious misassessment of the attitude of the GWR who proceeded to do everything they could to prevent the HHB being operated as a through route.

The evidence as to the sequence of events in the development of the Midland's position is confused, but it began with the 1860 HHB Deviation Act which permitted a south-facing junction with the NAH line from Barton to the S & H, and access to Barton Station. As far as we can tell, this link was constructed at an early stage, because there is a record of a claim for expenses from the GWR for the use of Barton Station during the time Savin was operating the

A charming study of the spacious Midland Railway goods shed at Moorfields, Hereford. The size and quality of this building suggests that Derby looked more favourably on infrastructure investment on the former HHB than on the Swansea Vale; *c.* 1900.

M. Lloyd

HHB, i.e. before 1865. Then, during the B & M train operations, for reasons which are not clear but perhaps to save money, the HHB used their station at Moorfields. This would certainly have been in accordance with GW wishes as it served to discourage any passenger wishing to make a through journey to or from Brecon; a 200-yard journey by bus was required between Moorfields and Barton. The south fork connection seems to have fallen into disuse, if not disrepair.

The other problem was the north fork at the NAH junction. This would be highly desirable if through trains, especially freight, from the HHB were to be operated to the Worcester or Shrewsbury lines. On 30 October 1863 Grierson wrote to his opposite number at the LNW concerning a request from the HHB for a meeting to discuss 'an extension into Barton station and a junction with the S & H'. Shortly afterwards, on 24 November, a sub-committee of the HHB board was appointed to deal with an approach from the LNW seeking 'friendly agreements', but this seems to have been fruitless and on 1 January 1864 the board approved the sub-committee's recommendation to make an agreement with the GW over Barton. On 10 May 1864 an agreement was made with the GW and LNW for the HHB to have access

Barr's Court Station forecourt with Midland Railway horse-drawn van; *c.* 1900.
National Tramway Museum

to Barr's Court Station, either by means of the north fork or a line, on the south side of Hereford, from the NAH to the Hereford, Ross & Gloucester line, known sometimes as the Hereford Curve. The whole was wrapped up in an overall agreement approved by the HHB on 30 May granting access to both stations at Hereford.

However, the LNW (Additional Powers) Bill as submitted to Parliament sought only to construct the south side branch in which the HHB had no interest, as it was a long way round to their objective; they therefore opposed it. This was to no avail as in 1866 Parliament approved the Bill, which authorised the line across the south of the city from the NAH to the Hereford Ross and Gloucester, enabling all trains from the south to run into Barr's Court without having to reverse. In an unusual gesture of co-operation, the GWR simultaneously inserted a third rail between the new junction and Barr's Court, and then converted the Ross line to standard gauge. This south side link survives in 1998 as part of the main line from Abergavenny to Barr's Court.

The north fork was excluded from the Act and thus remained unauthorised; at a HHB shareholders' meeting on 28 January 1865 it was reported that the line had been opened to Brecon on 19 September 1864; the report then went on: 'The loop line at Widemarsh [i.e. the north fork] has been proceeded with by the HHB, but, between there and Barr's Court, arrangements are pending we believe for proceeding with the works, but no operations have as yet been commenced by the GW and

LNW in accordance with the arrangements entered into with them. We trust shortly to have them completed and to be able to work the passenger traffic of your line into Barr's Court [this name was oddly deleted in the record, presumably because access was required to both stations] and thereby save the public the delays and inconvenience they now experience in getting from one station to another' (i.e. from Moorfields to Barton or Barr's Court).

Nothing appears to have been done throughout the period of the hiatus in the HHB affairs except that, in the deposited plans for the B & M (Arrangement) Act of 1868, the north fork was included. It was, however, withdrawn at the committee stage. This was either because of a shortage of funds or because the B & M was being extricated from HHB affairs at the end of that September; in either case the hand of the GWR can be imagined. On 17 August 1868 the board was told that the position at Hereford was still unresolved; the goods station at Moorfields was accordingly extended. At the next board meeting the chairman was asked to negotiate the passenger arrangements at Hereford with the other companies. This situation then seems to have continued right through into 1869; in that year a Bill was presented to construct the north fork.

In the plans deposited in connection with this Bill, the HHB formally applied for the north fork to connect the HHB to the old NAH. However, during the summer of 1869, in the course of the committee hearings and in the face of strong opposition from the GWR, it was agreed between the GW, LNW and HHB that this point would be sacrificed for the sake of the other more immediately vital clauses to do with re-financing and the granting of running powers as far as Brecon. Authority was obtained to acquire additional land to improve Moorfields Station, though it was not exercised. Specifically deleted from the Act was the right for the HHB to make arrangements with the LNW, GW or, significantly, the Midland. The GWR had again achieved a postponement of the

Barton Station, *c.* 1880. *Hereford City Library*

HHB's access to Barr's Court over a north fork, and furthermore had ensured that any arrangement between the HHB and the Midland would be confined to the Midland operating HHB trains, but not in their own name. In 1870 the north fork was shown as incomplete on the plans accompanying an aborted Bill.

Such was the situation when on 1 October 1869 the Midland started operating on the HHB. Some trouble at Hereford must have been expected because Bolden was there himself and witnessed the blocking of the first train from Brecon on the south fork. This prevented it from proceeding beyond Moorfields to Barton. He wrote immediately to Sir Daniel Gooch, chairman of the GWR, and told him how he had witnessed the placing of engines and coal wagons on the junction. He had himself heard the GW district manager declare that, if necessary, the rails would be pulled up to prevent traffic. No response from the GW was forthcoming so temporary passenger accommodation was installed at Moorfields.

A Midland train from Brecon is about to halt at the platform at Barton; 1892.

Hereford City Library/M. Lloyd

This second photograph was taken immediately after the train from Brecon had stopped. Passengers can be seen crossing the track to the shuttle awaiting departure for Barr's Court.

Hereford City Library

In December 1869 the HHB considered whether a writ of Mandamus could be obtained to compel the GW to concede access to the junction by the Midland. They then filed a writ in Chancery claiming access under the 1860 HHB Deviation Act and seeking an injunction to force the GW to restore the junction. Vice Chancellor James ruled that the GW could not obstruct the use of the junction because the HHB did not have to get new powers to permit the Midland to operate trains over it. Accordingly, on 18 April 1870 the Midland gave notice of its intention to move a train from the HHB; John Noble, assistant general manager of the Midland, was there in person. Again the GW placed obstructions in the way. On 3 January 1871 the Midland board approved a letter to the GWR indicating their intention to use the junction in the light of the Vice Chancellor's decision. The GW replied saying they were putting the matter in the hands of solicitors. The case again went to court and eventually Lord Romilly, Master of the Rolls, found against the Midland, arguing that a company could not delegate powers granted by Parliament without reference back to Parliament. Happily for the Midland, the Lords Justices of Appeal reversed this decision on the grounds that there was nothing in the agreement contrary to policy. However, it was now 1873 and a great hullabaloo was being created in Hereford by the mayor and townspeople, fed up with the bussing arrangements between Barton and Moorfields. The Midland was seen as the champion of the consumer; the GW was interested only in its shareholders.

Meanwhile a further complication had arisen over the north fork. At one stage in 1870 it looked as though the LNW had solved the problem by including in their 1870 so-called Omnibus Bill a schedule repeating the 1864 agreement, but when the HHB were required to hold a Wharncliffe meeting to endorse the Bill, Bolden refused to hold the meeting because a term of the agreement required the HHB to pay rent on the south side branch for which they had no use. When challenged later in committee that, if he had agreed at that time, the whole issue of the north fork could have been solved, he pointed out that a further problem had now arisen in that the original drawings would now require the moving of a pier in a new road bridge carrying the Leominster road out of Hereford, and the new alignment to avoid this pier would require GW consent. So nothing was done.

The Midland started using the south fork in 1873, but it was not until 1 September 1874 that they started using Barton for passenger trains through to Brecon. Thereafter they used it until 1893, reversing their trains and running a shuttle for through carriages from Worcester between Barr's Court and Barton.

The north end of Barr's Court Station with Castle Class 7027. The beginning of the Brecon Curve can be seen top left; 4 October 1962.
John Wiltshire

The style of Midland management, as revealed by the HHB books, is less purposeful than that displayed by the LNW in its dealings with the MTA, even more so with the Sirhowy. The HHB board were frustrated by what they saw as lethargy over taking the dispute with the GW to court, and the first evidence of Midland operating arrangements was unimpressive; traffic receipts in the first three months of Midland management were £4,625, down £220 on the same quarter under Mid-Wales management. However, Bolden himself said to the Lords' Committee in 1874 that he thought the Midland had done all they could in the circumstances. In 1871 he asked the Midland to convert the arrangement to a lease.

The Midland were endeavouring to form a view on the HHB. In April 1870 Allport was asked to report to the board on its profitability; on 2 August in the following year he was chased for the information, so it cannot have been a matter to which he attached the highest priority. In fact, it took until 3 December 1873, by which time John Lloyd had been appointed to represent the Midland on the HHB board, when it was Hodge who produced some figures for sales:

First half 1872 – £11,981.
First half 1873 – £11,050.

Hardly surprisingly he was tersely asked for some associated costs and profitability numbers for the next meeting. There is no evidence of this information appearing until 3 March 1875.

By 1874 the HHB infrastructure was getting seriously run-down; the Midland were only contracted to operate trains and, as we have seen, were unable to obtain the benefits of operating the HHB as a through line. Even when in 1873 the House of Lords found that the Midland were entitled to run through trains, it was insufficient to enable them to invest in the line; for this an Act of Parliament was required by which they could obtain title to the line by lease or purchase. Accordingly, the Midland sought approval to lease the HHB in 1874, and, despite predictable opposition from the GWR, this was granted; an agreement was made for a lease in perpetuity which led in 1886 to the full vesting of the HHB in the Midland.

Then a new factor had to be taken into account; by 1886 the Severn tunnel would enable the GWR to open a more competitive route from the north to Bristol. The LNW and GW had been in dispute over the rights of the LNW to pick up passengers south of Hereford; the case was eventually decided by the High Court in 1878 in the GW's favour, on the basis that the LNW had no more rights south of Hereford than the S & H had had. This paved the way for an attempt to resolve the Hereford Station problem, and Gooch paid a visit to Hereford which led to his recommending to his board that the GW and LNW concentrate at Barton. The LNW agreed subject to the Midland and the town council being satisfied. In February 1879 the Midland also agreed, but declared that they would not wish to be bound to Barton in perpetuity. By November 1880 something had occurred to make the GW change their mind, for they were now in favour of Barr's Court. Perhaps ease of contact with the Ross line and its short cut to Gloucester seemed more important than a connection with the Midland line to Brecon. The Midland were consistent in not wishing to leave Barton but in keeping their options open. Perhaps they saw maintaining their position at Barton as the best way to force the building of the 'north fork'. In 1883 the original Jacobean building of 1855/6 at Barr's Court was extended, Findlay having predicted the need for this as early as 1868. But Hereford still had two stations.

The final change was made in 1893 when what was called the Brecon Curve was inserted; this, with the north fork (now called the Barton Curve) put in at the same time, enabled trains from Brecon to run into Barr's Court. This eliminated the need for Barton, which, from 1 January 1893, became simply a goods station. The triangle was used for turning engines until 30 June 1894. Thereafter the NAH passenger terminal and offices were pulled down and the south fork cut off. Moorfields remained in use as a goods station, but at the end of a short branch. Much to the relief of the people of Hereford, they now, at last, had only one passenger station.

The demolition of Barton Station, *c.* 1895. *Hereford City Library*

Four trains at Three Cocks. The view is eastward. At about 1.50 p.m. two Cambrian trains were scheduled to cross at this junction, as were two Midland trains. Cambrian 4-4-0 No. 68 heads the 1.05 p.m. from Builth Road to Brecon, passing the 1.20 p.m. from Brecon to Moat Lane Junction. The Midland train, facing Hereford, had left Brecon just 10 minutes before the Cambrian train and was due at Three Cocks at 1.52 p.m. The Midland 0-4-4T, heading the Hereford to Brecon train, was due to depart at 1.58 p.m., a mere 6 minutes after No. 68 which was due to leave at 1.52 p.m; *c.* 1900.

W. Cartwright, Talgarth, courtesy Malcolm John

One oddity was the survival of the unlikely-looking platform which had appeared in the 1859 HHB Act at the point where the Brecon line was to leave the Shrewsbury line, just to the north of the junction of the S & H and NAH. It reappeared in deposited plans from the HHB in 1863 for a north fork, though on the other side of the track, and seems to have been used between about 1861 and 1869 for GWR trains from Worcester which were divided at the platform, one part continuing south through Barton and the other terminating at Barr's Court for connections with the line to Ross and Gloucester.

At this point it is worth pausing to examine the strategic issues which surfaced in the committee proceedings connected with both the 1869 HHB Act and the 1874 Midland Act, as they cast interesting light on the approach to south Wales by both the Midland and the LNWR. The 1869 Bill was motivated primarily by the need to restore the financial base of the HHB following its withdrawal from the B & M merger, but in order to have a free hand to work with the Midland, the HHB needed to recover the running powers between Three Cocks and Talyllyn, which they had lost when the B & M merger was unwound. Without them they could reach neither Brecon nor Dowlais, and the Midland had 62,000 tons a year of Northamptonshire iron ore to be moved to Dowlais, for which Hereford was the shortest route. What was even more important to the HHB was the fact that the Midland was the only one of the national companies who would use the HHB metals for this movement; the GW would take it by way of Quakers Yard and the LNW would use the MTA.

Three trains at Three Cocks. By 1962 some duplication had been avoided by terminating the Hereford train at Three Cocks. In other respects the timetable showed little change, despite the passage of 62 years. On the extreme left the 1.20 p.m. from Brecon to Moat Lane was due to leave Three Cocks at 1.55 p.m. The centre train, headed by No. 46401, had left Builth Road at 12.30 p.m. and was due to depart from Three Cocks for Brecon, also at 1.55 p.m. The train on the right had arrived from Hereford at 1.48 p.m. and was due to return to Hereford at 2.15 p.m; 8 August 1962.

T.B. Owen

The view along the Hereford platform at Three Cocks, looking towards Brecon; no date. *NMRW*

Under the agreement by which the Mid-Wales had operated the HHB for one year from 1 October 1868, it had been agreed that all traffic to or from places south of Three Cocks would be split between the parties, that to or from places north of an east/west line drawn through Shrewsbury going to the Mid-Wales, that to the south to the HHB. The Mid-Wales, just emerging from near bankcruptcy, were desperate to keep the HHB contract, but as Banks told the House of Lords committee, their hunger for traffic had led them to open discussions with the LNWR, who were already offering business out of Cardiff for the north of England over their ally the Rhymney; this then travelled over the B & M, and finally over the

Talgarth Station, facing Brecon; no date. *GBJ Coll.*

A Hereford train approaches Talgarth headed by No. 2218. The camera has caught the open fire door; 7 July 1962.
Alan Jarvis

Mid-Wales as far as the LNW's own Central Wales line at Builth Road. This Banks used to demonstrate in injured tone the regrettable need to discontinue the Mid-Wales contract.

The GWR was also keen to keep the Midland's hands off the HHB, arguing that as a result of the running powers from Worcester to Swansea, granted to the Midland as a price of their acquiescence in the West Midland merger, they had spent £86,000 doubling the track between Worcester and Hereford and between Quakers Yard and Middle Duffryn. This had been required by that agreement at the express request of the Midland, and they did not expect the Midland now to divert their traffic, especially when there was only 2 miles difference between the two routes from Hereford to Neath.

Where next?

The Midland had in the meantime been looking hard at its other options in south Wales. Both the B & M and the Monmouthshire Railway and Canal Co. (MRCC) occupied the area between Brecon, Dowlais and Newport. The B & M was an obvious target as it offered the attraction of direct access to Dowlais, albeit up a formidable mountain climb. On 1 January 1873 the Midland Chairman, now W.P. Price, made an agreement with the B & M Board to divide receipts and to produce £34,500 a year for the B & M, rising to £49,460 in perpetuity. The agreement would, however, require the consent of the B & M debenture holders to accepting a lower rate of interest. This was not forthcoming and on 3 December the Bill was withdrawn. The wisdom of this patriotic but perhaps financially unsound decision can be debated, but, on 7 May 1874, the Midland decided neither to lease nor buy the B & M, and, on 14 July, John Lloyd, who had been appointed to represent the Midland on the B & M board, resigned from it.

However, that was not quite the end of the matter. The Midland directors had inspected the Newport Docks in 1870 and an association was established with the MRCC. A meeting in the Queen's Hotel, Birmingham, on 5 December 1874, was attended by Ellis, Allport, Lloyd and Kenrick from the Midland and four representatives of the MRCC. This led to an agreement to make a joint offer to lease the B & M. The Midland appear to have been cautious. The

MRCC, not surprisingly, wanted to split the B & M between north and south and take the southern portion only. The Midland declined but did agree to frame terms whereby they would acquire the B & M, reserving certain powers to the MRCC; the whole was to be part of a Bill the MRCC were already preparing. Negotiations continued through January and February 1875, but in March the Midland decided not to proceed. The reason for what looks at first sight a hesitant performance is unclear, though the financial position of the B & M must have been discouraging. Furthermore, enthusiasm for the deal in the MRCC boardroom was shortly diluted by the GWR obtaining authorisation to build a revived Sirhowy Extension which, if built, would by-pass the MRCC altogether. On 27 May the MRCC board was told of a meeting with the chairman of the GWR. The following day the B & M called on the MRCC to air the possibility of reviving talks on the basis of the MRCC working the B & M, but, by then, the idea of falling into the arms of the GW had taken root. By 15 June, Heads of Agreement had been prepared and they were signed on the 28th, the very day the MRCC got wind of the LNW's purchase of the Sirhowy (see Chapter 3). The Midland found itself excluded, with no allies and no more worthwhile opportunities in that part of south Wales. The B & M as a result remained independent.

Attention had meanwhile focussed on Brecon which the Midland had reached by way of the operating agreement with the HHB from 1 October 1869. Brecon lies on the north bank of the Usk at a point where the river Honddu flows into it from the north, through a steep-sided valley. The town centre stands in the eastern angle of the two rivers, and the priory, latterly the cathedral, stands on high ground just to the north-west of the town centre, and west of the Honddu. This was another small county town which for a time enjoyed three separate stations. The first was at Watton, close to but to the north of the canal wharf which had been the site of the terminus of the Hay Tramway. In 1863 this became the terminus for the first trains operated by the B & M, which entered from the east. A year later the Mid-Wales and the HHB entered the same station. The second station was the Neath & Brecon's at Mount Street and the third, the ultimate joint station, was at Free Street.

The Neath & Brecon (N & B) approached from the west. It had been founded early in 1862 to build a line up the Dulais valley from Neath to haul coal from collieries in the Onllwyn valley. W.L. Banks was one of the promoters, as was Joshua Williams of the Vale of Neath. Green-Price became a director at a time when there was a possibility of linking with the Central Wales at Llangammarch.

Thoughts of extending to Brecon must have been in mind from an early stage because, in 1862, the N & B unsuccessfully promoted a Bill called the Swansea & N & B. This would have been a marvellously scenic route from the Vale of Neath at Glyn Neath to Ystradfellte, over the pass beneath Fan Fawr, and down Glyn Tarell to a point north of Brecon, near where the originally authorised HHB Brecon Station would have been. This met with opposition from the Vale of Neath. In September 1862, Banks tried again. With characteristic vision and enthusiasm for the grand plan, he held a meeting at which the HHB, B & M and Swansea Vale (SV) were all present to discuss linking Brecon with Swansea. They agreed to promote two routes: one from the Swansea Vale to Colbren, taking the pass to the west of Fan Gyhirych, and descending to Devynock and the Usk valley, thence to Brecon; the other to be an extension of the N & B to join the former line at Colbren and to make a link with the Swansea & Neath in Neath. This again met with opposition from the Vale of Neath and its minion the Swansea & Neath. Accordingly, the 1863 N & B Bill took the route which involved the least engineering and avoided controversy by extending the original line up the Dulais valley to Colbren, before descending to Devynock and Brecon. This received parliamentary blessing. It was a historic route following closely an old tramway which J. Palmer Budd had foreseen as a railway route in 1853 at the time of the Swansea Junction Bill and indeed earlier, in 1845, as part of the Welsh Midland.

Aerial view of Brecon showing the viaduct which carried the N & B over the river Honddu; *c.* 1957. *Tempest Coll./WIMM*

Devynock Station, looking towards Brecon; no date.
NMRW

A Midland freight train at Devynock bound for Swansea in 1902; at this time the line would have been at a peak of activity with as many as nine freight trains a day in each direction.
Tudor Watkins Coll.

Devynock and Sennybridge Station (as Devynock was called from 1913) with a Brecon-bound train; 23 June 1962.

Alan Jarvis

Cray Station, looking towards Brecon; no date.
Tudor Watkins Coll.

In 1864, the line from Colbren down to Ystradgynlais in the Tawe valley was revived independently by Banks and Benson of the SV as the Swansea Vale and Neath & Brecon Railway. This was to build a seven mile link from Ynysygeinon (near Ystradgynlais) to Colbren on the N & B, by climbing up the east side of the Tawe valley. A significant feature of the Act authorising this strategically important link line was that, not only did the N & B get running powers to Swansea, but, more importantly, the reciprocal rights for the Swansea Vale ran all the way to Brecon. The SV thus presented the Midland with a key to closing the gap between Brecon and Swansea without any entanglement with the financially fragile N & B.

Colbren Junction from the Swansea line platform, looking towards Brecon; April 1960.
Alan Jarvis

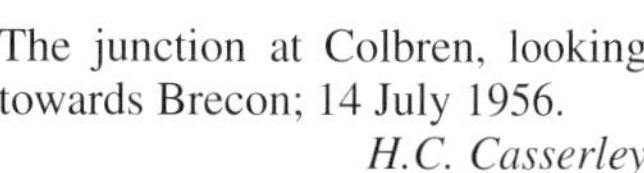

The junction at Colbren, looking towards Brecon; 14 July 1956.
H.C. Casserley

A pre-grouping photograph of Colbren Junction, looking towards Neath (left) and Swansea (right), with typical N & B and Midland trains of the period.

Lens of Sutton/Tudor Watkins Coll.

In 1864 another branch was projected to head north from Devynock for Llangammarch on the Central Wales Extension Railway. In 1866 the N & B agreed with the CWE that the latter would work their line once they reached Llandovery. If this had happened the N & B would have fallen into the LNW camp. During 1866, while a link with the Central Wales was still a possibility, Robertson opened discussions between the N & B, CWE and the SV about the eventual acquisition of the SV by the other two. No doubt the LNW were in the picture. However, the collapse of the project to get to Llangammarch on the CWE put paid to this idea and, instead of pursuing a take-over of the whole of the SV on their own, the N & B decided to go for control of part of their route to Swansea, and by the Neath & Brecon (Amalgamation & Arrangement) Act 1869, they became sole owners of the SV and N & B link line which eventually opened in 1873.

Completion of the line to Llangammarch was prevented by the financial uncertainty following the failure of bankers Overend Gurney in 1866; this led to the collapse of the N & B's contractor John Dickson in 1868. Besides blocking the LNW's chances of getting to Swansea over the SV, this nearly destroyed the N & B and certainly ruined its chances of getting from Neath along the coast to Swansea and Mumbles.

In March 1868 three new directors found serious problems: the railway, which had begun freight operations in 1866, was operating at a loss, was unable to pay rent on its hired vehicles, had been unable to pay for all the land in use, and needed to spend considerable sums on track and infrastructure safety. Work had halted on the projected line to link with the Swansea Vale as well as on the Llangammarch line. The 1869 Act gave a five year moritorium on debt repayments, converted much of the various forms of debt into debentures, and created preference shares, besides authorising the merger of the SV and N & B company with the N & B, mentioned in the previous paragraph. In 1870 Banks resigned from the board having already been dismissed as managing director.

LNWR penetration of south Wales in the early 1930s.

A Bowen-Cooke 0-8-0 makes its way 'light-engine' from Abergavenny to Brynmawr, past the defunct quarry at Llanelly Hill. This fascinating location still survives, almost untouched by time. [*GBJ*]

A Swansea-bound Midland Railway train at Brecon, depicted at the turn of the century from a building near Brecon Cathedral. [*GBJ*]

Returning to Brecon, the N & B line from the west was originally drawn as part of the Llanelly 1861 Bill for its line from Llandovery. It crossed the Usk to the west of Brecon and then, passing between the castle site and the cathedral, crossed the Honddu by means of a high stone viaduct. This viaduct, which dominated that part of the town had a keystone inscribed 'N & BR^{Y} 1866' which has more recently been placed in a wall near the site; it was, in fact, incomplete at that date as, in 1869, evidence in Parliament referred to £2,500 worth of work still to be done and the use of timber for at least part of the structure. Dickson, the contractor for the N & B, had designed the viaduct as stone arches with girder spans at either end, but in order to save money had built only the stone piers and had finished the top with wood. By 1872 the wood was beginning to rot, and that and the heavier traffic beginning to use it caused the N & B to decide to finish the job properly as a double track stone viaduct. With remarkable precision, this was now estimated to cost £3,185-8-6. The alterations were completed without having to close the line, though it was never laid with double track.

Keystone from the N & B viaduct, relocated in a wall near the site; 1997.

DD

It was this threat from the west and the possibility that the N & B might make a link to the HHB independent of the B & M which caused the B & M to decide to seek amalgamation with the HHB. Parliament authorised this logical move in 1865, whereupon William Banks, already chairman of the HHB and B & M, took over as chairman of the N & B as well.

From this unique position, Banks negotiated with the N & B an end-on junction at Brecon. To effect this the B & M laid a line across the north of Watton Station in a westward direction towards Free Street and the N & B viaduct; the N & B built a bridge over Free Street and met the B & M end-on just east of the bridge.

Brecon, Watton Station, looking west with No. 4679; Christmas Eve 1962. *J.M. Tolson, courtesy John Miles*

Watton Station, looking east; the line from Swansea to Hereford is indicated by the carriages; 29 August 1958. *V.R. Webster*

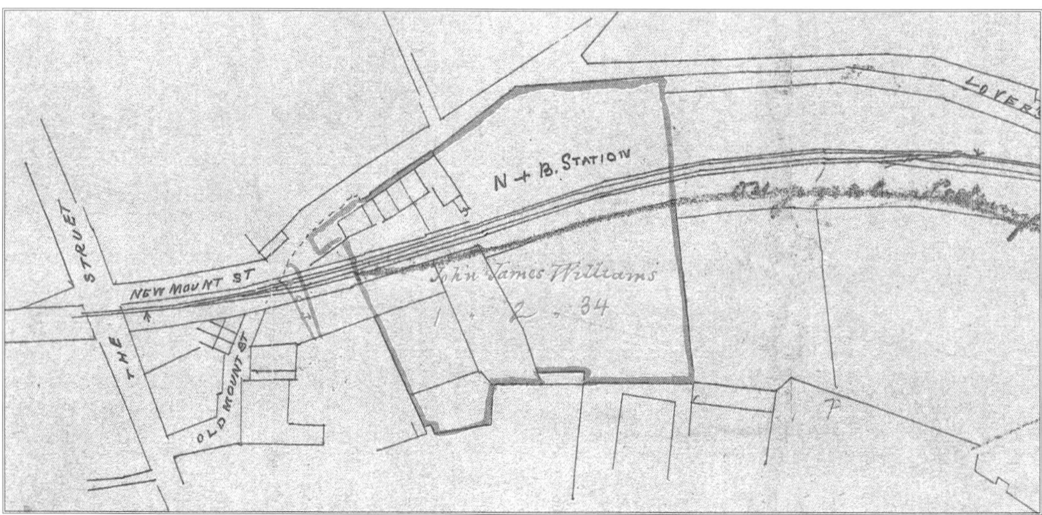

The solicitor's clerk who sketched this plan of Brecon in about 1869 would no doubt be surprised that it survived so long. It was probably drawn in connection with attempts to obtain additional land for Mount Street Station. *PRO RAIL 1057/1466*

Conybeare, the engineer to the B & M, had persuaded the B & M management to co-operate with the other companies in using one single joint station; the problem was to find the right site. Watton was ill-placed to expand to the size needed and in any case a new site was required if trains were to be able to run through Brecon from Hereford to Llandovery or Swansea. Accordingly, the N & B and B & M agreed in January 1867 to use a narrow site bordered by The Struet, Mount Street and the junction of their two lines. However, the Board of Trade considered the site too small for the purpose, and there was some difficulty in gaining possession of additional land. The N & B therefore built a temporary station for themselves which they called Mount Street, located between the viaduct and the Free Street bridge. It was to this station that they opened services from Neath on 8 June 1867. The house which was used as a station still stands, making Mount Street the only survivor of the three Brecon stations. The Mid-Wales shifted their trains from Watton to this station in 1868, though the Midland reverted to Watton from 1 October 1869 when they started working the HHB trains from Hereford. The reason for this is uncertain, though it may have been due to even less space being available at Mount Street than at Watton.

On the other hand, it may be that the Midland objected to the N & B's health and safety policy. In the absence of an alternative larger joint station, the N & B had no authority from the Board of Trade to convey passengers for stations to the east of Brecon beyond Mount Street. As a temporary expedient, they were therefore ferried on the footplate of a locomotive to a position just over the Free Street bridge and north of Watton, where they were deposited on the side of the line; at this point they were left to clamber over the track and down to Watton Station.

The house which accommodated Mount Street Station at Brecon; February 1998.

DD

A Midland train from Hereford approaches Brecon Free Street Station. Watton was to the left of the picture; *c.* 1922.

R.S. Carpenter

A cold Christmas Eve at Brecon in 1962, looking towards Hereford.

J.M. Tolson, courtesy John Miles

A Hereford train in the bay platform at Brecon Free Street in BR days. *Real Photographs/ N.T. Wassell Coll.*

Brecon Free Street, looking eastward; *c.* 1950. *L.G.R.P./ Tudor Watkins Coll.*

Eventually, on 1 March 1871, the B & M opened a new station at Free Street, east of the bridge, and just east of the boundary marking the junction between them and the N & B. This was available to all the companies, though the N & B went on using Mount Street until 6 March 1872, from which time it became a goods station, as did Watton. The Midland paid £2,150 a year rental for their use of Free Street, plus a handling fee on all goods moved in and out, as well as providing their own booking clerk. (cf. the LNW rental of £500 at Merthyr and their own £550 plus a one fifth share of running costs at Barr's Court).

SWANSEA AT LAST

The Midland had been turning its attention to the gap between Brecon and Swansea, and this time moved with a determination and effectiveness which appear quite different from the stumbling and fumbling in its simultaneous dealings to the south. Its first move, like a knight in a game of chess, was to hop over the immediate and obvious target, the N & B, and focus attention on capturing the Swansea Vale.

This was an independent and moderately successful though rather run down local company. The directors were a group of local businessmen under the chairmanship of Starling Benson, who was also chairman of the Swansea Harbour Trustees and sometime mayor of Swansea. Charles Smith, another Swansea noteable was deputy. Our old friend J. Palmer Budd was one of the directors, being keen to use any directorship he could get to further communications with his ironworks at Ystalyfera. Starling Benson was an old-Etonian who followed his father to Swansea from Surrey; he made a career in the town and was one of its benefactors. He did not marry but led a busy and sociable life, being hard working, capable, popular and highly respected. Like Henry Robertson, he was the best type of Victorian entrepreneur.

The Swansea Vale had begun life as a short mineral railway in 1845, without any parliamentary authorisation, but operating under a so-called 'deed of settlement'; it was approached by the projected Welsh Midland, of which J. Palmer Budd was deputy chairman, with the possibility of becoming a vehicle for that line's access to Swansea. Initially, it established a line up the east side of the Tawe to near Glais, but already in 1846 there were plans to build as far as Ystradgynlais and nearly to Abercrave. Discussions were held with both the Welsh Midland and the South Wales Railway, the SV directors being more interested in the connections than in running a railway. However, the South Wales broke off the discussions when it was discovered that the SV were also talking to the rival party; then, as noted in Chapter 1, the Welsh Midland venture failed. A Bill to authorise the SV as an independent line was presented to Parliament in 1846 but failed on a technicality raised by the Duke of Beaufort.

The SV then became involved in a somewhat farcical interplay with the South Wales. This broad gauge ally of the GWR was steadily pushing its line from Chepstow towards Fishguard, and with that goal dominant was proposing to pass to the north of Swansea. In August 1846 it was agreed, subject to the approval of the South Wales engineer, I.K. Brunel no less, that the SV would be sold to the South Wales for £70,000, payable in South Wales shares. However, Brunel, on his return, was not in favour of the deal and the chairman of the South Wales, Charles Russell, who was also Chairman of the GWR, was then involved in some serious back-tracking. Starling Benson not unreasonably stuck to his position that a deal had been done and that Brunel's agreement was merely a matter of form. By this time no South Wales shares were available as consideration for the purchase, and so a Bill was promoted for the purchase and extension of the SV under the name of a new company called the Swansea Valley Railway. An absurd situation then arose; the Swansea Valley was authorised by Parliament to lay a broad gauge railway along the line proposed by the SV and, where necessary was authorised to acquire land from and shares in the SV, but the Swansea Valley was only allowed to be sold to the South Wales once half the capital was paid up and actually used on constructing the railway. The Swansea Valley had the authorisation to acquire the SV but had no capital; and the South Wales had neither the authorisation to acquire the SV (even though it had agreed eventually to honour its earlier agreement so to do), nor indeed the funds, as payment in South Wales shares was no longer viable, the shares having fallen in value by nearly 75%.

In this position of stalemate, the SV remained independent and went on operating as a horse tramway, carrying coal over some 6 miles to the river at Swansea, while the South Wales continued the extension of its main line westward. In 1850 it reached the Swansea Vale, and a level crossing had to be made at Llansamlet. At the point of crossing, the SV had to be raised about two feet for some 400 yards. Starling Benson, when out for a walk along the line, was not surprisingly taken aback to find a team of South Wales workmen doing this without permission; their defence was that they were acting on the instructions of the South Wales management. In August 1851 the parliamentary authorisation of the Swansea Valley expired. At this point the SV gave up hope of selling on satisfactory terms to the South Wales, and decided instead to push their own line up valley, converting it to a railway and introducing steam locomotives.

The cross-over of the SV by the South Wales eventually became part of a complex of junctions and a fly-over. Here, in the 1950s, the SV is seen proceeding southward beneath the flyover at what became known as Six Pit. *N.C. Simmons/ John Miles Coll.*

Just north of Swansea St Thomas Station, the Swansea Vale sidings at Foxhole; no date. *N.T. Wassell Coll.*

In 1853 three options existed for taking a railway up the Tawe valley. As noted in Chapter 2, the NAH Swansea Junction Extension Bill projected a line from Quakers Yard to the head of the Tawe valley and down to Swansea. Secondly, the Swansea Valley was not yet dead and was attempting to get permission to revive its powers to build a broad gauge line over the same ground as the SV. And thirdly, there was the SV, with the advantage of being in possession. The SV's opposition to the NAH project no doubt contributed to its failure, but a Bill to authorise the extension of the SV also failed. A second attempt was made in 1854 and this too failed. It was not until 1855 that the SV was finally authorised by an Act which retroactively legitimised all that had gone on before.

The 1855 Swansea Vale Act authorised a line rather further than that later built, from Swansea to a point up the Tawe valley at Abercrave, behind the Red Lion and just before Abercrave House on the west side of the valley. This was beyond Pontardawe and Ystradgynlais and only a short distance from Capel Colbren, but at a much lower level. A line across the Tawe in Swansea to admit access to the North Dock was also included. Although narrow (standard) gauge itself, it was to construct a third rail for the broad gauge from the crossing of the South

Wales Railway main line to the docks and another up the valley, but only if three conditions were fulfilled:

1. If at least three owners of mineral rights required it.
2. If the Board of Trade considered it of public convenience.
3. If there was a 'fair prospect of reasonable remuneration'.

The Act also required the Swansea Vale trains to stop at the level crossing with the South Wales Railway. The price to be charged for this inconvenience in the interests of safety was £500 a year, but the South Wales was to seek approval to bridge the Swansea Vale. This the GWR subsequently did, with a complex fly-over and interchange. A characteristic of the Act is that 'guage' was so spelt throughout except when in the context of the 'Gauge Act'. The Oxford English Dictionary describes this variant as 'a mere blunder'.

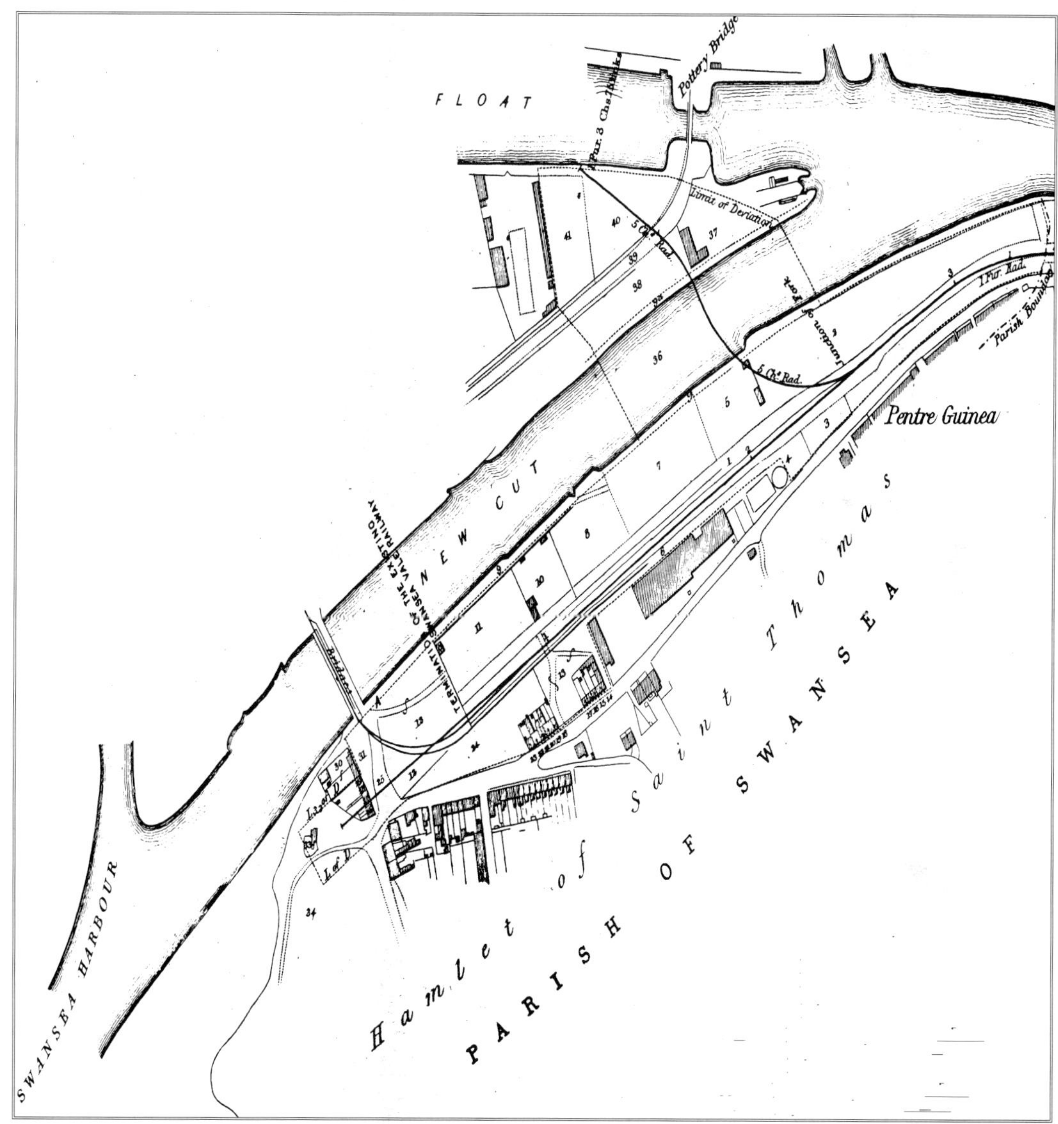

Plan of Swansea prepared for the 1855 Swansea Vale Railway Bill.

House of Lords Library

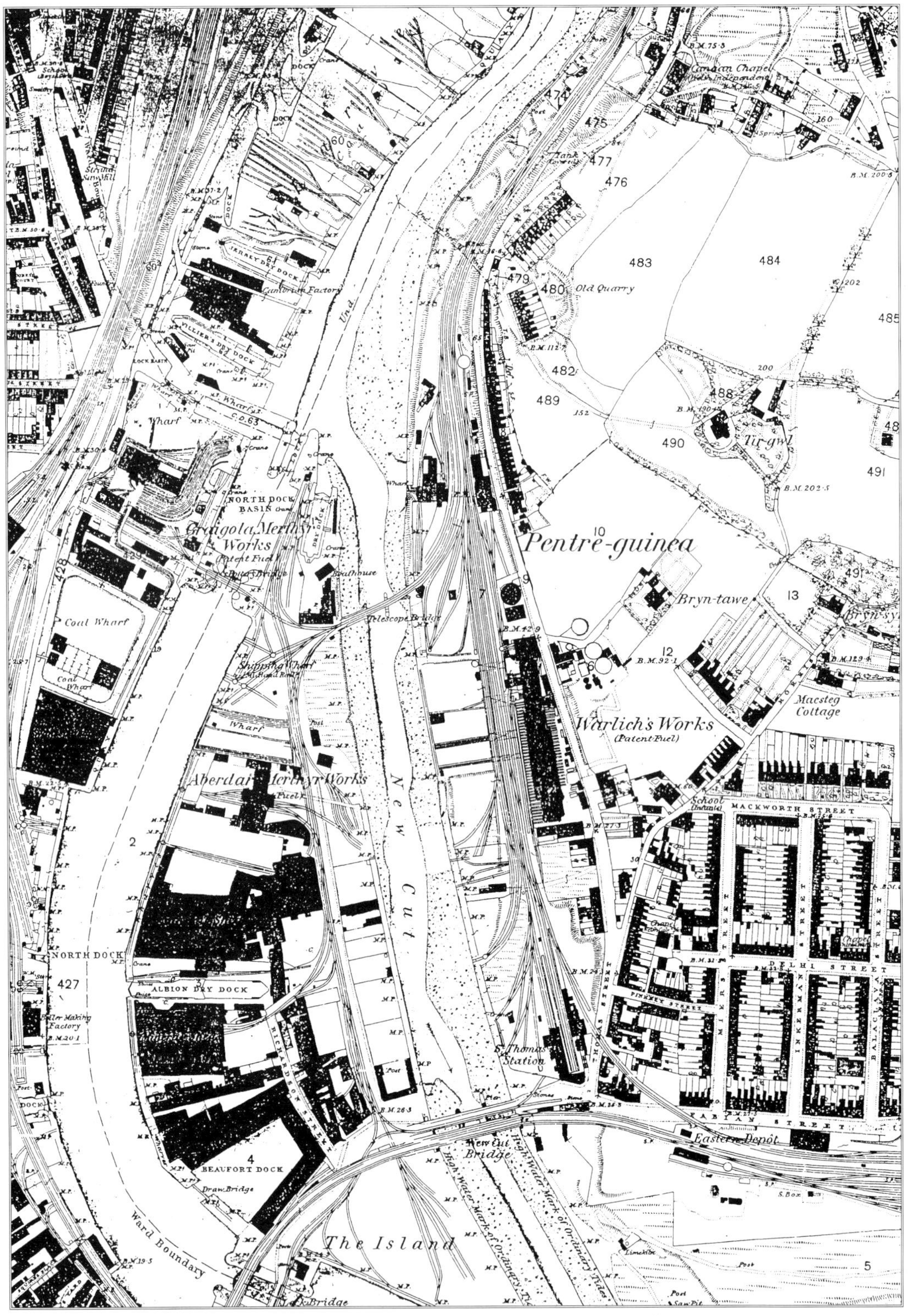

Plan of Swansea showing the later terminal connections of the Swansea Vale Railway.
Swansea City and County Library

The Swansea Vale progressively opened a line of railway over converted tramways up the Tawe valley to Pontardawe in 1860, and Ystalyfera in 1861, and over a pass to the west to Brynamman in 1863. Here it met head-on the Llanelly Railway with whom a joint station was suggested. It also built a loop line from Upper Bank through Morriston, Clydach and Glais, which subsequently, in 1875, became the passenger line; the original was then confined to goods traffic.

The approach to Pontardawe Station from the south; no date.
N.T. Wassell Coll.

The approach to Brynamman over the river Aman; 1961.
R.J. Essery/Tudor Watkins Coll.

Arrival of the line at Ystalyfera brought about the revealing events which led to J. Palmer Budd's resigning in unhappy circumstances from the SV board. He was a very active, if not pushing member of the board, and worked hard to get the line laid up to his ironworks. While work was in progress he was constantly checking and interfering, with his own interests always well to the fore. Accordingly, when he realised that the proposed station at the end of the line was to be some 300 yds from his home, Ynysydarren House, he arranged for it to be relocated more conveniently close to his drive. This necessitated a deeper cutting than originally planned and the relocation of a bridge under the

The station at Ystalyfera, looking towards Ynysydarren House and Swansea whence the 1.30 p.m. has just arrived; 2 June 1947.

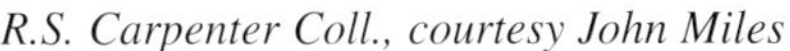

R.S. Carpenter Coll., courtesy John Miles

The station at Ystalyfera, looking down-valley; 1950. *LGRP 24757/NRM*

The back of Ynysydarren House, the home of J. Palmer Budd in Ystalyfera, seen from the railway; *c.* 1900. *Courtesy Mrs Margaret Watkins*

track for trucks carrying refuse from the ironworks. When he placed trestles and planks at the side of the track and used them to convey trucks across the track at the original location, 9 ft above the level of the rails, the Swansea Vale, not unreasonably, asked him to desist. Budd had the effrontery to blame the SV for having failed to provide the under-bridge, as though he had had nothing to do with the alterations, which had been made to suit his own personal wishes. After much correspondence and discussion the SV filed a suit in Chancery seeking an injunction and specific performance. By this time he had resigned from the board and was playing the part of the injured victim of other people's incompetence, choosing to ignore his own involvement. His duplicity was revealed in his evidence, where, for example, he denied knowledge of a manoeuvre, which he had admitted earlier, of diverting the line of the railway to preserve a shrubbery in his garden. The SV won the case.

When Moon and his party visited south Wales in 1867 and called on the Swansea Vale, relationships were friendly and two years previously the LNW had lent the Swansea Vale locomotives. They went up to Ystalyfera to see Budd who was one of their more important local customers. But by the time of the committee hearings for the N & B Bill in July 1869, it was widely rumoured that the Midland was on the march. In December that year the Midland made an agreement with the Swansea Vale whose contents are not revealed in the minute book, but it must have pointed to extensive cooperation for, by the end of the following year, directors' passes had been exchanged and a loan of £10,000 had been made in return for running powers and 5% preference stock; this was increased in two further tranches of £10,000 and £5,000. On the other hand, J. Palmer Budd was of the opinion that talk of the Midland entering Swansea was 'moonshine'. His former directorship of the Swansea Vale did not prevent him from cynically arguing that the Midland would bring no benefit to customers; he went on to give his opinion that, since all railway rates were fixed, there would be no cheaper rates available, and the frequency of trains would suffer due to the need for each company to accumulate full trains to optimise their operations. However, his opposition to the Midland did not prevent him from switching his business to them from the LNW when the 'moonshine' materialised in 1874.

Clydach-on-Tawe Station on the loop line, looking north, at the turn of the century.
Clydach Historical Society

Just north of Clydach Station were the extensive sidings of Player's Tin Plate Works and Hill's Cwm Clydach Colliery. Looking north on the main line; 12 September 1911.
R.J. Essery Coll., courtesy J. Miles

The view south from the location of the previous photograph; 12 September 1911.
J. Essery Coll., courtesy J. Miles

The 12.36 p.m. train from Brynamman to Swansea at Clydach; 27 August 1948.
H.C. Casserley/ Tudor Watkins Collection

The relationship between the Midland and the SV was cultivated steadily. By July 1871 Starling Benson was writing defensively to the chairman of the Midland, W.P. Price, no doubt as a result of Price hearing rumours of LNWR activity in the area: 'You may rest assured that no idea of departing from our understanding has arisen in the mind of any of our directors. The rumours (of which I was not aware) can only have arisen from the well known desire of the LNW to secure the increasing traffic of the valley and possibly from some attempt to ascertain if we are inclined to treat.' In March 1872 the Midland set up a sub-committee to negotiate the acquisition of the Swansea Vale. On 17 April Benson met Price, Ellis, Allport and Kenrick and on 3 May the Swansea Vale Board agreed that from 1 July both companies would exchange traffic, and the

The Midland's investment in infrastructure in the Swansea area was minimal, as this picture of Morriston Station bears out; 30 May 1954.
John Miles Coll.

Midland would pay out of the total receipts a preference dividend, fixed charges, and 6% on the ordinary Swansea Vale stock; within three years the Midland would seek parliamentary approval. As early as 6 August Price was asked to open discussion as to how management of the Swansea Vale could be brought more directly under Midland control. The Midland secretary advised against seeking parliamentary approval in November 1872 as being 'not expedient', but this was set in motion a year later. In the meantime several loans were made by the Midland against preference shares.

By March 1874 the Midland was already quoting rates between Swansea and Brecon over the Swansea Vale. The Swansea Vale had started goods trains through from Swansea to Brecon on 1 February, only four months after completion of the SV/N & B link line. From 1 October 1873, when it opened, the N & B had been operating four trains a day from Swansea through to Brecon.

This was distressing for the LNWR who had been seeing their once burgeoning traffic over the Swansea Vale start to decline, after an encouraging start, thus:

1870	8,086 tons
1871	9,032 tons
1872	18,103 tons
1873	16,008 tons

So it was not only J. Palmer Budd who was shifting allegience.

The parliamentary evidence for and against the Midland's take-over revealed some interesting arguments. Starling Benson was of the opinion that a small independent railway could not profitably continue, in particular because of the problem with waggons; many customers required waggons to be provided and, if the company had no control of these once they were in England, they were likely to be lost, or, even if returned, would be empty on the return run and not earning, whereas the large companies could earn on both runs. The N & B objected that they would lose their freedom of choice for the routeing of through traffic, but Benson argued that the Midland was by far the most competitive line for the midlands and Birmingham, and that in case of the Midland being less competitive, as for example to Birkenhead, where the extra mileage in England would reduce the proportion due to the N & B, arbitration was available to determine a fair rate.

Effective from 1 September 1874, the Midland was authorised to take a lease of the Swansea Vale. That day Allport, Samuel Johnson, Crossley and Hodge inspected both the new acquisitions, the SV and the HHB. In their report they commented on the assets and the staff changes proposed. Both lines were to be operated directly as part of the Midland. The Swansea line's permanent way was badly worn and needed to be replaced within two years. That on the HHB was in a fair state but the

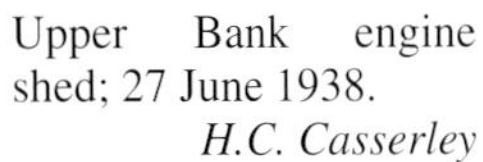
Upper Bank engine shed; 27 June 1938.
H.C. Casserley

stations, being mainly of wood, were in serious need of repair. It was noted that a locomotive shed for 18 engines would be needed at Swansea and that the newly constructed Morriston loop was in need of some minor alterations. More accommodation for goods traffic would be needed at Hereford.

On 3 March 1875 results of the two new lines for the second half of 1874 were reported as follows:

HHB proceeds	£10,600
less guaranteed rental/interest	£6,838
SV proceeds	£24,000
less guaranteed rental/interest	£11,768

This is the first evidence of a full answer to the request made originally in April 1870, shortly after the start of Midland operations over the HHB.

The Midland then negotiated the take-over of all through traffic on the 29 miles between Ynysygeinon Junction and Brecon, paying the N & B 30% of gross receipts; the Midland was responsible for track repair and staffing. This left the N & B with no operations of its own to Brecon and confined it to the line between Neath and Colbren Junction. Through Midland goods services were started in 1876. A typical consequence of this situation, where one company owned the track and another operated

Looking south at Abercrave Station on the link line which, when opened in 1873, made clear the Midland's path to Swansea; no date. *NMRW*

the trains, was that when the public campaigned for a new station as they did at Abercrave in 1889, the N & B had to write to the Midland to ask them if they would guarantee to stop their trains there if a station were built. Noble replied that they would do what they apparently already did at Ynyscedwyn (later called Ystradgynlais), i.e. stop their trains but not guarantee to do so. Nevertheless the station was built.

This arrangement continued until June 1889 when, in the course of negotiations for a new term, the Midland withdrew their traffic and shifted it to the Vale of Neath line, over which they still had running powers. Sir Edward Watkin had become chairman of the N & B early that year and had pressed the Midland for 50% of gross receipts. He arranged for the Manchester, Sheffield & Lincolnshire Railway, of which he was also chairman, to assist the N & B to fill the resulting shortage of plant and manpower. The Midland were taken to court and the arbitrator found against them and fined them over £6,000. They resumed their through operations on 22 July, the N & B henceforth handling local coal traffic on the link line between Colbren Junction and Ynysygeinon, as well as over the Onllwyn valley to Neath. Watkin brought vigour to the N & B affairs and as early as February 1889 was seeking shareholders' agreement to a Bill to authorise arrangements between an amazing collection of still independent companies, including his own Manchester, Sheffield and Lincolnshire, and such diverse players as the Taff Vale, Barry, B & M, Cambrian, Wirral and the Mersey. Like other of Watkin's grandiose plans, this came to nothing.

Having reached Swansea it would perhaps be useful to retrace our steps to Hereford and review what exactly the Midland had acquired.

St. Thomas Station in Midland days. *R.M. Casserley Coll.*

The evening train to Brynamman hauled by No. 7479; 24 April 1948.

W.A. Camwell/Tudor Watkins Coll.

A Midland 0-4-4T at Swansea in 1906. *Perkins Coll./ Tudor Watkins*

By 1874 they had access to the former NAH station at Barton, though that still entailed a reversal out of the station for trains to or from the former HHB line. There was then an easy run up the Wye valley to Hay, and on to a point just short of Three Cocks, over their own former HHB single track line; from here running powers over the Mid-Wales, later the Cambrian, took them through Three Cocks over a pass along the western flank of the Black Mountains to Talyllyn Junction, at which point they transferred to the B & M line through the ancient Talyllyn tunnel into Brecon Free Street Station. This was a handsome mid-Victorian building at which each of the tenants had their own booking-office, set on the north side of the station with an east-facing bay platform; an island platform with passenger access on the level served westbound trains. From here to the former Mount Street Station was the only double track section throughout from Hereford to Upper Bank, just north of Swansea.

Talyllyn Junction, looking towards Brecon. The Talyllyn tunnel is obscured by the distant smoke; 29 April 1961. *R.M. Casserley, courtesy John Miles*

Pannier tank No. 3661 on the turntable at Free Street; 8 June 1962.

Alan Jarvis

The first station out of Swansea was Upper Bank where the loop line diverged to the left, in the distance; 8 September 1951.

H.C. Casserley

They then moved on to the N & B, over the Honddu viaduct, and then over the Usk and up the Usk valley, turning south at Devynock to climb up over the pass to the plateau at the head of the Tawe valley. This entailed a climb of over seven miles at 1:50 through spectacular mountain scenery, with picturesque rocky outcrops and the formidable glowering presence of Fan Gyhirych to the left. Just beyond the summit was Penwyllt Station with the private waiting-room for Madame Patti, the renowned opera singer. Her castle, Craig-y-nos, stood on the other side of the valley some two miles away. Happily, the station still stands with its two platforms, which at one time echoed to the excited arrivals and departures of people from another world.

Penwyllt Station, known as Craig-y-nos from 1907, after Madame Patti's nearby castle, looking towards Swansea.

Lens of Sutton

Craig-y-nos Station from a similar viewpoint in 1997.
DD

At Colbren Junction, set on a bleak and windy plateau, the route divided, the N & B original line going off to the left to descend to Neath, while the link line swung to the right to descend for seven miles at around 1:50 down to Ystradgynlais. The line dropped down the east side of the Tawe valley, with fine views across to the river and the hills on the far side. Below Ystradgynlais the line from Brynamman came in through a shallow trough in the steep hillside on the right, through Ystalyfera, while to the left rose the stark, craggy side of Mynydd Craig Llywel. The two lines converged at Ynysygeinon Junction. The rest of the route lay through the dense industrial activity of the lower Tawe valley, relieved only by the striking spire of Pontardawe church, rising high above the town and factories, and said to have been so built at the request of its benefactor, William Parsons, in order to be higher than the highest

Ystradgynlais Station, looking up the link line towards Abercrave; 14 July 1956.
H.C. Casserley

The link line approached the Brynamman branch (seen on the right) at Ynysygeinon Junction; 14 July 1956.
H.C. Casserley

The junction at Ynysygeinon looking north, with the Brecon line diverging to the right; the centre line formed a loop.

N.C. Simmons/ John Miles Coll.

industrial chimney. At Glais the line split, freight continuing straight ahead down the original route, while passenger trains swung to the right down the Morriston Loop through Clydach. The loop rejoined the original at Upper Bank and entered Swansea along the east bank of the river, through scenes of the most intense industrial activity. It ended at the modest two-platformed St. Thomas Station, located on the opposite side of the river from the centre of Swansea.

The tall chimneys of Pontardawe compete in height with the spire of St. Peter's Church in the distance.

J.E. Martin/WIMM

Glais Station at the northern end of the loop; 30 May 1954.
R.M. Casserley Coll.

The Midland loop line heading south towards Morriston is seen at the point of crossing by the later GW Morriston branch. To the right is the Swansea Canal; 21 September 1963.
P.J. Garland Coll., courtesy R.S. Carpenter

Brynamman, the Midland's outpost in Carmarthenshire, had an odd railway system which is best explained by delving into the history. The Llanelly had built a line eastward from Pantyffynnon in 1842 for the carriage of anthracite down the Aman valley. This terminated at a point east of the north-south turnpike road in the centre of the small town, having passed under it by means of a single-track stone arch. In June 1863 the Swansea Vale was planning station accommodation at Brynamman for its line approaching from the east; the Llanelly rejected the proposal to build a single station for both companies, and by October the newcomer had made physical connection with the Llanelly. Terms were agreed in August; the signalman was to be positioned on the Llanelly side of the road bridge and was to be a Llanelly man paid for by the SV. Discussion of running powers, with the possibility of the Llanelly getting down to

The Midland station at Brynamman, with the GW station visible through the arch beneath the road. *GW/WIMM*

The platform at the Midland station at Brynamman in 1950.
NMRW

A LMS auto train at Brynamman; 27 August 1948. *N.T. Wassell Coll.*

Ystalyfera for J. Palmer Budd's ironworks, seems to have reached no conclusion. The SV went ahead with the construction of their own station on the east side of the turnpike and must have built a wall between their station and the joint siding as in May 1865 it was removed and replaced by a platform.

In June 1864 the Llanelly decided to obtain Board of Trade clearance of their branch for passengers, and to cost the widening of the bridge to accommodate double track under the turnpike road. In July the Llanelly decided to move the station shed from Garnant to provide carriage accommodation at Brynamman, and, on 13 December 1864, the two parties agreed to the following programme:

The stations at Brynamman were separated by a turnpike road across the centre of the picture. The GWR station is in the foreground while the Midland counterpart is just visible beyond the road.

GW/WIMM

The GWR (former Llanelly) station at Brynamman; no date. *Lens of Sutton*

1. The SV would widen the bridge under the road in order to enable it to accommodate two tracks. The second line would be at joint expense.
2. The SV was to have free access to the Gwtter Level Colliery on the Llanelly side of the bridge.
3. The Llanelly was to have access to the SV station for a nominal charge.

Not one of these actions was implemented.

The Llanelly started passenger trains on their branch in March 1865, still without a proper station at Brynamman; this led the Swansea Vale to complain when Llanelly passengers were found deposited on Swansea Vale land, presumably on the SV side of the road bridge. A dispute over the ownership of a siding appears to have prevented any substantial progress on an agreement until March 1867, when the SV made another proposal:

1. SV to widen the arch: Llanelly were agreeable.
2. Double track from the SV station through the bridge at joint expense for joint use: Llanelly said SV should pay as they (the Llanelly) already had a line, but agreed to joint user.
3. Joint use of station, Llanelly to pay rent of 5% of initial cost: Llanelly agreed.
4. The Llanelly to have free access to the Amman Company's yard: Llanelly said this right was theirs already.
5. SV to have free access to Amman Co. Colliery. Llanelly demanded 6d. a ton.

A LMS 0-6-0T enters the bridge under the road at Brynamman from the GWR side. The carriages in the distance are standing at the old Midland station; no date.
J.J. Davis/HMRS

This produced a stalemate until May 1868 when discussions were reopened about the interchange siding on the SV side of the bridge and the possibility of the Llanelly constructing further sidings on SV land. It was eventually agreed in July that the Llanelly could go ahead, paying a rental of £10 a year, the SV paying 3d. a ton for moving coal over the Llanelly and the Llanelly 6d. over the SV.

By 1871 the use of the SV station for Llanelly passengers seems to have become regularised as the Llanelly were seriously in arrears with their rent. At a meeting in June that year the SV threatened to exclude the Llanelly if they did not pay by 1 July. On 29 August the Llanelly decided to discontinue use of the SV station and to deposit their passengers on their own land on their side of the road bridge, thus saving the rent to the SV. But they did pay the £200 overdue.

Eventually, after the Llanelly had become part of the GW, a second station was built on the Llanelly side of the road bridge on the still single through siding. Thus it remained even into the period of nationalisation. The SV station was closed in 1950 whereupon, until its closure in 1958, the Llanelly station handled the Swansea traffic which was switched to Victoria over the former Llanelly and LNWR.

The SV's Brynamman branch ran through what was hardly a tourist area. Mining, industry and housing surrounded the train most of the way. After Ynisygeinon Junction, where the N & B line continued up the east bank of the Tawe, the Brynamman line crossed the river on a girder bridge and passed through Ystalyfera. At Gurnos Junction, just beyond Ystalyfera, the line bore to the left, away from the goods line which continued up the Tawe valley for another mile. The main line headed up the Twrch valley through Gwys and Cwmllynfell, winding in places between steep rocks, interspersed with housing and chapels. Surprisingly, what was in essence a suburban commuter line became almost picturesque as it wound its way up the steep and narrow valley, before emerging on the plateau which divides the valleys and whose boggy grass conceals the source of the Aman. From Cwmllynfell a tramroad led over to the colliery complex at Gwaun-Cae-Gurwen (GCG for short) which, much to the irritation of the GWR, enabled the Midland to tap this source.

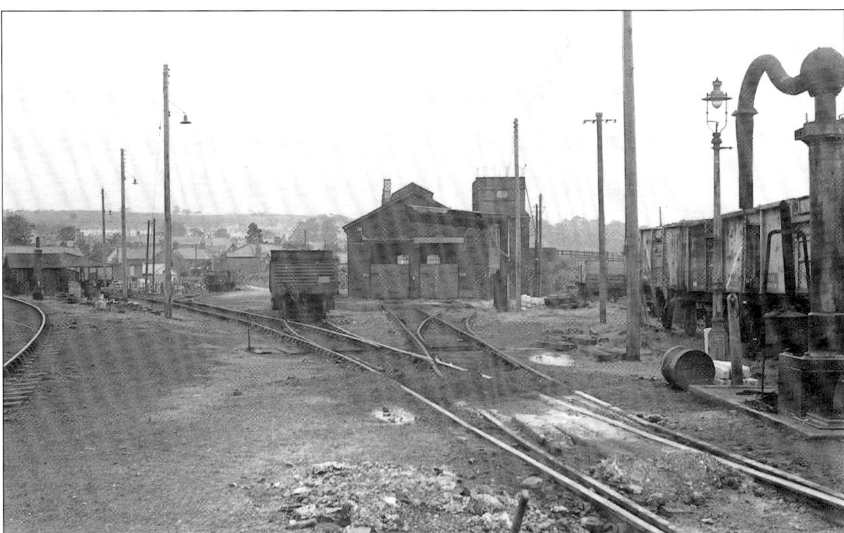

The sub-shed at Gurnos was in the fork between the Brynamman branch, just visible to the left, and a mineral feeder line; 22 April 1962. *R. S. Carpenter*

Gwys Station, looking up the Twrch valley towards Cwmllynfell; 1956. *Mowat Coll./ John Miles*

At Cwmllynfell, on the plateau at the head of the Aman valley, looking back towards Gwys.
Lens of Sutton

The bleak surroundings of Cwmllynfell Station are revealed in this view looking towards Brynamman.
Mowat Coll./ N.T. Wassell

Brynamman itself lies a little way down the Aman valley at a point where the sides become steeper; its location is picturesque even if it was seriously blemished during the life of the railway. Even the trains were unlikely to inspire great enthusiasm, being hauled exclusively by 0-6-0 tank engines and consisting of a sparse service of passenger trains made up of elderly and undistinguished carriages and an intense mineral traffic. Nor did the timetable offer great interest; three trains a day were the norm for many years. But there is something irresistible about this far-flung and detached outpost of the Midland, with its proliferation of station and junction names beginning with the letters 'Y' and 'G', and the single track winding through the heart of industrial south Wales to an end-on confrontation with the opposition.

And so matters stood. However, by the 1890s the structure of the railway system around Swansea was revealing the defects of its origins. The South Wales, it will be remembered, was originally concerned only to reach a port for Ireland, so the GWR simply inherited a line across the north of Swansea, with a branch to High Street Terminus. From the Llanelly it acquired access to the Aman valley, and from the Vale of Neath it had acquired the route along the shore, built by the Swansea & Neath in 1863. The Midland was well placed, but its line was of limited capacity, and the LNWR was definitely confined to the west side. The Eastern Docks were under development and the coal-field south west of Brynamman was still unexploited. In 1895 a group of local business-men obtained an Act to build what was was accurately but long-windedly called the Neath, Pontardawe & Brynamman Railway (NPB). In the following year Parliament authorised the company to enter into working arrangements with the GWR. In 1898 an extension of time was granted and the GWR actually agreed to

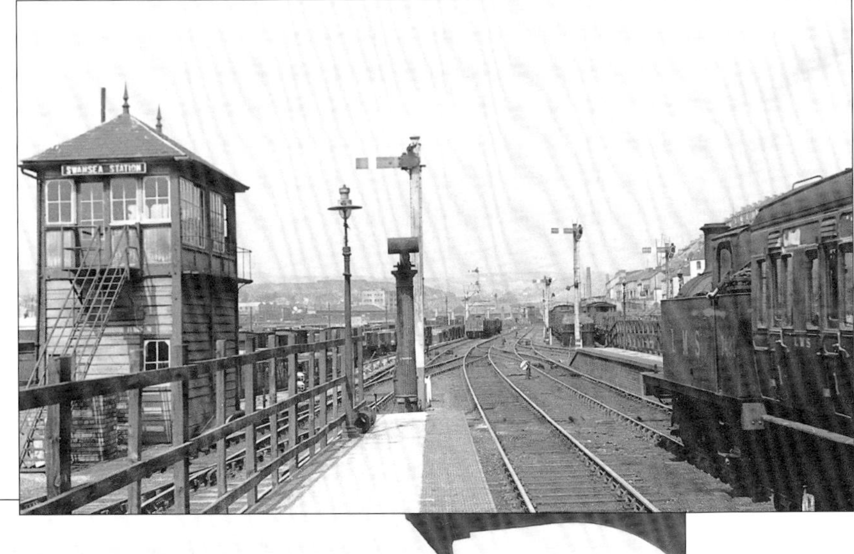

St. Thomas Station, looking up the line; 27 August 1948.
H.C. Casserley

The 8.20 a.m. to Brynamman; 7 March 1948.
W.A. Camwell/ Tudor Watkins Coll.

St. Thomas Station with a Brynamman train disappearing in the middle distance. The man in the raincoat was presented with a long wait for another; 1950.
LGRP 24782/NRM

buy the company. This was revealed as a stalling tactic, as, by 1901, nothing had been done and the powers lapsed. In 1903 a revived scheme was put to Parliament at which the GWR put in an overlapping scheme of their own. Parliament decided that there was no reason to renegue on the earlier authorisation and the NPB set about raising capital. Unfortunately, this coincided with the start of the Russo-Japanese War and financial markets were uncertain. The Midland were invited to participate but advised against investing at that time. There was another lull. In 1907 the project was revived, this time with financial support from the arch-maverick, the Barry. The GWR recruited to their side the Rhondda & Swansea Bay and Port Talbot Railways, who had hitherto been supporters of the project, and the scene was set for a battle royal.

The committee proceedings contain some interesting arguments which alone justify mention of this topic. The GWR were alarmed at the possibility of the Barry entering the Swansea hinterland. They argued that it was wrong and without precedent for a railway company to finance a line with which it had no physical connection. This had been precisely the argument of the minority on the LNWR board opposed to involvement with the NAH. The position of the LNW and Midland at Swansea was distinguished on the grounds that, by means of joint lines and running powers, they were linked to Swansea as though they had their own line all the way. The counter argument, for which there was a parallel in Scotland where the Highland had been allowed to operate the Fort Augustus Branch, with which it had no physical connection, was rebutted on the grounds that the Highland had an interest in stimulating transport from the Great Glen to Inverness, even if it were partly by road. Parliament, no doubt impressed by what the Barry had already done for the movement of coal in south Wales, gave the project another extension of 18 months, but nothing came of it. The GWR got away with building only a small part of it.

The Midland also obtained approval for its own additional line in 1911. This was to run from Llansamlet down the east side of Swansea, through a major tunnel under Kilvey Hill, and end at the East Dock, but it was never built. Instead, improvements were made to the existing connections, and the Midland maintained its low level of infrastructure investment in the Swansea area.

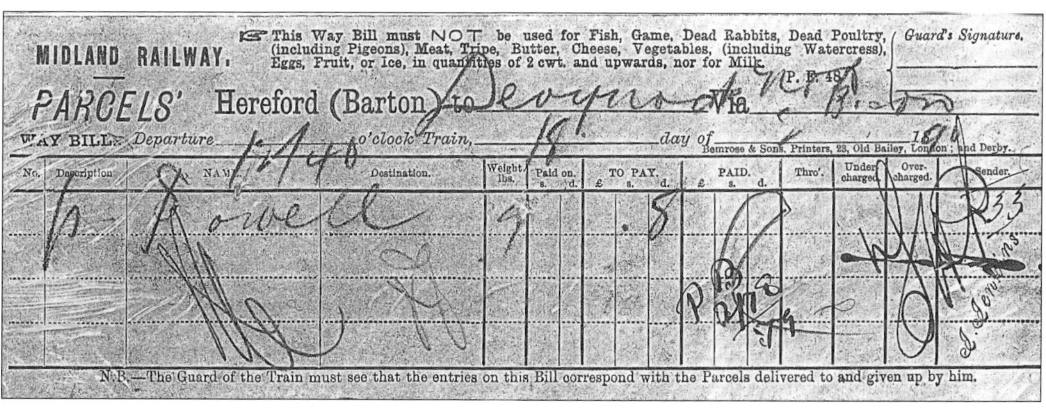

MIDLAND RAILWAY.

This Way Bill must NOT be used for Fish, Game, Dead Rabbits, Dead Poultry, (including Pigeons), Meat, Tripe, Butter, Cheese, Vegetables, (including Watercress), Eggs, Fruit, or Ice, in quantities of 2 cwt. and upwards, nor for Milk.

Guard's Signature.

P. F. 48

PARCELS' Hereford (Barton) to ______ Via ______

WAY BILL. Departure ______ o'clock Train, ______ day of ______ 189

Bemrose & Sons, Printers, 23, Old Bailey, London; and Derby.

No.	Description	NAME	Destination.	Weight. lbs.	Paid on. s. d.	TO PAY. £ s. d.	PAID. £ s. d.	Thro'.	Under charged.	Over-charged.	Sender.

N.B.—The Guard of the Train must see that the entries on this Bill correspond with the Parcels delivered to and given up by him.

Waybill.

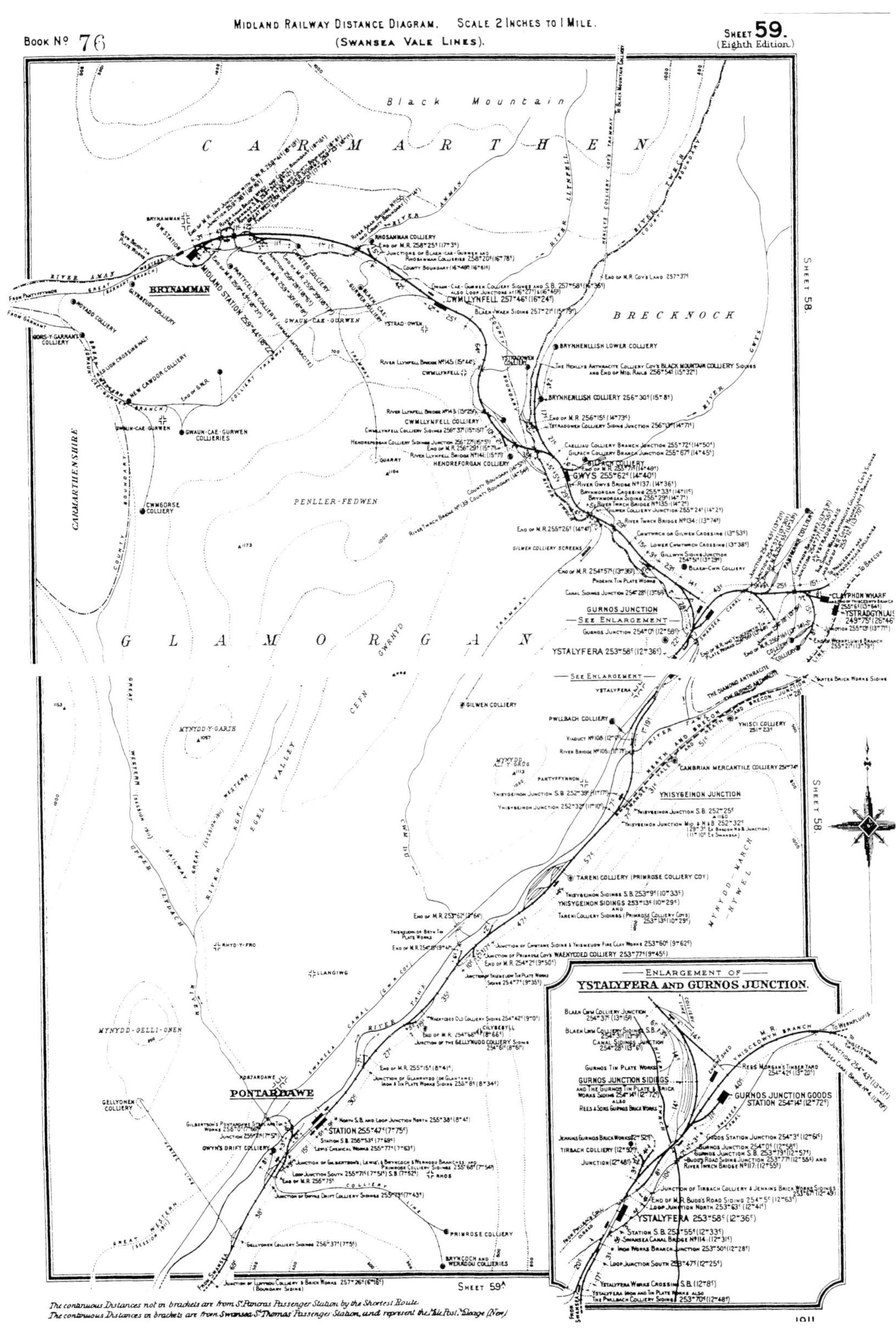

Midland Railway plan of the upper Swansea Vale; 1911. *Courtesy Peter Kay*

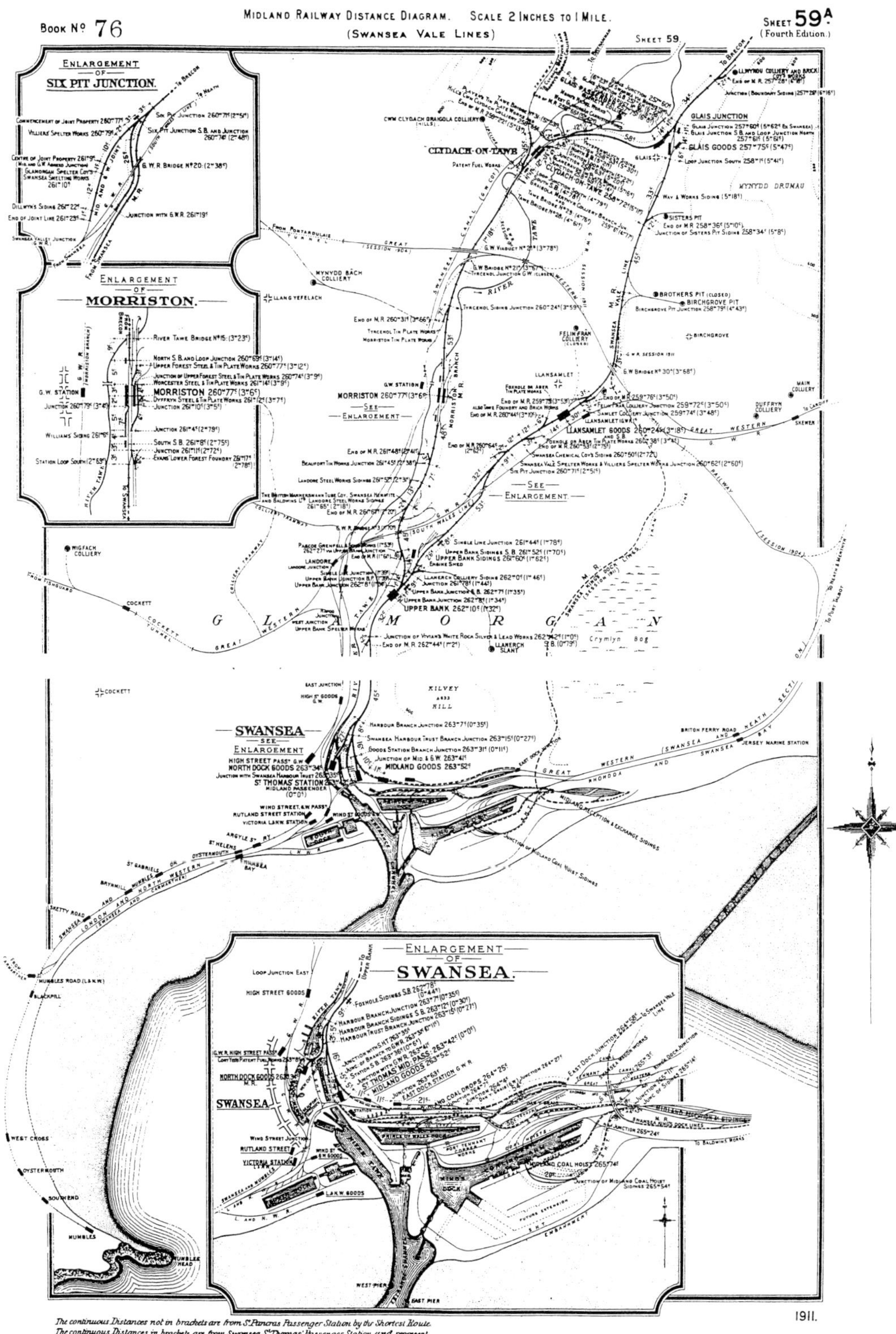

A similar plan of the Swansea area; 1911. At that time the new line under Kilvey Hill was a sufficiently firm intention to be included. *Courtesy Peter Kay*

Chapter 7

THE HARVEST

Having witnessed the story of the hard-fought entry by both the Midland and the LNW, it would be interesting to be able to calculate the benefit to their shareholders of the resulting tortuous connections over difficult terrain. Unfortunately, this is virtually impossible. Even if records of profitability analysis or even of capital employed ever existed, they seem to be lost, and consequently it is only the tonnages transported which can provide a sense of the relative commercial importance of these south Wales lines. In the case of the Midland we are fortunate in having records of income from passenger trade by station, together with station costs. The freight trade is only given in tons and no figures are provided for train operating costs, but a slightly clearer picture can be created.

At a time when competitors were able to threaten them by attacking them in their heartlands, both companies had stated that the grounds for penetrating south Wales were to feed their existing core networks and to protect their shareholders' investment. South Wales was not the only part of the country which served this purpose, but its growth and mineral wealth justified the prolonged management effort described in the previous chapters. In 1852 Moon and Tootal had been enthusiastic about the market's potential and, as revealed in Chapter 2, wrote a very upbeat report, though it was not backed by any very sophisticated statistics; in the second half of the last century there was an underlying optimism about economic growth and the unending availability and demand for minerals. This overcame the economic downturns which in fact occurred. In spite of the decline of the old iron industry in the latter part of the century, the closures of coalmines as seams were exhausted, and despite the massive unemployment resulting in the

Coal sidings at Clydach. *GWR/WIMM*

Cwm Clydach Graigola Colliery, 1911. *GWR/WIMM*

early part of the twentieth century as coal production declined from its 1913 peak, even as late as the fifties and sixties new housing estates were being built on top of the mountains, as though it would never stop.

The statistics are dramatic; the population of Wales grew from just over half a million in 1801 to two million in 1901, mainly in the south. From 1801 to 1851 the population of Glamorgan trebled; in the rest of the century it grew fivefold to over a million. Monmouthshire grew to something just under half a million. Meanwhile several rural counties were seeing a decline, as indeed did Merthyr, which had grown in the first half of the century to be the largest town in Wales with some 70,000 people; it dropped to 50,000 by the end of the century, while Cardiff and Swansea were rising to about 100,000 each.

Behind the population figures was the economic growth. In the first half of the century iron production was mainly near the heads of the valleys at Merthyr, Dowlais, Hirwaun, Sirhowy, Tredegar, Nantyglo and Blaenavon; this led the growth and stimulated both coal-mining and stone quarrying. The invention of steel in the 1850s meant the gradual decline of these early works, which were expensive to convert to steel-making. As iron-ore stocks declined, the need to turn to import forced new plant to be located near the sea. Meanwhile rising coal demand for uses other than iron manufacture caused a major growth of activity in the lower valleys of Glamorgan and Monmouthshire, and an important trade in Scandinavian pit-props was established. 1913 was the peak year for Welsh coal production and, at that time, one third of total world trade in coal was supplied from south Wales. Steam coal for locomotives and ships was richly available in the Rhondda and Aberdare valleys and in the western valleys of Monmouthshire. Blaenavon was an outstanding source of steam coal, and the Sirhowy valley yielded supplies

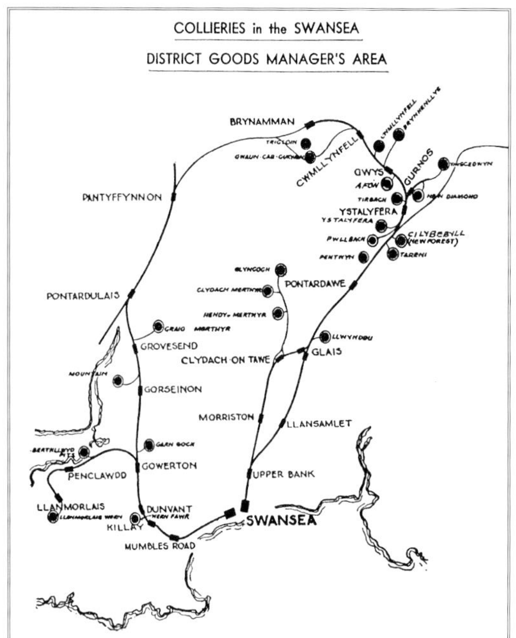

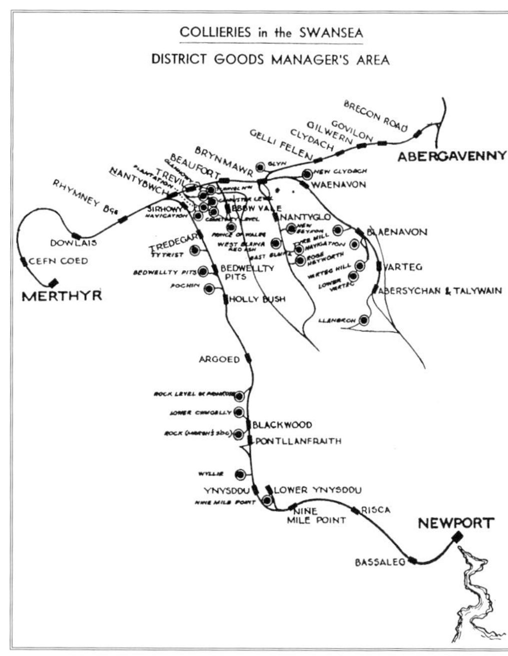

Maps showing the connections between the collieries and the LMS system in south Wales; July 1937.
PRO RAIL 421/182

consistently, even through the bad times and nearly to the end. Further west, the Aman valley and surrounding hills were rich in anthracite, a hard non-bituminous fuel particularly suitable for stoves and furnaces. (Anthracite, derived from the Greek 'anthrax', meaning 'coal'.)

Swansea first produced minerals in the fourteenth century when readily accessible outcrops of coal were found. This was the key to its success. In the seventeenth century there were 153 houses clustered round the castle on the banks of the Tawe. Because of its ready accessibility, the coal was exported to south-west England and copper ore was brought back on the ballast run. The first copper smelter was set up at Landore in 1717. During the nineteenth century nine tenths of British copper was produced in the Swansea area. Copper declined in the 1870s but was replaced by silver and zinc, of which three quarters of British production was located near Swansea. The Mond nickel works at Clydach just north of Swansea was the largest in the world when it was built in 1902. Tin-plate production grew in the nineteenth century alongside iron and by 1913 there were 106 tin-plate works producing over 800,000 tons, of which over 500,000 tons were exported. In 1869 the German company

Pontardawe Station, looking south towards the sinister shapes of an early industrial complex; *c.* 1904.
Tudor Watkins Coll.

Siemens opened their Landore steelworks and by 1873 this was the fourth largest in the world. Evidence in the committee hearings of the 1861 Llanelly Bill referred to the important trade with South America, importing silver and copper ore in return for bituminous coal. In the same hearings in Westminster the chairman of the committee impatiently stopped evidence of the trade of Swansea, saying the importance of Swansea was so well known that it was not necessary to take such evidence.

Heavy industries encroach upon the river Tawe near Hafod, just north of Swansea. Vivian & Sons Beyer Garrett is seen outside the shed, probably in the 1920s.

Librarian, City and County of Swansea

Industrial detritus at Upper Bank; 27 June 1938. *H.C. Casserley*

The concentration of industrial activity was all too readily discernible. In 1854 Thomas Williams wrote in poetic vein, 'The scene fills the eye of the spectator standing on the Landore viaduct, on a tranquil summer's night fall, when the beams of the down-going sun are fringeing with fire and gold the revolving clouds which veil the blackness of the slag mountains, and multiply by shadowing the forests of chimneys; peering above the slattered roofs of the vast 'sheds' dubiously looming in the darkness of the valley is really grand, if not awe-striking; sublime if not terrific.' The winner of a railway carriage eisteddfod held on a return journey from Newport was more earthy:

> It came to pass in days of yore,
> The Devil chanced upon Landore,
> Quoth he, by all this fume and stink,
> I can't be far from home, I think.

As early as 1848 the smoke of Swansea was visible 50 miles away. In 1861 a report to the Royal School of Mines described how 'Swansea smelters enjoy the privilege of pouring dense volumes of thick sulphurous and arsenical smoke from comparatively low chimneys into the atmosphere . . . which would not be allowed in many other parts of the kingdom.' In 1880 S.C. Ganwell described Landore as, 'A spot rich in the renown of its metal and chemical works but, to the casual visitor, ugly with all the ugliness of grime and dust, and mud and smoke and indescribable tastes and odours.' Swansea was thriving, but at a terrible price.

The following paragraphs examine how the railway traffic, passenger and goods, developed over each of the lines and at the key centres up until the demise of the LMS. But first we look at the locomotives employed. Considering the nature of the terrain over which both the LNW and the Midland had to operate in south Wales, it is hardly surprising that in some cases special types of locomotives had to be engaged.

The view from the station bridge at Gorseinon, looking north, with two LNWR trains and a great deal of industrial activity; date unknown.

Courtesy N.T. Wassell

This fine engraving of Swansea illustrates the heavy industrial activity in the lower tawe valley. Prominent in the middle distance is the GWR Landore viaduct. St. Thomas Station is in the centre. Victoria is on the extreme left; 1876.

ILN

Over the straightforward line from Shrewsbury to Newport no unusual locomotive types were needed, but we know that the Prince of Wales class of 4-6-0s were used on passenger trains. Goods engines used included the 19 ins 4-6-0 and the compound and non-compound 0-8-0s. A characteristic locomotive of south Wales was the 0-6-2T 'coal tank' introduced in 1890. This took the place on the MTA of some so-called 'special tanks' of 0-6-0ST wheel arrangement, which had been introduced in the 1870s for the extension of the line to Rhymney Bridge. The MTA saw 0-8-0 locomotives right to the end as they combined power with respect for the track; for service on the MTA many of them were fitted with tender cabs. Some of the 0-8-2T locomotives found their way to Blaenavon and just after the end of the LNW's existence the 0-8-4Ts arrived, the second type designed especially for the MTA Sirhowy and Blaenavon lines. Their tendency to abuse the track and to become derailed limited their appeal, and some of them were moved on to the Central Wales line and to the north-west. Much has been written about the tendency of these locomotives to become derailed on the tight

A Stanier trio at Swansea; 27 August 1948.
H.C. Casserley

Fowler tank engine No. 42307 at Paxton Street; 17 April 1955. *T.B. Owen*

Swansea Paxton Street shed with ex-LNWR No. 49035; 17 April 1955. *T.B. Owen*

General view of Paxton Street shed with former LNWR locomotives flanking LMS Class 5 No. 5191; 27 June 1938.
H.C. Casserley

A dramatic demonstration of the inherent problem with the Beames 0-8-4T; date and location unknown.
Nigel Lewis Coll.

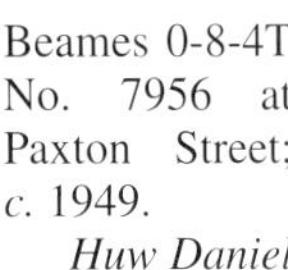
Beames 0-8-4T No. 7956 at Paxton Street; *c.* 1949.
Huw Daniel

curves of the MTA; it has even been suggested that the problem also arose when the locomotives were actually stationary in a siding and were shaken off the rails by the vibrations caused by heavily laiden trains rattling over adjacent unstable track. They were outlasted on the MTA by 'coal tanks' and 0-8-0s. These two types also handled the Cardiff traffic, since the GWR banned the 0-8-4Ts from the former Rhymney lines. All these types were used on both passenger and goods trains on the MTA and Sirhowy.

On the Central Wales line there was a greater variety over the years. At the beginning, the Ramsbottom DX 0-6-0 handled most of the goods traffic and was superceded by the Webb 'Cauliflower' in 1880. These were replaced on passenger trains by Webb's 'Precedent' 2-4-0 and, in the early 1900s, by his 2-4-2T. When the 4-6-2T arrived in 1911, the 2-4-2Ts were relegated to the Llandilo/Carmarthen line and other local services, together with the 'Coal Tanks'. Then there was a significant increase in locomotive size with the introduction in 1912 of the 0-8-0, in 1913 the 19 ins 4-6-0 goods, then the 0-8-2T and finally the 0-8-4T which were used particularly for banking purposes, based at Knighton and Llandovery.

0-8-4T No. 7941 on banking duty at Llandovery; date uncertain.
G.A. Hookham/ N.T. Wassell Coll.

During the 1920s some Fowler 2-6-0 'Crabs' found their way to Swansea. In spite of an appearance which many people find distinctly plain, they were popular with the operating staff. At the end of the '20s under LMS management, the Fowler 2-6-4T replaced the 4-6-2T on passenger duties, and in 1936 the first 'Black Five' 4-6-0 appeared, followed in 1937 by the 8F 2-8-0. During the Second World War the 'Austerity' 2-8-0 type was used on the line, with some brief appearances of the American 2-8-0.

The HHB had no locomotives and the SV only 0-6-0STs, so for passenger trains the Midland used 0-4-4T engines with specially enlarged water tanks, boilers and fireboxes; goods trains were handled by the Kirtley double framed 0-6-0. They then introduced the 'South Wales tank engine', a 0-6-0T which had a specially designed cab and large boiler and firebox. This type eventually monopolised the line and indeed survived on the Brynamman branch until the end, sharing the task with the later LMS development known as 'Jinties'. These locomotives were accommodated at two sheds, Upper Bank and Gurnos. The former was by far the larger and survives in part as a base for railway preservationists. The standard of construction of these buildings was said to be markedly superior to the rather shoddy and run-down former LNW affair at Paxton Street.

The Midland's principal engine shed was just north of the station at Upper Bank; 27 August 1948. *H.C. Casserley*

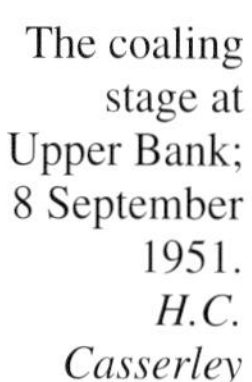

The coaling stage at Upper Bank; 8 September 1951. *H.C. Casserley*

Turning now to the passenger and goods traffic, it is clear that passenger traffic was not of prime importance; it was the movement of minerals that drove the operations. Passenger traffic was fairly specialised, with local and workmen's trains, excursion trains, through long distance carriages attached to other trains, and, only on the Central Wales line, mainline through trains. Between Shrewsbury and Newport, most were operated by the GW. Goods traffic was dominated by the movement of coal and iron, though Swansea generated other mineral traffic, and the whole area saw a level of general goods traffic appropriate to such a densely populated and industrialised part of the country.

Parcels traffic at Nantybwch and further examples of the variety of carriages found on this line; no date.
R.C. Riley

Hereford is a convenient place to start and was the only place where the south Wales operations of the Midland and LNW met. In Swansea, the only place in Wales where both were present, they were largely insulated from one another. At Hereford the LNWR were mainly involved in goods traffic. Such was the complexity of the development of railway services through Hereford that it will be desirable to take a step by step approach to understand what happened.

1853 The S & H opened in December with a service from Shrewsbury to Barr's Court. At this stage the station was a terminus and consisted of a small single platform.

1854 The NAH arrived in January at Barton and ran some four trains a day in each direction between Hereford and Newport; at least one of these had through carriages which were shunted between the two stations; half an hour was allowed for this process, since it involved reversal outside Barr's Court.

1855 The broad gauge Hereford Ross & Gloucester arrived at the south end of Barr's Court.

1861 The OWW, by then part of the West Midland, and soon to be GW, operated from Worcester over the newly opened W & H to Barton. The S & H started to use Barton as well as Barr's Court, having acquired running powers over the NAH (now West Midland).

1862 The GW and LNW, now joint owners of the S & H, operated through trains from Shrewsbury to Newport; by splitting the trains at Hereford Junction, the through portion served Barton, and Barr's Court acted as a terminus. These trains were operated by the GWR though until 1879 the LNWR operated its own passenger trains from time to time. (see page 230).

1864 The HHB opened to Eardisley with four trains a day from Moorfields. The GW started through trains to Swansea over the Vale of Neath line. This ceased in 1873.

1865 For about a year the HHB through trains to Brecon used Barton.

1866 The LNW's south link enabled through running of GW/LNW Shrewsbury to Newport trains via Barr's Court, avoiding Barton.

Of GW Worcester trains, four served Barton, two Barr's Court. In the opposite direction, two were from Barton and four from Barr's Court.

1868 On completion of the doubling of the W & H, for three years the Midland operated its own passenger trains from Worcester which terminated at Barton. From 1 October the HHB was operated by the Mid-Wales from Moorfields.

1869 The HHB was run by the Midland from Moorfields.

1870 The one GW train from Paddington via Worcester used Barton.

1871 The Midland ceased operating their own trains from Worcester and attached carriages to GW trains.

1873 MR carriages for Brecon were shunted between Barr's Court and Moorfields by a Midland shunting engine kept at Hereford for the purpose.

1874 Midland carriages started operating from Birmingham to Brecon via Barton. Between Barr's Court and Barton, carriages were still shunted.

1876 The Midland started operating Birmingham to Swansea, still using both stations. Moorfields was closed to passenger traffic.

1893 The Brecon and Barton Curves being built, Barton was closed. Midland trains switched to Barr's Court.

In 1876 the Midland started a service of some five trains a day between Hereford and Swansea, conveying through carriages between Birmingham and Swansea once a day. This journey took the best part of seven and a half hours, but must have been a fascinating experience. It survived until 1916. From that time the only Midland through trains were two a day from Hereford to Swansea. This was cut back to a local service between Hereford and Brecon at the end of 1930; from this time the N & B trains from Brecon to Neath provided a service which made connection at Colbren Junction with trains over the old SV and N & B from Ynysygeinon Junction. This survived until 12 September 1932 whereupon the only LMS services out of Swansea St. Thomas were the local trains to Brynamman. From the same year this route also lost its through goods trains which were diverted to the Vale of Neath line.

Jack Simmons recalls a journey in the mid-1920s from Bedford to Clydach via Birmingham and Hereford which necessitated a 9.00 a.m. departure and arrival 10 hours later. The journey was normally made via Paddington which took three hours less. He recalls travelling in an extremely uncomfortable and un-lit non-bogie carriage, with sepia photographs in the compartment illustrating places served by the Midland Railway.

Jack Simmons also recalls in the *Oxford Companion to British Railway History* that in 1889 a through carriage was operating from St. Pancras to Brecon by way of Hereford.

The goods traffic was rather more interesting as the Midland had a policy of cutting rates in order to overcome any disadvantage they suffered due to mileage. They therefore succeeded in attracting copper and anthracite traffic, and, in addition, iron and iron ore; J. Palmer Budd's enthusiasm for rail links with England was partly based on the importance he attached to blending ores to achieve quality. Although the line from Swansea to Brecon was expensive to operate, at its peak, in 1909, it handled some 500,000 tons in a year. Trains were restricted to 18 waggons and two locomotives were required, both ascending and (as an additional brake) descending, besides two brake vans. The nine or ten trains a day in each direction over mainly single track required careful planning.

It was on the former Swansea Vale lines that the Midland really found wealth. The density of coalmining and mineral works in the relatively short distances in the lower Tawe valley was such that, at one time, there were 70 private sidings. As early as 1861, 300,000 tons of coal and minerals were being moved to the docks by the SV. The Midland had their own coal tippers on the north side of the Prince of Wales Dock and on the south side of King's Dock, both reached along GW and Swansea Harbour Trust metals. By 1907 the former SV was handling over 4.5 million tons of coal and minerals; this

44 Third Class Tickets are issued by all Trains on the Midland Railway.

TABLE 39.]

SWANSEA, BRECON, & HEREFORD,

WORCESTER, BIRMINGHAM, & THE NORTH.

STATIONS.	WEEKDAYS. 1w	2w	3w	4w	5w	6	7
SWANSEA (S. V. Sta.).. dep.	..	8 0	11 0	3 40	6 20	..	—
Upper Bank	....	8 6	11 6	3 46	6 26	....	....
Morriston	..	8 11	11 11	3 51	6 31	..	..
Cwm Clydach	....	8 18	11 18	3 58	6 38	....	....
Glais (New Station)	..	8 23	11 23	4 3	6 43	—	..
Pontardawe	....	8 30	11 30	4 10	6 51	....	....
Ystalyfera	—	8 49	11 49	4 20	7 5	..	..
Gwys	....	8 58	11 58	4 41	....	....	....
BRYNAMMAN arr.	..	9 7	12 7	4 50	..	..	..
Yniscedwyn	....	8 50	11 50	4 30	....	....	....
NEATH (N. & B. Sta.) arr.	—	10 10	..	7 3	..	..	.
NEATH (N. & B. Sta.) dep.	....	8 15	....	3 55	....	....	....
Colbren Junction	..	9 3	12 3	4 42	..	..	..
Penwyllt	....	9 14	12 14	4 52	....	....	....
Cray	..	9 30	12 30	5 8	..	..	..
Devynock	....	9 40	12 40	5 18	....	....	....
Aberbran	..	9 51	12 51	5 29	..	..	..
Cradoc	..	9 58	12 58	5 36	..	..	..
BRECON arr.	....	10 5	1 5	5 43	....	....	....
B. & M. — **NEWPORT** (Dock St.).. dep.	....	7 50	....	12 40	..	..	..
B. & M. — Dowlais ,,	....	9 35	12 15	2 10	....	....	....
B. & M. — Cardiff (T. V.) ,,	—	8 10	....	..	..	..	..
B. & M. — Merthyr (V. of N. Sta.) ,,	....	9 35	12 25	....	....	....	....
B. & M. — Cefn ,,	—	9 45	12 33	..	..	..	..
B. & M. — Talybont ,,	....	10 32	1 11	3 10	....	....	....
BRECON dep	7 10	10 30	1 10	5 50	..	..	..
Talyllyn Junction ,,	7 20	10 45	1 25	6 0	....	....	....
Talgarth ,,	7 33	10 57	1 38	6 15	..	..	..
ABERYSTWITH .... dep	....	....	8 0	12 30	....	....	....
Mid Wales — Llanidloes ,,	—	6 35	11 30	4 35	..	.	..
Mid Wales — Rhayader ,,	....	7 7	12 8	5 8	....	....	....
Mid Wales — Builth (Wells) ,,	..	10 5	1 0	5 45	—	—	..
Three Cocks Junction dep.	7 41	11 10	1 55	6 25	....	....	....
Glasbury	7 47	11 14	1 59	6 30	..	—	..
HAY	7 57	11 24	2 5	6 40	....	....	....
Whitney	8 6	11 33	2 18	6 49	..	..	..
Eardisley	8 15	11 40	2 25	6 56	....	....	....
Kinnersley	8 20	11 45	2 30	7 2	..	—	..
Moorhampton	8 28	11 52	2 37	7 9	....	....	....
Credenhill	8 37	12 0	2 45	7 18	..	—	..
HEREFORD (Barton) .. arr.	8 50	12 12	2 57	7 30	....	....	....
Hereford (Barton) dep.	9 37	12 35	3 42	7 40	..	..	..
Ledbury arr	10 23	1 16	4 13	8 21	....	....	....
Great Malvern ,,	10 49	1 40	4 36	8 44	..	..	..
Bath (via Malvern) ,,	2 40	....	....	....	....	....	....
BRISTOL (v. Malvern) ,,	2 5	..	12 20	..	..	..	..
Malvern Link ,,	10 54	1 45	4 41	8 49	....	....	....
Worcester ,,	11 20	2 3	4 5[illegible]	9 10	..	—	..
BIRMINGHAM (NewSt.) ,,	1 25	3 35	3 40	10 18	....	....	....
Leicester ,,	3 57	6 15	8 5	1 44	..	..	..
LONDON (St. Pancras) ,,	6 30	8 55	12 30	4 15	....	....	....
Derby ,,	2 45	6 0	8 0	11 45	..	..	..
MANCHESTER ,,	5 0	8 10	9 45	5 10	....	....	....
LIVERPOOL (RanelaghSt.) ,,	6 0	9 0	10 40	6 0	....	....	....
Nottingham ,,	3 30	7 5	9 5	1 30	..	..	..
Sheffield ,,	4 1	7 32	10 15	12 46	....	....	....
LEEDS ,,	5 25	9 15	—	2 15	..	..	..
Bradford ,,	6 5	9 50	....	2 37	....	....	....
Hull ,,	8 0	11 15	..	4 32	..	..	..
York ,,	6 45	10 20	....	3 36	....	....	....
Newcastle ,,	11 20	12 45	..	5 58	..	..	..
Carlisle ,,	....	....	....	5 0	....	....	....
Edinburgh (Wav. Bridge) ,,	—	—	..	7 45	..	..	..
Glasgow (St. Enoch) ,,	....	....	....	8 0	....	....	....

STATIONS.	WEEKDAYS. 1w	2w	3w (B)	4w	5w	6w	7
Glasgow (St. Enoch) dep.	—	4 30	9 15	..	—	..	—
Edinburgh (Wav. Bridge) ,,	....	4 25	9 20	....	....	....	....
Carlisle ,,	..	8 10	12 10	..	—	8 20	..
Newcastle ,,	....	7 8	11 20	....	1 30	10 5	....
Hull ,,	..	8 50	....	..	5 45	10 30	..
York ,,	....	9 38	1 55	....	6 50	12 50	....
Bradford ,,	..	10 30	2 25	..	8 15	12 30	..
LEEDS ,,	....	11 30	2 25	....	8 50	1 20	....
Sheffield ,,	..	12 34	4 25	..	10 10	2 28	..
Nottingham ,,	....	11 40	..	....	10 50	2 35	....
LIVERPOOL (RanelaghSt.) ,,	..	10 40	....	..	9 0	12 0	..
MANCHESTER ,,	....	11 30	..	....	9 50	1 0	..
Derby ,,	....	1 45	6 40	....	11 35	3 40	....
LONDON (St. Pancras) ,,	..	9 15	—	—	5 15	12 0	..
Leicester ,,	....	11 42	....	....	8 10	2 55	....
BIRMINGHAM (NewSt.) ,,	..	2 45	8 40	..	12 40	4 45	..
Worcester ,,	....	7 30	10 20	....	2 5	6 15	....
Malvern Link ,,	..	7 55	10 46	—	2 25	6 33	—
BRISTOL (v. Malvern) ,,	....	....	8 5	....	....	3 20	....
Bath (via Malvern) ,,	..	—	7 45	..	..	3 0	—
Great Malvern ,,	....	8 3	10 52	....	2 32	6 43	....
Ledbury ,,	..	8 27	11 16	..	2 55	7 4	..
Hereford (Barton) arr.	....	9 5	11 55	....	3 34	7 35	....
HEREFORD (Barton) ..dep.	..	9 25	12 30	..	3 40	8 0	..
Credenhill	....	9 35	12 40	....	3 50	8 10	....
Moorhampton	..	9 43	12 48	..	3 58	8 20	..
Kinnersley	....	9 50	12 56	....	4 5	8 28	....
Eardisley	..	9 55	1 2	..	4 11	8 34	..
Whitney	....	10 3	1 10	....	4 19	8 44	....
HAY	..	10 15	1 18	..	4 27	8 54	..
Glasbury	....	10 23	1 32	....	4 39	9 4	....
Three Cocks Junction arr.	..	10 27	1 37	—	4 45	9 9	..
Mid Wales — Builth (Wells) arr.	—	11 50	2 19	..	6 22	—	—
Mid Wales — Rhayader ,,	....	....	2 55	....	6 54	....	....
Mid Wales — Llanidloes ,,	..	..	3 30	..	7 30	—	..
ABERYSTWITH ,,	....	....	6 24	....	....	....	....
Talgarth arr.	....	10 34	1 52	....	4 56	9 16	....
Talyllyn Junction ,,	—	10 45	2 5	..	5 8	9 32	..
BRECON ,,	....	11 5	2 20	....	5 20	9 45	....
B. & M. — Talybont arr.	..	..	2 25	..	5 22	....	....
B. & M. — Cefn ,,	....	....	3 15	....	6 20	—	..
B. & M. — Merthyr (V. of N. Stn.) ,,	..	..	3 25	..	6 30	....	....
B. & M. — Cardiff (T. V.) ,,	....	....	4 52	....	8 0	—	..
B. & M. — Dowlais ,,	..	..	3 20	..	6 27	....	....
B. & M. — **NEWPORT** (Dock St.) ,,	....	....	4 45	....	7 55	—	..
BRECON dep.	8 20	11 20	—	....	5 40	....	....
Cradoc	8 30	11 30	....	....	5 51	....	....
Aberbran	8 37	11 37	..	..	5 58	..	..
Devynock	8 48	11 48	....	....	6 9	....	....
Cray	8 58	11 58	—	..	6 19	..	..
Penwyllt	9 14	12 14	....	....	6 35	....	....
Colbren Junction	9 24	12 24	—	..	6 45	—	..
NEATH (N. & B. Sta.) arr.	10 10	....	....	....	7 30	....	....
NEATH (N. & B. Sta.) dep.	8 15	..	..	..	3 55	..	..
Yniscedwyn	9 36	12 36	....	....	6 57	....	....
BRYNAMMAN dep.	9 17	12 17	—	5 0	..	—	..
Gwys	9 27	12 27	....	5 10	....	....	....
Ystalyfera	9 36	12 36	—	5 20	..	..	—
Pontardawe	9 55	12 54	....	5 34	7 11	....	....
Glais (New Station)	10 3	1 2	—	5 42	7 19	..	..
Cwm Clydach	10 8	1 7	....	5 47	7 23	....	....
Morriston	10 15	1 14	..	5 54	7 30	—	..
Upper Bank	10 20	1 20	....	6 0	7 35	....	....
SWANSEA (S. V. Sta.).. arr.	10 25	1 25	..	6 5	7 40	—	..

A MARKET TRAIN for HAY and intermediate Stations leaves HEREFORD (Barton Station) at 5.10 p.m. on WEDNESDAYS.

THROUGH CARRIAGES are run between Birmingham, Worcester, Malvern, Hereford, Brecon, and Swansea, as follows:—

Between Birmingham and Swansea by 12.40 p.m. from Birmingham, and 8.0 and 11.0 a.m. Trains from Swansea; between Birmingham and Brecon by 8.40 a.m. and 4.45 p.m. from Birmingham, and 7.10 a.m. from Brecon; between Worcester and Swansea by 7.30 a.m. from Worcester and 0 p.m. from Swansea.

Third Class Tickets are issued by all the above Trains, with the exception of Aberystwith, and Third Class Passengers are booked there as under:—

B—From Bristol, Bath, Hereford and Hay to Aberystwith.

Passengers travelling to Swansea by the Midland Route, and requiring cabs on arrival at that Station, can have them provided by informing the the Station Master at Brecon before the departure of the Trains.

THIRD CLASS MARKET TICKETS, at about a Fare and a Half for the Double Journey, are issued from Brynamman and intermediate Stations to Swansea on Saturdays, by all Trains, available for Return by any Train on that day only. Holders of these Tickets will not be required to pay the Bridge Toll at Swansea.

[1] NOTE—The Times from Noon to Midnight are distinguished by the Thin Line between the Hour & Minute Figures

By 1877 through carriages were available from Birmingham to Swansea. *PRO RAIL 962/9*

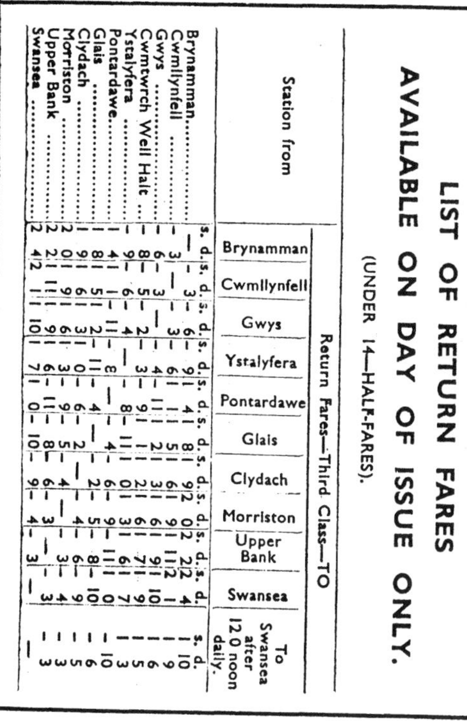

LIST OF RETURN FARES AVAILABLE ON DAY OF ISSUE ONLY.

(UNDER 14—HALF-FARES).

Station from	Return Fares—Third Class—TO: Brynamman	Cwmllynfell	Gwys	Ystalyfera	Pontardawe	Glais	Clydach	Morriston	Upper Bank	Swansea	To Swansea after 12 0 noon daily.
	s. d.	s. d.	s. d.	s. d.	s. d.	s. d.	s. d.	s. d.	s. d.	s. d.	s. d.
Brynamman	—	– 3	– 6	– 9	1 4	1 8	1 9	2 0	2 2	2 4	1 10
Cwmllynfell	– 3	—	– 3	– 6	1 1	1 5	1 6	1 9	1 11	2 1	1 9
Gwys	– 6	– 3	—	– 4	– 11	1 2	1 3	1 6	1 9	1 10	1 6
Cwmtwrch Well Halt	– 8	– 5	– 2	– 3	– 9	1 1	1 2	1 6	1 7	1 9	1 5
Ystalyfera	– 9	– 6	– 4	—	– 8	– 11	1 0	1 3	1 6	1 7	1 3
Pontardawe	1 4	1 1	– 11	– 8	—	– 4	– 6	– 9	– 11	1 0	– 10
Glais	1 8	1 5	1 2	– 11	– 4	—	– 2	– 5	– 8	– 10	– 6
Clydach	1 9	1 6	1 3	1 0	– 6	– 2	—	– 4	– 6	– 9	– 5
Morriston	2 0	1 9	1 6	1 3	– 9	– 5	– 4	—	– 3	– 4	– 3
Upper Bank	2 2	1 11	1 9	1 6	– 11	– 8	– 6	– 3	—	– 3	– 3
Swansea	2 4	2 1	1 10	1 7	1 0	– 10	– 9	– 4	– 3	—	—

CHEAP TICKETS

AND

WINTER TRAIN SERVICES

SEPTEMBER 28th, 1936,

until further notice.

O/1444. E.R.O. 53506/228 McC., Newton.

SWANSEA and BRYNAMMAN.

WEEK DAYS.

				FSX	FO	SO	SX
	a. m.	a.m.		a.m.	a.m.	a.m.	p.m.
Swansea (St. T.) dep	...	**8 10**	...	**11 0**	**11 0**	**11 0**	**1 3**
Upper Bank	...	8 15	...	11 5	11 5	11 5	1 8
Morriston	...	8 19	...	11 9	11 9	11 9	1 13
Clydach-on-Tawe	...	8 24	...	11 15	11 16	11 16	1 19
Glais	...	8 28	...	11 19	11 20	11 20	1 23
Pontardawe	...	8 35	...	11 26	11 27	11 27	1 30
Ystalyfera	7 10	8 49	...	11 40	11 45	11 47	1 43
CwmtwrchW. Halt	...	8 54	...	11 45	11 50	11 52	1 48
Gwys	7 16	8 57	...	11 49	11 54	11 56	1 51
Cwmllynfell	7 22	9 3	...	11 56	12 1	12 3	1 57
Brynamman arr.	**7 28**	**9 9**	...	**12 2**	**12 7**	**12 9**	**2 3**
	SO	**SX**	**SO**	**SX**	**SO**	**SX**	**SO**
	p.m.	p.m.	p.m.	p.m.	p.m.	p.m.	p.m.
Swansea (St.T.)dep.	**1 3**	**3 55**	**3 55**	**5 29**	**6 0**	**6 30**	**7 40**
Upper Bank	1 8	4 0	4 0	5 34	6 5	6 35	7 45
Morriston	1 13	4 4	4 4	5 38	6 10	6 39	7 49
Clydach-on-Tawe	1 19	4 9	4 9	5 44	6 15	6 44	7 55
Glais	1 23	4 13	4 13	5 49	6 19	6 48	8 0
Pontardawe	1 30	4 20	4 20	5 56	6 27	6 55	8 8
Ystalyfera	1 48	4 33	4 38	6 6	6 45	7 8	8 23
CwmtwrchW. Halt	1 53	4 39	4 44	...	6 51	7 14	...
Gwys	1 56	4 42	4 47	...	6 54	7 17	...
Cwmllynfell	2 2	4 49	4 52	...	7 1	7 23	...
Brynamman arr.	**2 8**	**4 55**	**4 58**	...	**7 7**	**7 29**	...
	SO	**SX**	**SO**	**SO**	**SO**	**SO**	
	p.m.	p.m.	p.m.	p.m.	p.m.	p.m.	
Swansea (St.T.)dep.	**9 5**	**9 20**	**9 20**	**9 50**	**10 15**	**11 0**	...
Upper Bank	9 10	9 25	9 25	...	10 20	11 5	...
Morriston	9 17	9 29	9 31	...	...	...	...
Clydach-on-Tawe	9 23	9 34	9 37	...	10 28	11 13	...
Glais	9 30	9 38	9 44	...	10 32	11 18	...
Pontardawe	9 37	9 45	9 52	10 12	10 39	11 25	...
Ystalyfera	...	9 55	10 16	10 34	...	11 35	...
CwmtwrchW. Halt	...	...	10 20	10 40	...	...	...
Gwys	...	...	10 25	10 44	...	...	...
Cwmllynfell	...	...	10 33	10 52	...	...	...
Brynamman arr.	...	...	**10 39**	**10 58**	...	...	...

FO—Fridays only. **FSX**—Fridays and Saturdays excepted.
SO—Saturdays only. **SX**—Saturdays excepted.

BRYNAMMAN and SWANSEA.

WEEK DAYS.

						SO	SX
	a.m.	a.m.		a.m.		p.m.	p.m.
Brynamman dep.	**7 43**	...	...	**9 25**	...	**12 21**	**12 26**
Cwmllynfell	7 47	...	...	9 29	...	12 25	12 31
Gwys	7 53	...	...	9 35	...	12 31	12 36
CwmtwrchW. Halt	7 56	...	...	9 38	...	12 35	12 39
Ystalyfera	8 2	9 1	...	9 44	...	12 42	12 45
Pontardawe	8 14	9 10	...	9 56	...	12 56	12 56
Glais	8 20	9 16	...	10 1	...	1 2	1 2
Clydach-on-Tawe	8 25	9 20	...	10 5	...	1 8	1 7
Morriston	8 31	9 25	...	10 10	...	1 11	1 12
Upper Bank	8 36	9 30	...	10 16	...	1 19	1 17
Swansea (St.T.) arr.	**8 43**	**9 37**	...	**10 22**	...	**1 27**	**1 25**
	SO B	**SO** A	**SX**	**SO**	**SX**		**SO**
			p.m.	p.m.	p.m.		p.m.
Brynamman dep.	p.m.	p.m.	**2 15**	**2 20**	...	...	...
Cwmllynfell	...	...	2 19	2 24	...	...	...
Gwys	...	...	2 25	2 30	...	...	...
CwmtwrchW. Halt	...	...	2 28	2 33	...	...	...
Ystalyfera	1 20	1 55	2 34	2 40	4 8	...	4 8
Pontardawe	1 32	2 5	2 44	2 54	4 18	...	4 18
Glais	1 39	2 11	2 50	3 0	4 25	...	4 26
Clydach-on-Tawe	1 43	2 16	2 54	3 5	4 29	...	4 32
Morriston	1 48	2 21	2 59	3 11	4 34	...	4 39
Upper Bank	1 53	2 26	3 4	3 16	4 40	...	4 44
Swansea (St.T.) arr.	**2 0**	**2 34**	**3 11**	**3 24**	**4 46**	...	**4 52**
	SX	**SO**	**SO**	**SX**	**SO**	**SO**	
	p.m.	p.m.	p.m.	p.m.	p.m.	p.m.	
Brynamman dep.	**5 2**	**5 10**	**7 35**	**7 50**	...	**11 30**	...
Cwmllynfell	5 6	5 15	7 40	7 54	...	11 37	...
Gwys	5 12	5 21	7 46	8 0	...	...	...
CwmtwrchW. Halt	5 15	5 25	7 50	8 3	...	...	...
Ystalyfera	5 21	5 31	7 56	8 9	8 35	...	...
Pontardawe	5 32	5 47	8 10	8 20	8 46	...	...
Glais	5 38	5 54	8 17	8 26	8 52	...	...
Clydach-on-Tawe	5 44	6 1	8 21	8 30	8 56	...	...
Morriston	5 49	6 10	8 26	8 34	9 1	...	...
Upper Bank	5 54	6 17	8 31	8 40	9 6	...	...
Swansea (St. T.) arr.	**6 2**	**6 23**	**8 38**	**8 46**	**9 13**	...	...

A—Will not run Nov. 14, 1936, until Feb. 20, 1937 inclus.
B—Runs November 14, 1936, until February 20, 1937 Inclus.
SO—Saturdays only **SX**—Saturdavs excepted.

LMS timetable for the Swansea Vale line, 1936. *Courtesy Keith Evans*

Excursion train from Swansea arriving at Brecon with former Midland 0-6-0 No. 3389; July 1939.
G.A. Hookham, courtesy R.H. Marrows

peaked in 1913 at over 5 million. Nearly 2 million of this was generated at Swansea alone with another million at Gurnos. Ystalyfera, on the other hand, declined from some 60,000 tons in 1876 until by 1922 it was handling no coal at all. Pontardawe saw an opposite trend, rising to a peak of 500,000 tons in 1922, half of which was minerals. H.C.H. Burgess who worked on the LMS in Swansea recalls how in the 1920s two trains a day of 90 loaded coal waggons would be hauled the twelve miles from Gurnos to Llansamlet, with two 0-6-0 tank engines hauling the 1,200-1,300 tons, amounting then to about one million tons a year. At the Six Pit marshalling yard these trains were split for hauling by Swansea Harbour Trust locomotives to the hydraulic coal hoists at the East Dock.

Passenger numbers were also high. In 1907, for example, the SV lines moved 630,000; in the same year St. Pancras handled 900,000. Operating costs at stations were in similar proportion at £20,000 and £28,000 respectively. The position was not as healthy on the former HHB where in the same year only 140,000 passengers were moved; here the goods trade was insignificant, but the station costs were roughly proportional at only £5,000. The SV peaked in 1916 at over 800,000 passengers.

'Coaching income' which was the Midland's term for the total receipts from passengers and 'parcels, horses, carriages, dogs, etc.' had started to decline from the 1916 peak by the time of the grouping. In 1922 HHB income was £28,000 against station costs of £10,000,

The approach to St. Thomas Station from the street; *c.* 1903.
Lens of Sutton/ Tudor Watkins Coll.

St. Thomas Station entrance, mid-1956.
Mowat Coll./ John Miles

The gentleman in the boater reading his newspaper at Pontardawe Station would, no doubt, be surprised if he knew in how many publications he had appeared some 80 or 90 years later. Swansea was to his right.
Tudor Watkins Coll.

whereas on the SV the comparable figures were £40,000 and £32,000, no doubt reflecting the shorter journeys. In that year Swansea handled 118,000 passengers after a peak in 1919 of 229,000. Brynamman was down to 52,000 from 67,000. Ystalyfera was at 88,000, down from 127,000 and the pattern was similar at Pontardawe. In 1913 the train services which conveyed these large numbers were nine a day all the way to Brynamman and four only as far as Ystalyfera. By 1925 these had fallen to five, with as many as eight 'Saturdays only' trains over part of the line, for instance from Ystalyfera to Brynamman and down to Swansea.

Turning now to the LNWR, we have a much more extensive operation but rather less statistical information available. From the north, access to Newport was achieved first in 1862 through Abergavenny and over the old NAH and Monmouthshire Railways; the second route came in 1875 down the Sirhowy valley, the third in 1879 from Brynmawr, through Blaenavon and the Eastern Valley, and the fourth, also from Brynmawr, but down the Western Valley from 1905.

Until the rationalisation, which took place after the conversion of the broad gauge in 1872 and the acquisition of the MRCC by the GW in 1875, Newport had three stations, High Street, Dock Street and Mill Street. High Street was on the South Wales main line and was broad gauge until 1872. Dock Street was the terminus for the Western Valleys trains of the MRCC and the Sirhowy Railway. Mill Street was the terminus for the Eastern Valley trains of the MRCC and the NAH line trains from Hereford.

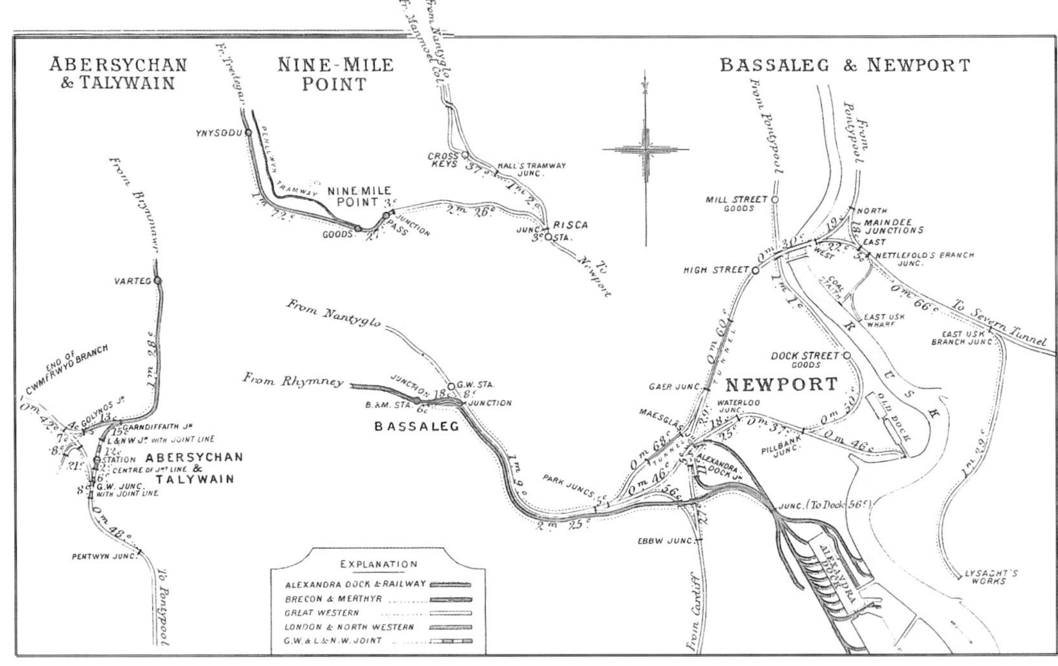

The railways of Newport, 1913. *Railway Clearing House*

1. MRCC ROUTE

The Monmouthshire Railway opened its Newport and Pontypool Eastern Valleys line on 30 June 1852 from a temporary station in Newport at Marshes Gate. This was superceded by Mill Street from November the following year; when the NAH started operations from Hereford to Newport on 2 January 1854, this was the station they used. Running powers had been negotiated between Newport and a junction south of Pontypool at Coed-y-gric, but these powers were not backed by any parliamentary Act. The first test train over the line on 9 November 1853 had in fact consisted of LNWR carriages, as Thomas Brassey was contracted to run the NAH using LNWR rolling stock until 1855. From April 1854 goods traffic ran through Mill Street station to terminate at the docks.

The next sign of the LNWR occurred on the 1 January 1862 when it announced the operating of through carriages from the rest of its system over the S & H and West Midland, in exercise of the running powers being acquired with the purchase of the lease of the S & H. It looks as though this was jumping the gun. For a start, Brassey's lease of the S & H did not expire until the 1st April, and secondly the S & H had running powers over the NAH only as far as Pontypool Road; the NAH was in no position to grant the S & H running powers south of Pontypool Road since it was itself dependent not on an Act of Parliament but on bilateral negotiation. Not surprisingly, therefore, the WestMR disputed the LNW's right to haul these trains with its own engines and actually placed a locomotive blocking the track at Hereford. With effect from 1 June 1862 this was resolved as part of the Act authorising the lease of the S & H to the GW, LNW and WestMR. Initially, the GW operated the passenger trains but in 1863 the LNW negotiated running powers over the MRCC and, until the end of 1865, ran its own trains into Newport hauled by its own engines. Thereafter LNWR carriages were hauled by the GW until August 1873, when one passenger train a day ran to and from Liverpool, and continued until 1879. On 18 March 1874 it was decided to start fast trains from Newport Mill Street, once the PCN was completed. This PCN, the Pontypool, Caerleon & Newport, provided the GW with a direct line from

Pontypool to High Street Station and diverted most of the traffic off the old MRCC line. From 1875, three LNW trains between Shrewsbury and Hereford were extended to Newport, but they too ceased in 1879 in favour of a rationalised service with the GWR. From 1880 High Street superceded Mill Street which closed altogether. Several goods trains ran through to the Dock station and this traffic continued into LMS days.

2. SIRHOWY ROUTE

The second route to Newport lay down the Sirhowy valley. The upper Sirhowy valley was rich in coal and, at the head, Tredegar was one of the early iron centres. However, the movement of coal and iron products down to Newport was handicapped by the fact that the MRCC and, from 1875, the GWR controlled access to Newport south of Nine Mile Point. Until the grouping most of the south-bound mineral traffic was taken out of the valley at Bird-in-Hand Junction on the Vale of Neath line and switched down the Rhymney valley at Hengoed to Aber sidings, where trains for Newport were marshalled and handed over to the Alexandra Docks Railway for completion of the journey. Coal bound for Cardiff docks also found its way on to the Rhymney at this point. A complementary movement was made by the GWR, which moved Aberdare coal trains, bound for southern England, onto the Sirhowy line at Bird-in-Hand, thus by-passing Pontypool Road. After the grouping Sirhowy valley coal was taken directly through Nine Mile Point, where a GWR locomotive took over the train.

Passenger trains were able to serve Newport directly over the MRCC lines, and from the four trains a day with three on Sundays operated by the Sirhowy, the LNW built up to a pattern of some eight trains a day in each direction, most of them all the way to Nantybwch, though with

Sirhowy valley train at Newport headed by LMS 0-6-0T No. 41204 (after 1934, No. 7394) and before the introduction of bogie carriages.

H.T. Hobbs/R.C. Riley Coll.

Some twenty years later, BR No. 41204 heads the 9.05 a.m. to Nantybwch at Newport; 13 September 1951.

H.C. Casserley

none on Sundays. Until 1880 the LNW went on using Dock Street as its terminus in Newport for the Sirhowy line, but in 1879 a connecting line from Park Junction through the Gaer tunnel enabled trains from the Western Valleys to gain access to High Street. Dock Street became a goods station. Thus, for that five year period from 1875 to 1880, the LNW was in the unusual position of having access to two terminal stations, Dock Street and Mill Street, in the same town, little more than a mile apart and facing in opposite directions. In 1932 there was an effort on the Sirhowy branch to improve the service; in order to attempt to meet competition from buses, the services were increased to 12 trains a day. Simultaneously corridor coaches appeared on the MTA. In 1935 the four-wheeled LNW carriages, until then used for scheduled trains on the Sirhowy, were replaced by corridor carriages.

In addition to scheduled trains there were a number of excursion trains. Before the First

Brynmawr Station, facing Abergavenny, photographed from the bay platform used for Western Valley trains. What at first sight appears to be graffiti is, in fact, an advertisement for excursion trains to Barry Island via the Sirhowy Valley (fare 5/8d). It was at this platform that the directors' special train was parked overnight on 18 July 1945; 13 July 1958.

H.C. Casserley

An excursion train of the type advertised in white paint on the fence at Brynmawr winds its intricate way from Tredegar to Barry through Beddau Loop Junction; no date.

Derek Chaplin

World War these were mainly to the north and Scotland; a sleeping car for the trains to Edinburgh would normally be added at Abergavenny. After the war the excursions were directed mainly to the seaside at Barry, with as many as five trains on a summer Saturday; there were also special trains to and from international rugby matches. In addition, there was a considerable commuter service for coal miners; any one colliery could well require as many as a thousand men to travel to work by train.

Carriages reserved for miners' trains on the carriage sidings at Brynmawr. This set was composed of former North London Railway first-class four wheelers; 13 September 1951.

H.C. Casserley

The journey from Newport to Nantybwch was full of interest as the Sirhowy valley is scenic, with steep hills on both sides of the river for much of the way, and at one time there was impressive industrial activity, especially in the area to the south of Tredegar.

The LMS train standing in the platform at Newport was very much a visitor on alien territory, Newport sharing with Merthyr, Carmarthen and Brecon the characteristic of hosting LMS as well as GW trains. D.S.M. Barrie described a journey from here to Nantybwch which contributes to the following exercise in historical reconstruction. The journey started southward in the direction of Cardiff through the tunnel at the western end of Newport Station. The GW main line was left shortly after the tunnel as the line for the Western Valleys bore away to the right and through another tunnel, to a junction with the old MRCC line from the dock area; this was then visible on the left. At this point, the so-called 'Park Mile' began, over which a toll was payable to the owners of Tredegar Park. In the 1930s there were six tracks, as traffic from the Sirhowy and Western Valleys shared the line with traffic from the B & M and Pontypridd. After Bassaleg, where the Alexandra and B & M diverged to the left, the tracks were reduced to four, as the line followed the wide valley of the Ebbw past the extensive coal sidings at Rogerstone.

At Risca the mountains begin to close in and it is not obvious where the railway was able to find its way around the steep and massive slopes which fill the scene on three sides. The Western Valleys line made its way sharply right after the station and the Sirhowy followed the eponymous river to the left, closely hugging the slopes of Machen mountain on the left-hand side. Just over two miles up the narrow valley was Nine Mile Point where the ownership of the line changed to LMS. Nine miles was the distance from the original tramroad terminal in

Nine Mile Point, looking up-valley; 12 July 1958.
R.M. Casserley

Newport. The station had both GW and LMS signal boxes though the station itself was LMS. At this point was a junction for the Penllwyn Tramway which was acquired by the LNW as part of the Sirhowy. From here the railway climbed up the side of the mountain on the western side of the steep valley and the Penllwyn Tramway ran parallel on the other side of the river, lower down in the valley. Past the Wyllie Colliery the line emerged onto a wide area of more level ground prior to crossing the Vale of Neath line at Pontllanfraith.

Ynysddu Station, looking down-valley; 11 July 1958.
H.C. Casserley

Wyllie Halt on a wet day, looking down-valley; 12 July 1958.
H.C. Casserley

It was here that the line crossed the GW, with complicated connections to and from it at a junction, originally called Tredegar Junction. Later this became a series of junctions, Sirhowy Junction, Tredegar Junction Lower, and Bird-in-Hand. Past Pontllanfraith High Level Station, the valley became narrow and steep-sided again, and the railway climbed up the west side, high above the river, through Blackwood, Argoed and Hollybush. On the other side of the valley, Hall's Tramroad was visible on the side of the steep mountain. Then the evidence of mining returned; Pochin and Bedwellty Pits filled the valley with men, machines, smoke and tips.

Argoed, looking south, after closure.
NMRW

Argoed, looking north; 1939.
LGRP 11352/ R.M. Casserley Coll.

Hollybush Station, looking up-valley. The works appear to be demolition rather than repair, suggesting a date after closure to passengers.
NMRW

Winter I—at Bedwellty Pits Halt in January 1960.
Alan Jarvis

Winter II—at Tredegar with a train from Newport; January 1960.
Alan Jarvis

Tredegar Station, looking north; 13 July 1958.
H.C. Casserley

At Tredegar the valley broadens again, and the rows of houses and modern warehouses of the 1990s give little clue to the industrial toil and sweat which produced coal and iron on the very edge of the town, and filled the place with noise, dirt and smoke. The line had been doubled all the way to just south of Tredegar in the 1890s, but from here to Nantybwch it was single until the end. Tredegar Station was rebuilt by the LMS in 1932; the single-storey brick building was not unprepossessing and was quite an improvement on the previous wooden shed. There was also an engine shed housing, in the 1930s, some 15 locomotives. At that time most of the trains both passenger and goods were worked by 'Coal Tanks' or 0-8-4Ts. Beyond Tredegar the line climbed steeply at 1:42 past the Tredegar ironworks on the left and the ruins of the old Sirhowy works on the right. Sirhowy Station had two platforms. Just over a mile further on the line joined the MTA at Nantybwch, a desolate location in the midst of the mountains, where even today, in spite of rows of houses and a children's playground, it is possible to sense the contrast between the teeming industry down the valley and the wilderness out on the top.

This industrial activity generated a heavy freight traffic, with 50 to 60 trains a day operating in each direction over all or part of the line from the 1870s until well into the 1950s. Assuming 20 12-ton waggons per train for 250 days a year, that amounts to about 2½ million tons. As a cross-check, J.M. Dunn counted 33,560 waggons moved on the line during March 1928, of which 8,559 moved in and out of the Tredegar Iron & Coal Co. On a rough calculation and assuming 12 ton waggons of which half were empty that also represents some 2½ million tons a year. Not all of this was routed northward, part going to Newport and part to Cardiff.

3. Blaenavon route

The third route to Newport lay over the high point at Waunavon where, from 1912, the GWR provided a passenger service between Newport and Brynmawr on behalf of both companies. This was closed in 1941. The LNW's High Level Blaenavon Station was located at some distance from the town, on the other side of the valley, and so passenger traffic was never very busy. More important was the coal traffic, from the rich steam-coal mines around Blaenavon; it reached a peak of 1 million tons a year, but the LMS locomotive shed was closed in 1942 due to the decline in traffic. The Blaenavon Iron & Steel Works also closed in the 1930s. J.M. Dunn was in charge of the locomotives at Blaenavon in the late 1920s, and in his *Reflections* he wrote a graphic description of the operation of the massive 0-8-4T engines on the Blaenavon line and of the hardships in winter.

On 14 January 1961 locomotive No. 7241 was photographed at various locations on the line, here at Furnace sidings just above Blaenavon. Before nationalisation the GW handled traffic south of Abersychan and Talywain.

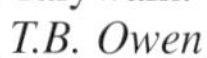

T.B. Owen

Empty waggons at Furnace sidings.
T. B. Owen

7210 takes water at the former joint LNWR/GWR station at Abersychan and Talywain.
T.B. Owen

Climbing towards Abersychan on the former GWR line lower down the valley.
T.B. Owen

4. Brynmawr & Western Valleys

The passenger service over the fourth route was also operated by the GWR starting from Brynmawr over the Brynmawr & Western Valleys Railway, the 1¼ mile jointly owned link between Brynmawr and the old MRCC line at Nantyglo. The nearby goods line was important to the LNWR as it served the Rose Heyworth Colliery which supplied much of the LNW and later LMS steam coal.

The LNWR also operated coal trains from the Sirhowy valley to Cardiff. This was achieved by transferring to the Rhymney valley at Ystrad Mynach, after running on the Taff Vale Extension of the old NAH from Tredegar Junction. These amounted to some 9 trains a day at the peak in 1913, perhaps 1 million tons a year, and comparable to the volume carried by the GWR over the Vale of Neath line to England for many years. The pure LNW goods activity based on the Tyndall Street depot was confined to general merchandise, and until the First World War some six trains a day were run over the Rhymney to and from the LNW's own territory, hauled by LNWR engines. The LNWR also kept a 'coal tank' stationed at the Rhymney's depot in Cardiff docks to haul trains on the half mile branch to Tyndall Street. This was closed in 1933 as part of a general harmonisation of facilities between the GWR and LMS.

Passenger train operations to Cardiff were interesting though minimal. As soon as the joint line from Nantybwch was in operation in 1871, trains from Abergavenny terminated at Rhymney at a bay platform at the north end of the up platform. This service continued until the LNW reached Dowlais Top in 1873. Cardiff (R.R.) was quoted as a destination in LNW timetables from the early 1860s.

The north bay at Rhymney Station was for a short time the terminus of MTA trains from Abergavenny. The locomotive is RR No. 37; 25 July 1922.
R.S. Carpenter

Long-distance workings consisted initially of up to three LNW carriages attached and detached at Rhymney Bridge, and connecting Cardiff with Liverpool twice a day with a journey time of nearly nine hours. These carriages had to be adapted for two braking systems. This service then became once a day to both Manchester and Liverpool and two to Crewe, but ceased for good in the First World War. It must have been an interesting ride out of Cardiff, up to the Caerphilly tunnel, through Caerphilly and up the Rhymney valley, all the way to the top at Rhymney Bridge and then onto the MTA. But it was no bonanza for the LNW. For a time between the wars it was replaced by an LMS through carriage from Leeds and Manchester to Cardiff via Pontypool Road and Newport. For a time there was also a through train from Liverpool and Birkenhead to Cardiff over the same route.

Turning to the hard fought western end of the MTA line from Rhymney Bridge to Dowlais and Merthyr, it is doubtful how remunerative this proved to be. It was certainly much less busy than the eastern end, and the rate of locomotive coal consumption over the whole of the MTA was twice the national average. Freight traffic was mainly iron ore and products in connection with the works at Dowlais, but, already in 1891, part of the production had moved to Cardiff, and the plant closed completely in 1930. In 1909, the working timetable showed only one mineral train a day from Merthyr, out of the 13 scheduled to pass through Abergavenny Junction. The Cwm Bargoed branch tapped opencast workings, and Merthyr was a source of general goods traffic. It was also the terminus for most passenger trains on the line. These amounted to eight or nine a day in each direction for many years. Apart from these purely local trains, the LNW and later the LMS operated one through train a day from Shrewsbury to Merthyr which changed engines at Abergavenny Brecon Road. By 1934 this was reduced to a through carriage attached to a GWR train from Shrewsbury to Abergavenny. Oddly, the return journey started at Dowlais High Street. On summer Saturdays there was also for many years a train from Merthyr to Blackpool.

Passenger train operations centred on Brynmawr, which had an intense service for many years with some eight or nine trains to Merthyr and as many as eleven to Abergavenny, some starting at Tredegar. The Merthyr trains connected at Nantybwch for Tredegar and Newport, and at Rhymney Bridge for Cardiff. For many years Ebbw Vale enjoyed a service of seven trains a day which in the 1920s was boosted to 18 and, by 1934, 21, in an attempt to combat the bus. The Blaenavon line had four or five GW and LNW trains as far as Abersychan and Talywain. In the 1930s, by which time the GW had taken over the service, it was extended to Newport with six or seven trains a day. The GW also operated a service of as many as 18 trains down the Western Valley line, either to Aberbeeg or all the way to Newport. Thus at one time it was possible to find over 30 services a day from Brynmawr down a choice of three valleys to Newport, where, as Barrie records, as many as 750,000 tickets (including GWR) were sold in a year.

The carriage sidings at Brynmawr. The date of the picture is uncertain but is probably *c.* 1930.
Old Bakehouse Publications

Our focus now shifts to the west, to Swansea and the Central Wales line. Until 1863 the LNW had no access to Swansea. The Midland

LNW 0-8-0 No. 8945 with a Swansea-bound train, 15 August 1927.
H.T. Hobbs/R.W. Kidner Coll.

publicised a through route via Gloucester from the South Wales Railway to towns in the midlands, but this was only a ticketing arrangement. At that date, running powers, which had been negotiated in 1863 over the Vale of Neath Railway, combined with the S & H running powers over the NAH Taff Vale Extension, enabled both the LNWR and the Midland to reach Swansea, but these powers were only exercised by the LNW and for freight. Even this ceased in 1868 when the Central Wales line opened throughout. The Midland made no attempt to develop the route. From 1868 and until some time early in the twentieth century they were exercised by the LNW only once a year. In 1874 the Midland agreed with the LNW not to exercise its rights, and was in breach for only a few weeks in 1889 during a dispute with the Neath & Brecon (see Chapter 6).

The opening of services over the Central Wales line enabled the LNW to by-pass the Vale of Neath route. The first LNW passenger train into Swansea over the new route was in 1868. The first through service was between Craven Arms and Swansea and four trains a day each

At Llandilo Station, an ex-LNWR 'Prince of Wales' tank engine No. 6986 heads a train for Swansea in 1928. The bay platform, to the right, accommodated trains for Carmarthen.
LGRP 16009/NRM

way were provided, taking between four and five hours. By 1913 two of these trains ran from Shrewsbury. An engine shed with capacity for 50 locomotives was constructed on the south side of the track just outside Victoria at Paxton Street and remained in use until the end of steam. The Llanelly Railway opened a freight service between Llandilo and Carmarthen in November 1864, followed by passenger trains from 1 June 1865. From 1t June 1868 the LNWR obtained running powers over the Llanelly which included the line to Carmarthen, and it seems that the first step was to introduce a through carriage once a day from London to Carmarthen.

The busy platform at Llandrindod Wells with a crowd waiting to board the Birmingham train; *c.* 1905.
Warwick County Archives

The next developments followed the growth of the spas. When the Central Wales first reached Llandrindod, it was a minor resort, known for its health-giving waters, but inaccessible and little used. The railway suddenly made possible travel from all parts of the country and during the next two decades holiday facilities were built. In 1883 Llangammarch, Llanwrtyd and Llandrindod all had 'Wells' added to their station names. By the turn of the century Llandrindod, the largest of them, was receiving some 100,000 people every year. The sight of Eastbourne transposed into the Welsh hills can, at first, strike the unsuspecting visitor as odd, but an impressive town was built to entertain a wealthy clientele, who mainly arrived by rail, and who kept the economy booming through into the period between the wars. Today, the high brick mansions and elaborate hotel façades, set in formal gardens, mainly serve to accommodate the administrators of Radnor and Powys, but they still have some of the style and atmosphere of the late Victorians who built them.

The through carriage for Birmingham behind a 2-4-2T locomotive about to depart from Llandrindod Wells, *c.* 1905.
Warwick County Archives

Another busy scene at Llandrindod Wells in 1905. The Shrewsbury train is hauled by two 2-4-2Ts.

National Railway Museum

FOUR WELSH SPAS

LLANDRINDOD STATION.

INTRODUCTION.

To "Take the Waters." An excuse sufficient to allay the conscience of the most busy of men and the most home-devoted of women, sufficient for contented resignation to a holiday otherwise begrudged. An added interest to the pleasure seeker, and a necessity to the poor in health, presented to them all in the most exquisite of settings. Here in Wales, at our very doors, these springs—the flowing crystal jewels of Earth—arise in sun-lit valleys, spread with flowers and cut by glistening brooks and rock-strewn rivers, whose banks are fringed by trees and fresh green undergrowth listening to the ever murmuring voices of the running, tumbling waters. Upwards from the valleys roll the slopes of hills with dark toned grass and sombre firs to the distant mountains, in their mantles of purple, cloud clad and mysterious. From above come the song of birds and the sweet breezes sweeping between the blue sky and the green earth.

TOILET.

This is the land of LLANDRINDOD, BUILTH, LLANGAMMARCH, and LLANWRTYD, the "Four Welsh Spas," which are increasing in popularity as fashionable health resorts year by year. Renowned since many years amongst the Welsh residents, the waters of these Spas equal, if they do not even excel, those of the famous English and Continental resorts to which thousands flock every year, and rival them in beauty and variety of scenery. Here can thousands meet, and yet attain rest and quiet in the lovely solitudes of these hills and

FOLDING TABLE.

THROUGH CORRIDOR LAVATORY CARRIAGE.

An example of the LNWR's exuberant publicity for the Central Wales line. The well-known photograph, which appears on the previous page, was probably taken expressly for publicity purposes and has been cleverely adapted by the photographic processor.

PRO RAIL 410/1991

At summer weekends, special trains were run to the new resorts from Birmingham and Wolverhampton. Through carriages were introduced between Swansea and Manchester, Liverpool, York and Euston. The fare charged to Euston was the same as by the GWR to Paddington, in spite of the much greater distance. There was also a daily through carriage between Manchester and Carmarthen, and on summer Saturdays a through carriage from Liverpool to Pembroke Dock. The York carriage from Swansea gave the name of the 'York Mail' to its train, and, by 1922, was picking up a mail van from Carmarthen at Llandilo. These facilities were promoted heavily with advertisements and a variety of publications.

Morning departure from Swansea with BR Standard Class 5 No. 73035 on 9 March 1961. *Huw Daniel*

When the LMS took over in 1923 they made little change, though in 1924 a through train a day each way between Euston and Carmarthen was introduced. Six trains a day were run between Shrewsbury and Swansea. Through carriages to English cities ceased in the Second World War, though the 'York Mail' survived until nationalisation.

Besides these through services, there were local trains, between Craven Arms and Knighton, Llandovery and Builth Road, and at the other end of the line, between Swansea and Pontardulais and Gowerton and Llanmorlais. The GWR operated trains between Llandovery, Pontardulais and Llanelly. An intermediate engine shed was built at Llandovery and for a time housed the 0-8-4T locomotives used for banking up to Sugar Loaf summit. An earlier Vale of Towy shed became first Llanelly then GW property and closed in 1935. There was also a small shed at Builth Road.

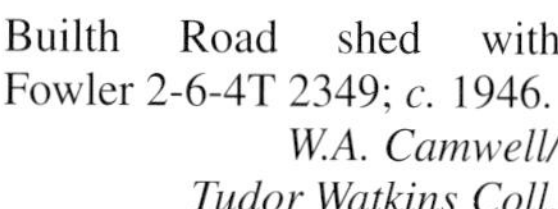
Builth Road shed with Fowler 2-6-4T 2349; *c.* 1946. *W.A. Camwell/ Tudor Watkins Coll.*

The former LNW locomotive shed at Llandovery; 15 May 1964. *Alan Jarvis*

Goods traffic was also developed. By 1913 there were some five through trains a day in each direction for minerals, coal or general goods. Through trains operated daily between Swansea and Liverpool and Burton-on-Trent. Fish trains from Swansea and Milford Haven were marshalled at Llandilo. Carmarthen market generated a considerable cattle traffic and there were intermediate local goods services for example to Llandovery and to Llandrindod, from Shrewsbury or Craven Arms.

Although the Carmarthen line was used spasmodically as a through trunk line, it was mainly a rural branch. The five or six trains a day in each direction were reduced to three in the Second World War, but five were restored after the war. Until grouping, the carriages used were ancient six-wheelers, but after grouping some bogie carriages from the North Stafford found their way to the line. It remained something of an anomoly until final closure in 1963.

To assess the LNWR's trade in south Wales we have to take a macro view. As we noted earlier, 1913 was the peak year of Welsh coal production. At 57 million tons, this was coincidentally the tonnage of freight of all kinds carried by the LNWR across the whole of Britain in that same year. At least half of Welsh coal production was exported, leaving a balance of some 20 million tons for inland consumption in Wales and England. While total production gradually declined, the inland share remained at a fairly constant level, with a boost during the Second World War. During the war, the Central Wales line peaked at about a million tons of freight, from a norm of only two thirds that size. Its normal tonnage was not much more than the 400,000 tons of iron ore hauled by the GWR up to Dowlais over the joint Bargoed Taff line. By contrast, during the first half of this century the Sirhowy valley generated as much as 2.5 million tons of coal traffic and the Blaenavon area another million. Between Ebbw Vale and Beaufort, the mountains were peppered with mine shafts, though their production peaked earlier, and was shared with the GWR. W.W. Tasker quotes a peak activity of 5,000 tons of coal a day being moved northward through Abergavenny in 1916. This is some 1.5 million tons a year in about 20 trains a day. The working timetables suggest that this level of activity was sustained from the 1880s through to the 1920s. With another 1 million tons through Cardiff and probably no less through Newport, some 5 million tons of coal and minerals were probably being moved by the LNW throughout that period. This approximate equality between Abergavenny Junction, Newport and Cardiff as exit points for coal and minerals is borne out by the 1909 Working Timetable which lists 13 trains down to Tredegar Junction, and another 13 down the Eastern Valley to Talywain, as well as the 13 to Abergavenny mentioned earlier. In addition, there would have been unscheduled coal trains. At this level the tonnages were of great importance even if the management did not know how profitable they were. At the peak, the tonnages were remarkably similar to those on the Midland, but the costs were greater, more being hauled against the gradient, and the distances were longer; accordingly the profitability was probably less.

On 17 July 1945, the chairman and board of the LMS made what proved to be a farewell tour of south Wales. The special train consisted of a brake first, 1st Class sleeper No. 308, a 1st Class diner, and saloon No. 45005. It left Euston at seven o'clock in the evening, and the first overnight stop was on a siding at Newport (Salop). The next day, they went down the Central Wales line to Swansea, arriving just after lunch. They were then taken back to Craven Arms, down to Abergavenny and up to Brynmawr, where they arrived at five to eleven. There they spent the second night, alongside the bay platform for the Western Valley trains. Next day they visited Merthyr and then travelled back to Nantybwch and down to Nine Mile Point and Newport. The former Midland lines were omitted, though the return to London had a strong Midland flavour being by way of Gloucester, Cheltenham, Evesham, Stratford, and Bedford, ending at St. Pancras. The management brief, complete with hand-drawn and coloured map, was informative, not only about the industrial and commercial situation, but it also included choice pieces of relevant local and national history, spiced with literary allusions written by F.H. Fisher. He even offered an explanation of the name 'Ystalyfera', meaning, he suggested, 'Go, catch that haystack'. This was believed to originate in a period of flood, when a local farmer saw his haystack being washed away and told his dog to go after it. Sadly, this imaginative explanation finds little favour with Welsh speakers.

The effect of the war had been mixed; for instance, on the Central Wales line there were now 11 freight trains a day of up to 37 waggons (approx. 1 m. tons a year) while before the war there had been only seven. The Midland line had seen little war traffic, mainly because of the gradients, but there had been some additional coal movements from the Neath valley to Peterborough, avoiding London. In 1909, as noted earlier, this line had moved an average of 3,900 waggons a month (say 500,000 tons a year or 9 trains a day). Waunavon was producing 900 tons of coal a day for movement by the LMS, expected to rise shortly to 15,000 per week (750,000 tons a year). Blaenavon was shipping 5,000 tons a week, as was Tredegar, but this was only 60% of pre-war volumes. Pochin shipped 4,000 tons a week. On the Central Wales, Gorseinon and Gowerton steel-works were expected to become obsolete, and the outlook was dismal for the Swansea valley tin-plate works. The number of private sidings, once 70, was down to 45 and the anthracite fields were seriously depleted.

War damage had been limited to Swansea, St. Thomas suffering from blast and Victoria from a direct hit on the telegraph office and on the main line, all in 1943. The resulting damage to the glass of the overall roof was never fully repaired. Capital investment had been required to meet increased traffic density by providing more siding capacity at Craven Arms and a crossing loop at Sugar Loaf summit. Now, a turntable large enough for 2-8-0 locomotives was needed at Llandovery.

Passenger bookings in 1944 had been:

Builth Rd.	8,556
Nantybwch	11,160
Abergavenny (Brecon Rd)	16,934
Knighton	18,983
Llanwrtyd	21,703
Llandrindod	21,703
Swansea Victoria	40,395
Brynmawr	96,794

So Brynmawr, besides being at the heart of the largest freight operations, was also top of

This familiar photograph illustrates how busy Brynmawr Station was. At the bay on the left is the 4.58 p.m. to Pontypool Crane Street by way of the Blaenavon line. In the centre distance, in the other bay, is a train for the Western Valley. To the right is the 4.30 p.m. from Tredegar to Abergavenny; 7 July 1938.

H.C. Casserley

Railway Station--Time Table.

Arriving	From *	Departing	To
6.30 a.m.	Abergavenny & North	*6.35 a.m.	Cardiff, Merthyr
6.53 ,,	.. Ebbw Vale		& Newport
7.5 ,,	.. Aberbeeg	7.1 ,,	.. Abergavenny
7.18 ,,	.. Blaenavon	7.20 ,,	.. Western Valley
7.22 ,,	Merthyr & Cardiff	7.30 ,,	Abergavenny & North
8.24 ,,	..Abergavenny	8.30 ,,	Cardiff & Merthyr
8.25 ,,	.. Ebbw Vale	8.35 ,,	.. Ebbw Vale
8.28 ,,	..Newport, &c.	E8.45 ,,	.. Newport, &c.
8.40 ,,	.. Merthyr	9.15 ,,	.. Western Valley
9.0 ,,	Western Valley	10.0 ,,	Abergavenny & North
9.40 ,,	Western Valley	10.14 ,,	Newport & Tredegar
9.46 ,,	.. Ebbw Vale	10.20 ,,	.. Ebbw Vale
9.56 ,,	.. Merthyr	*10.20 ,,	.. Abergavenny
10.0 ,,	..Abergavenny	10.32 ,,	Abergavenny & North
10.9 ,,	.. Abersychan	10.52 ,,	Car., Mer., & Newport
10.27 ,,	Car., Mer., & Newport	10.55 ,,	.. Ebbw Vale
10.43 ,,	Western Valley	10.55 ,,	.. Abersychan
10.47 ,,	Abergavenny & North	11.1 ,,	.. Western Valley
10.48 ,,	.. Ebbw Vale	12.15 p.m.	.. Western Valley
11.53 ,,	Western Valley	1.4 ,,	.. Western Valley
12.48 p.m.	Western Valley	*1.35 ,,	Dowlais & Tredegar
*1.30 ,,	Abergavenny	2.8 ,,	Abergavenny & North
1.50 ,,	.. Ebbw Vale	2.20 ,,	Cardiff & Merthyr
E1.56 ,,	..Newport, &c.	E2.35 ,,	.. Newport, &c.
2.4 ,,	Car., Mer., & Newport	2.53 ,,	.. Western Valley
2.17 ,,	Abergavenny & North	3.28 ,,	Abergavenny & North
2.28 ,,	Western Valley	3.57 ,,	.. Western Valley
3.15 ,,	.. Ebbw Vale	4.20 ,,	.. Ebbw Vale
3.26 ,,	.. Merthyr	4.20 ,,	Car., Mer., & Newport
3.44 ,,	Western Valley	4.55 ,,	.. Abergavenny
4.0 ,,	.. Newport	4.59 ,,	.. Western Valley
4.15 ,,	..Abergavenny	5.41 ,,	Cardiff and Merthyr
4.41 ,,	Western Valley	5.55 ,,	.. Ebbw Vale
E5.32 ,,	.. Newport	6.7 ,,	Abergavenny & North
5.40 ,,	Abergavenny & North	E6.20 ,,	.. Newport, &c.
5.43 ,,	.. Ebbw Vale	6.49 ,,	.. Western Valley
6.4 ,,	Car., Mer., & Newport	7.39 ,,	Cardiff & Merthyr
6.39 ,,	Western Valley	7.45 ,,	.. Ebbw Vale
7.33 ,,	.. Ebbw Vale	7.50 ,,	.. Abergavenny
7.34 ,,	Abergavenny & North	7.55 ,,	.. Abersychan
7.36 ,,	.. Abersychan	8.24 ,,	.. Western Valley
7.47 ,,	Cardiff & Merthyr	9.37 ,,	Cardiff & Merthyr
8.6 ,,	Western Valley	10.5 ,,	.. Ebbw Vale
S9.25 ,,	.. Abersychan	*10.5 ,,	.. Blaenavon
9.32 ,,	Abergavenny & North	S10.5 ,,	.. Abersychan
9.45 ,,	.. Ebbw Vale	10.13 ,,	.. Abergavenny
9.50 ,,	Western Valley	10.53 ,,	.. Western Valley
10.10 ,,	Car., Mer., & Newport	W—Wednesdays and Saturdays only.	
10.36 ,,	Western Valley	*—Tuesdays only.	
11.30 ,,	Western Valley	S—Saturdays only.	
W12.20 ,,	Western Valley	E—Eastern Valley.	

Stationmaster, Mr. Kavenagh. Goods Agent, Mr. Humphreys.

This local timetable, advertised in Brynmawr in 1909, demonstrates the level of activity at this station. Mr Kavenagh, the station master mentioned, was a long serving LNWR employee who retired sick in July 1914. He was succeeded by Mr Humphreys.

Old Bakehouse Publications

the league by a long way for passengers, though almost certainly the tickets sold were for short journeys and many at so-called 'workman's' rates. Brynmawr Station must have been a busy place in the early years of the twentieth century.

With all that activity at Brynmawr, it may seem odd that the directors chose to spend the night there. But at 1,200 ft, in the middle of the mid-summer night, after the last train had left, and they had sipped their nightcaps and toddled along to the sleeping carriage, they may well have found an unexpected tranquillity, disturbed only by their collective snores; all the worries of their inheritance from Bailey, Banks, Batt, Benson, Biddulph, Bolden and Budd banished for the night.

The decline of the Welsh extractive industries started in earnest after the LMS had disappeared, and only those lines which have a strategic freight and passenger-carrying role survived to the end of the twentieth century; the old NAH main line and the MRCC which provided the LNW with running powers between Hereford and Newport, together with the Shrewsbury and Hereford, form part of the rail link between north and south Wales. Perversely, and triumphantly, the Central Wales line survives against the odds, rather like some of the more remote lines in Scotland. But of the Midland there is nothing left. The pioneers would hardly be surprised; they were clear-thinking businessmen who saw the railways as a way of reducing transport costs. They might be rather more surprised to see how many railways are preserved around Britain for reasons that have nothing whatsoever to do with economics.

Evening light at Abergavenny Junction, July 1951. *John Beardsmore*

BIBLIOGRAPHY AND SOURCES

Most of the material upon which this book is based lies in the Public Record Office at Kew and in the House of Lords Record Office. In addition, there is relevant material in the Brecon Museum, the Hereford Reference Library and Carmarthen Museum, and in the County Record Offices of Carmarthen, Glamorgan, Hereford and Gwent. The following publications also contain helpful and relevant material:

D.S.M. Barrie. *The Brecon & Merthyr Railway*. Oakwood. 1957.
D.S.M. Barrie. *The Rhymney Railway*. Oakwood. 1952.
D.S.M. Barrie. *South Wales Regional History*. David & Charles. 1980 (revised 1994).
D. Bayliffe & J. Harding. *Starling Benson of Swansea*. D. Brown. 1996.
H.C.H. Burgess. *Working with LMS Steam*. Bradford Barton. 1983.
R.V.J. Butt. *The Directory of Railway Stations*. Patrick Stephens. 1995.
W. Bradney. *History of Monmouthshire*. 1907
A. Byles. *The History of the Monmouthshire Railway & Canal Co*. Village Publishing. 1982.
R.A. Cook & C.R. Clinker. *Early Railways between Abergavenny & Hereford*. RCHS. 1984.
J.H. Davies. *History of Pontardawe and District*. Christopher Davies. 1967.
A. Doughty. *The Central Wales Line*. OPC. 1997.
J.M. Dunn. *Reflections on a Railway Career*. Ian Allan. 1966.
G.B. Jones & D. Dunstone. *The Vale of Neath Line*. Gomer. 1996.
H. Morgan. *South Wales Branch Lines*. Ian Allan. 1986.
G. Rattenbury & R. Cook. *The Hay & Kington Railways*. RCHS. 1996.
M.C. Reed. *The LNWR*. Atlantic. 1996.
J.B. Sinclair & R.W.D. Fenn. *A Kington Family*. Mid-Border Books. 1992
J.B. Sinclair & R.W.D. Fenn. *The Facility of Locomotion*. Mid-Border Books. 1991.
D.J. Smith. *Shrewsbury to Swansea*. Town & Country Press. 1971.
M. Smith. *Portrait of the Central Wales Line*. Ian Allan. 1995.
W.L. Steel. *History of the LNWR*. 1914.
C.E. Stretton. *History of the Midland Railway*. 1901.
W. Tasker. *The Merthyr, Tredegar & Abergavenny Railway*. OPC. 1986.
W. Tasker. *Railways in the Sirhowy Valley*. Oakwood. 1992.
Transactions of the Radnorshire Society. Vol. LV. 1985.

INDEX

A

Abercrave 17, 197
Aberdare 13, 37
Abergavenny 9, 10-11, 14, 51, 54, 119, 246
  Brecon Road engine shed 56-59, 119
  Brecon Road Station 53-54, 58, 70, 119
  Junction 35-36, 58, 62, 66, 69, 70-73, 119, 247, 249
Abersychan & Talywain 74, 76, 230, 238
Act of Parliament
  Brecon & Merthyr 1862 98
  Brecon & Merthyr 1863 98
  Brecon & Merthyr (Arrangement) 1868 170
  Brecon & Merthyr (Extensions) 1860 97
  Brecon & Merthyr (Extensions) 1861 88
  Brecon & Merthyr Junction 1859 96
  Brecon & Merthyr (New Lines) 1864 99
  Brecon & Merthyr No.1 1864 99
  Brecon & Merthyr (Various Powers) 1865 99
  Central Wales Railway 1859 152
  Central Wales & Carmarthen Junction Railway 132, 155
  GWR (West Midland) 1863 168, 177
  Hereford & Brecon Railway 1859 159, 175
  Hereford, Hay & Brecon Railway 1869 170
  Hereford, Hay & Brecon (Deviation) 1860 159, 168
  Llanelly Railway & Dock1861 127
  Llanelly Railway & Dock1862 128
  Llanelly Railway & Dock1863 128
  Llanelly Railway & Dock (Capital) 1865 131
  LNWR (Additional Powers) 1866 169
  LNWR (Additional Powers) 1870 99
  LNWR (Joint & Various Powers) 1877 93
  LNWR (New Lines) 1867 70, 91, 99
  LNWR (New Lines & Additional Powers) 1875 103
  LNWR (Sirhowy Railway Vesting) 1876 87
  LNWR (Wales) 1874 103
  Merthyr, Tredegar & Abergavenny 1859 54, 98
  Merthyr, Tredegar & Abergavenny 1863 67
  Merthyr, Tredegar & Abergavenny 1866 70
  Merthyr, Tredegar & Abergavenny (Lease) 1862 60
  Midland Railway 1874 175
  Neath & Brecon Railway (Amalgamation & Arrangement) 1869 182
  Rhymney Railway (New Lines) 1866 91
  Rhymney Railway (Northern Lines) 1864 90
  Rumney & B & M 1863 98
  Shrewsbury & Hereford (Leasing) 1860 145
  Sirhowy Railway 1860 76
  Sirhowy Railway 1865 76, 84
  Swansea & Carmarthen Railway 1871 147
  Swansea Vale 1855 188, 189
  Worcester & Hereford 1853 29-31
Argoed 79, 235

B

Bailey, Crawshay 11, 52-53, 55, 57, 59, 70, 73, 119
Banks, W.L 19, 124, 160-61, 163, 177-78, 181-83
Bargoed Rhymney 88, 97-98, 111
Bargoed Taff 96, 246
Barry Railway 211
Batt, solicitor 54, 57, 62
Beaufort 21, 61, 114
Beaufort, Duke of 40, 135, 139, 187
Bedwellty Pits Halt 236
Benson, Starling 18-19, 181, 187, 195-96
Biddulph, John 19, 123-124, 126, 130, 135, 139, 144, 147, 151-52
Birkenhead 27, 196
Birmingham 37, 196, 225, 242
Birmingham & Gloucester Railway 15, 18, 24
Bishop, John 71, 87, 147
Bishop of St. David's 128
Black Mountain 11
Black Mountains 51, 199
Blackwood 79, 82-83, 235
Blaenavon 3, 11, 74-75, 78, 237
Blaen-y-cwm viaduct 66, 113
Board of Trade 64, 81, 84
Bolden 165-66, 168, 171-73
Boyle, John 88-91
Brecknock & Abergavenny Canal 51-52, 119, 159
Brecon 9-10, 16, 125-27, 157, 159, 178-79, 225
  Free Street 183, 185-86, 199, 200
  Mount Street 178, 184-86, 199
  Watton 178, 183-86
Brecon & Merthyr Railway 11, 46, 60, 67, 84, 88, 90, 96, 100, 102-03, 159, 161, 163, 165, 170, 176-178, 183-84, 186
Brecon Beacons 11, 38, 51, 95, 104

Breconshire Railway & Canal Co. 10
Bristol Channel 11, 96
Broad gauge 13, 34, 37, 40, 46, 86
Brown, Thomas 19, 25-26, 53, 55-57, 70
Brynamman 122, 130, 150, 191, 201, 203-04, 206-09, 225
Brynmawr 5, 52, 69, 115-16, 120, 232, 240, 247-48
Brynmawr & Blaenavon Railway 74
Brynmawr & Western Valleys Railway 88, 120, 239
Brunel, I.K. 25, 46, 187
Budd, J. Palmer 17, 19, 37, 44, 61, 123, 150, 159, 178, 187, 191, 193
Builth Road 142-43, 177, 245
Bute, Marquis of 40, 94

C

Cardiff 11-12, 14, 89, 91-94, 239, 246-47
Carmarthen 11-12, 14, 16, 124-28, 158, 242, 246
Carmarthen & Cardigan Railway 128
Carmarthen Fan 12
Carriages 43, 132
Cawdor, Lord 18
Cawkwell 62, 89, 147, 150
Cefn Coed 101, 103, 105, 106
Central Wales & Carmarthen Junction Railway (CW & CJ) 9, 155, 157
Central Wales Extension Railway (CWE) 129-30, 144-46, 152, 182
Central Wales Line 19, 23, 45, 47, 121, 139, 177, 241, 247, 249
Central Wales Railway (CWR) 45, 124, 130, 144-45
Chester & Holyhead Railway 15
Clydach 66, 68, 118
Clydach-on-Tawe 191, 194-95, 202
Clydach gorge 9, 13, 51, 56, 60, 62, 68, 73-74, 116-17
Coal traffic 14, 41, 43, 65, 86-87, 123, 135, 214-16, 224-225, 228, 231, 237, 239, 246-47
Colbren Junction 17, 37, 178, 181, 188, 201, 225
Conybeare 98, 126, 184
Craig-y-nos, *see* Penwyllt
Craven Arms 23, 130, 144, 241, 247
Cray 12, 181
Creden Hill 162
Cwmllynfell 208-09
Cynghordy 20, 47

D

Devynock 178, 180, 200
Dickson, John 132, 182-83
Dowlais 88, 93, 95-96, 99, 100, 177
  High Street 101, 109, 111
  Lloyd Street/Central 99-101, 107, 109
  Top 11, 100, 110-12
Dowlais Railway 95, 97-98
Dryslwyn 156
Dunvant 132

E

Eardisley 161
Ebbw Vale 65, 114, 240
Excursion trains 232-33

F

Fan Gyhirych 17, 200
Fforest Fawr 11-12, 38
Findlay, Sir George 45-46, 61, 64-65, 68, 87, 93, 96, 139, 147, 149-50

G

Gardner, John 55, 57, 60, 64, 74, 76, 98, 101
Gauge Commission 13
Gelli-felen 2, 60, 62, 71, 73, 116-17
Gilwern 9, 61, 66, 118
Glais 191, 202-03
Glasbury 161-62
Glascodine 147
Gloucester 13
Golden Valley line 36, 139
Gooch, Sir Daniel 86, 171
Goods traffic 47, 224-25, 230, 247
Gorseinon 218
Govilon 51-52, 54-55, 60, 118
Gower Road 128, 131
Gowerton (formerly Gower Road) 136, 154
Great Northern Railway 14
Great Western Railway (GWR) 13, 23-24, 26-27, 37, 41, 44-46, 65, 81, 84, 86-87, 94, 96, 144, 151, 159, 165, 168, 172-173, 175, 177, 207, 209, 211, 224-25, 230
Green-Price, Sir Richard 19, 139, 143-44, 178
Grierson 165, 169
Grundy, Frank 147, 157-58

Gurnos 208, 223, 228
Gwaen-Cae-Gurwen (GCG) 208
Gwys 208-09

H

Hay 166-67, 199
Hay Tramway 161, 178
Hereford 9, 13-14, 16, 21-22, 24, 27-30, 46, 159, 172, 197, 224, 225
  Barr's Court 22, 27-30, 169, 170-73, 175, 224-25
  Barton 22, 27-30, 159, 163, 168-75, 199, 224-25
  Moorfields 163, 168-71, 173, 224-25
Hereford, Hay & Brecon Railway (HHB) 9, 20, 46, 55, 146, 159, 160, 163, 165-66, 168-73, 183, 185, 196
Hereford, Ross & Gloucester Railway 30, 32, 40, 169, 224
Herefordshire & Gloucestershire Canal 18, 25, 30
Hill, Captain J.C. 54, 57, 60, 70
Hollybush 20, 87, 235
Homfray, Samuel 19, 78
Honddu viaduct 179, 183, 200
House of Commons 17, 20, 24, 29
House of Lords 20, 24, 27, 142, 151, 173
Huish, Capt. Mark 15, 29, 35, 41, 43

I

Iron trade 26, 52, 96, 214-15, 225, 240, 246-47
Iron works
  Blaenavon 237
  Cyfarthfa 95, 98
  Dowlais/Ivor 95-97, 99, 215
  Penydarren 95-96, 105
  Plymouth 95
  Sirhowy 215, 237
  Tredegar 215, 237

J

Johns 125-26

K

Killay 132
Knighton Railway 45, 124, 130, 144-45, 152

L

Lancashire & Yorkshire Railway 14
Liddell, Charles 24, 40-41, 43, 53
Liverpool 27
Llandilo 16, 18, 120, 122-23, 150-51, 156
Llandilo bridge 157
Llandovery 16, 120, 123-24, 145-46, 151, 160, 246
Llandrindod Wells 145-46, 242-44
Llanelly 13, 121, 151
Llanelly (Clydach gorge) 55, 57, 116
Llanelly Railway & Dock Co. 9, 11, 19, 37, 121, 124-25, 129-30, 135, 139, 142-44, 146, 150-52, 203, 205, 207, 242
Llanfoist 11
Llangammarch 178, 182
Llanvihangel Railway 51, 56
Llanwrtyd 142, 149
Locomotives
  BR — Class 5 142, 245
    2-6-0 161-162, 164, 167, 175
  Cambrian — 4-4-0 174
  GWR — 'Castle' class 34, 172
    'Hall' class 33
    0-6-0 33, 167, 177
    0-6-0T 136, 157
    2-8-0T 75
    2-8-2T 237-38
  LMS — 0-6-0T 134, 149, 223
    2-6-0 223
    2-6-2T 104
    2-6-4T 140, 220, 223
    Class 5 119, 121, 133, 142, 153, 221, 223
    'Jubilee' class 133
    2-8-0 223
  LNWR — 0-6-0 154, 222
    0-6-0ST 73, 220
    0-6-2T 57-58, 61, 79, 84, 94, 104, 113, 116, 129, 140-41, 220, 222, 237, 248
    0-8-0 2, 34, 58, 67, 69, 141-42, 220-22, 232, 241
    0-8-0 (compound) 59
    0-8-2T 220, 222
    0-8-4T 55, 59, 78, 113, 116, 220-22, 237, 245
    2-4-0 134, 222
    2-4-2T 130, 146, 155-56, 222, 242, 243
    4-6-0 34, 46, 220
    4-6-2T 222-23, 241

LYR 0-6-0 27-28, 46
Midland 0-4-4T 171, 174
0-6-0 228
0-6-0T 180, 223
RR 0-6-2T 89, 94
London 14, 23
London & Birmingham Railway 14, 16, 18
London & North Western Railway (LNWR) 9, 11-12, 14, 16, 19, 23-24, 26-27, 29, 32, 34-37, 40-47, 59-62, 64-65, 67-70, 74, 76, 81, 86, 88, 91-92, 94, 96, 98, 100, 103, 125, 130, 139, 142, 144-47, 150, 157-58, 165, 169, 173, 175, 176, 178, 182, 186, 209, 224-25, 229-31, 241, 246
London Financial Association 135, 137, 146-47
London, Midland & Scottish Railway (LMS) 12, 94, 144, 247
Lundie, Cornelius 91

M

Malvern 24, 26-27
Manchester, Sheffield & Lincolnshire Railway 14, 198
McCormick & Co. 57, 59-60, 163
Merthyr 11-13, 21, 93, 95, 98, 100, 102, 104
Merthyr, Tredegar & Abergavenny Railway (MTA) 9, 11, 19, 21, 45, 47, 52-60, 64-5, 67-70, 91, 96, 98, 105
Midland Railway 9, 12, 14-16, 18-19, 24, 26-7, 30, 32, 34, 39, 41, 43-4, 47, 87, 158-59, 166, 168, 172-73, 175, 177-78, 181, 185-86, 193, 195-97, 209, 211-13, 224-25
Mid-Wales Railway 130, 135, 143, 145, 159, 161, 176, 185
Mineral trade 216-17, 225, 246247
Monmouthshire Railway & Canal Co. 22, 37, 43, 47, 62, 74, 81-2, 84, 86-7, 177-78, 229, 231
Moon, Sir Richard 23, 35-37, 43-5, 59-60, 62, 66, 70-71, 73, 86-91, 93, 96, 139, 142-43, 147, 149, 150-52, 192, 214
Moorhampton 162-63
Morlais tunnel 100, 103, 107-08
Morris, George Byng 127, 139
Morriston 191, 195, 203
Mumbles 131-32
Mumbles Road 133
Mumbles tram 16
Mynydd Llangynidr 11

N

Nantybwch 54, 60, 62-64, 86, 88-91, 96, 98, 113, 224, 237
Nantyglo 51-52, 88, 115, 120, 239
Neath 13
Neath & Brecon Railway (N &B) 9, 12, 17-18, 38, 132, 159, 178, 181-83, 185-86, 197, 201, 225
Neath, Pontardawe & Brynamman Railway 209
Newport 11-13, 22, 37, 96, 229-30, 246-47
Dock Street 82, 232
Mill Street 229-32
High Street 229, 231-33
Newport, Abergavenny & Hereford Railway (NAH) 9, 16-17, 22, 24, 27, 29-30, 34-37, 41-42, 44, 51, 53, 55, 159, 224
Nine Mile Point 78, 81-82, 84, 88, 230-31, 233-34

O

'Old Rumney' Railway 46, 88, 98-99
Overend 130, 134
Overend Gurney 135, 182
Oxford, Worcester & Wolverhampton Railway (OWW) 15, 18, 23-24, 26, 32, 36, 40, 224
Oystermouth 16
Oystermouth Railway 127-28, 132, 139

P

Pant 98-101, 107
Pantyffynnon 122, 148-50
Pantyscallog 109, 111
Parliament 14, 16-19, 21, 24, 32, 34, 40-41, 44-46, 53, 67, 69-70, 76, 89, 94, 124, 126, 131, 146, 150, 172, 211
Passenger traffic 42, 209, 224-33, 237, 239, 240, 242-45, 247-48
Pembroke & Tenby Railway 157-58
Penclawdd 127, 154-55
Penson, R.K. 124, 131, 147, 160
Penwyllt 12-13, 17, 200-01
Pontardawe 188, 191, 201, 216, 229
Pontardulais 17, 122, 131, 135, 147-48, 150-51
Pontllanfraith 80-81, 234-35
Pontsarn 101, 103, 107
Pontypool 16, 22, 24
Pontypool, Caerleon & Newport line (PCN) 84, 230
Population figures 95, 215

Port Talbot Railway 211
Price, W.P. 25, 177, 195-96

Q

Quakers Yard 16, 37, 96

R

Rhondda & Swansea Bay Railway 211
Rhymney 89-91, 176
Rhymney Bridge 66-67, 73, 89-91, 96, 112-13
Rhymney Railway 66-67, 88, 90-91, 94, 96-97
Rich, Captain 81-82
Robertson, Henry 19, 22, 25, 27, 29, 59, 124-25, 130, 139, 143-46, 152, 182
Rose Heyworth Colliery 88, 107, 239

S

Savin, Thomas 19, 46, 101, 103, 124-26, 131, 161, 163, 168
Shrewsbury 13-14, 16, 22, 44, 121, 144
Shrewsbury & Crewe line 22-23, 45, 121, 144
Shrewsbury & Hereford Railway 19, 22, 24, 27, 29-30, 40, 45-46, 59, 130, 144-45, 152, 224, 230
Sirhowy 79-80, 237
Sirhowy Railway 19, 62, 65-67, 76-79, 81-86, 91, 94, 178
Six Pit 129, 187-89
Stoke Junction 18, 26
South Wales Railway (SWR) 15, 46, 123, 131, 187, 189, 241
Sugar Loaf (Abergavenny) 13, 116
Sugar Loaf (Central Wales) 145-46, 245, 247
Swansea 12-14, 16-17, 37, 39, 87, 121, 124, 127, 129, 131, 135-140, 144-45, 151, 160, 189, 190, 216-19, 225, 240
  Paxton Street shed 152, 221, 223, 242
  St. Thomas 8, 137, 198-99, 202, 210, 228-29, 247
  Victoria 121, 130, 137-38, 140, 152-53, 247
Swansea & Carmarthen Railway 147, 150, 155
Swansea Bay 16, 126-27
Swansea Junction Extension Railway 18, 37, 38-39, 41, 121, 159, 188
Swansea Vale and Neath & Brecon Railway 17, 181, 225
Swansea Vale Railway (SV) 9, 18, 43, 130, 178, 181-82, 186-91, 195-96, 203, 205, 207, 225
Swansea Valley Railway 37, 187-88

T

Taff Vale Extension (TVE) 34, 37, 41, 44, 46, 74, 96
Taff Vale Railway (TVR) 11, 37, 45, 95-98
Talgarth 176
Talyllyn Junction 159, 161, 163-65, 199
Tareni Colliery 14-15
Tawe valley 14, 16-17, 37, 181, 188, 201, 208
Three Cocks Junction 159, 163, 174-76, 199
Tickets 48-50
Tootal, Edward 35-37, 44, 214
Tredegar 62, 78-79, 82, 84, 86, 236-37
Tredegar Junction 62, 65, 79-80, 82-84, 86, 235

U

Upper Bank 15, 191, 199-200, 202, 217, 223
Usk river 11, 51, 119, 178, 200

V

Vale of Neath line 9, 81, 197, 224, 231, 234, 239, 241
Vale of Neath Railway 40, 43, 46, 60, 71, 96, 98, 104, 159, 178, 209, 241
Vale of Towy Railway 123, 130, 143-45, 151-52

W

Waggons 44, 135, 150, 196
Watkin, Sir Edward 160, 197-98
Watson & Overend 131
Waunavon 74, 76-77, 237
Welsh Midland Railway 16-17, 123, 187
West Midland Railway 21, 32, 45-46, 55, 60, 62, 83, 144, 159, 160, 224, 230
Whitney 165-66
Williams, Joshua 71, 96, 178
Wolverhampton 13
Worcester 13-14, 16, 18, 23-27, 44, 168
Worcester & Hereford Railway 18, 24, 27, 29, 30, 32, 35-37, 39, 224
Wyllie Halt 234

Y

Yockney 64-65, 79, 84, 86
Ynysddu 234
Ynysygeinon Junction 14, 17, 181, 201-02, 208, 225
Ystalyfera 17-18, 37, 43, 150, 187, 191-93, 201, 205, 208, 247
Ystradgynlais 181, 187-88, 201

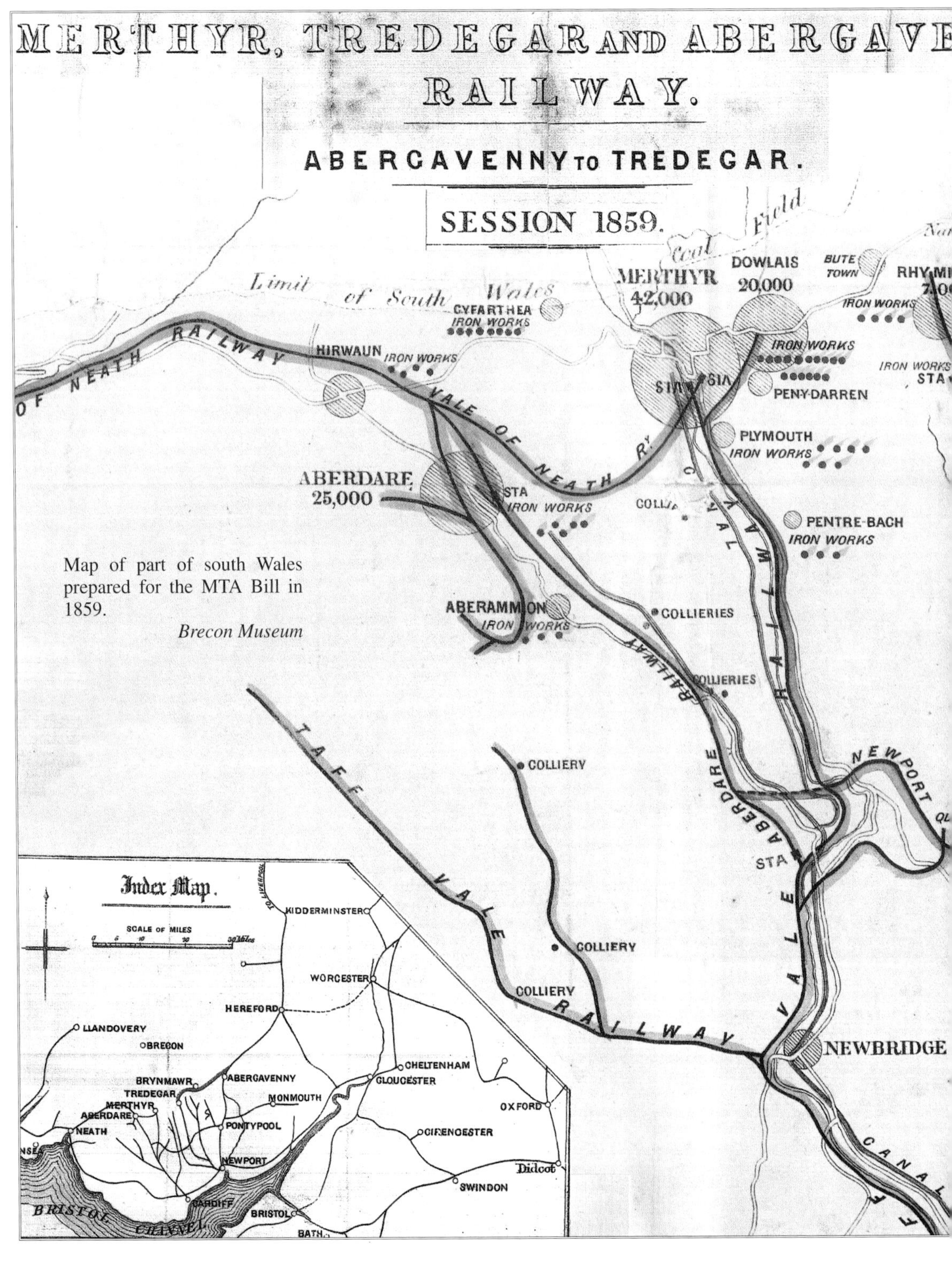

Map of part of south Wales prepared for the MTA Bill in 1859.

Brecon Museum